Henry N.S. Teignmouth

Three Pleasant Springs in Portugal

Henry N.S. Teignmouth

Three Pleasant Springs in Portugal

ISBN/EAN: 9783337288853

Printed in Europe, USA, Canada, Australia, Japan

Cover: Foto ©Andreas Hilbeck / pixelio.de

More available books at **www.hansebooks.com**

THREE PLEASANT SPRINGS IN PORTUGAL

BY COMMANDER THE HON.

HENRY N. SHORE, R.N.

AUTHOR OF
'SMUGGLING DAYS AND SMUGGLING WAYS'

WITH A SKETCH MAP
AND 15 FULL-PAGE ILLUSTRATIONS
FROM THE AUTHOR'S DRAWINGS

LONDON
SAMPSON LOW, MARSTON & COMPANY
LIMITED
St. Dunstan's House
FETTER LANE, FLEET STREET, E.C.
1899

CONTENTS

	PAGE
SPRING THE FIRST	1
SPRING THE SECOND	159
SPRING THE THIRD	315
INDEX	391

LIST OF ILLUSTRATIONS

THE GLORY OF PORTUGAL	*frontispiece*
THE ROCK OF LISBON AND CINTRA MOUNTAINS, FROM OFF CASCAES	*facing page* 10
VIEW FROM THE PEDRA DO ALVIDRAR, NEAR CINTRA	,, 16
ANCIENT AQUEDUCT OVER THE RIVER ZIZANDRO AT TORRES VEDRAS	,, 48
OBYDOS, FROM THE CALDAS ROAD . .	,, 100
MAP OF PORTUGAL . .	,, 104
A STREET IN CINTRA . .	,, 112
VIEWS OF OPORTO	,, 160
ART POTTERY .	,, 208
BOM JESUS	,, 224
'THE RIVER OF OBLIVION,' FROM PONTE DE LIMA	,, 240
PONTE DE LIMA	,, 248
BUSSACO : SHOWING THE GROUND TRAVERSED BY THE RIGHT COLUMN OF ATTACK . .	,, 272
BUSSACO : SCENE OF THE RIGHT ATTACK . .	,, 288
LISBON, FROM THE SOUTH SIDE . . .	,, 304
IN THE DREARY WASTES OF THE ALEMTEJO	,, 378

THREE PLEASANT SPRINGS IN PORTUGAL

SPRING THE FIRST

'So you have been to Portugal! How very interesting!' was the exclamation of a friend; and he added, 'Portugal is a country one hears nothing about, nowadays: why is that?'

Why, indeed? I have often wondered; for Portugal is not an unexplored corner of the 'dark continent': its position is clearly defined on the map of Europe; and it is but a couple of days' steam from our shores. While even statesmen, whose knowledge of geography is apt to be more extensive than profound, have been known to refer to it as 'our ancient ally,'—a compliment, by the way, which gives mortal offence. For the fidalgos of Lusitania scorn the idea of ever having stood in need of help, much less of alliance with an effete and perfidious power like Great Britain; they even affect to regard us with aversion.

This indifference concerning a country which has played a by no means insignificant part in history, and whose wines we still drink, is the more singular seeing that a hundred years ago Portugal was all the vogue—with consumptive patients especially, who flocked to Lisbon and

Cintra, as they now do to Madeira and the Canaries, making no more fuss over the voyage than people do nowadays over a trip to the States.

Perhaps the change of fashion is due to the prevalence of a mistaken idea that Portugal is merely an inferior edition of Spain—Spain stripped of all that lends interest and zest to travel; that it possesses neither architecture nor scenery; that hotels are non-existent; that native cookery is a compound of garlic and oil; and that its inhabitants are a set of fierce and rapacious savages.

The following plain story of our experiences during three delightful tours in Portugal may perchance do something to correct these erroneous ideas, and to shed a little light on sundry other matters pertaining to a much misunderstood country. It may even induce roving Britons, satiated with the conventionalities of present-day continental travel, and sighing for fresh fields and pastures new, to spurn the stupid old tyrant, Custom, which, as Bacon truly says, 'doth make dotards of us all,' and try the experiment of a trip to 'Fair Lusitania.'

To be sure, Portugal has been thrust into rather an out-of-the-way corner of the world, and leads to nowhere. But the facilities of access, to say nothing of travel in the country itself, are far greater than is commonly supposed; while those who seek for information will find plenty of literature; for Portugal is a country which has been much written about, from the day when those sturdy warriors, Drake and Norris, sallied forth to capture Lisbon (1588), up to more recent times.

'Oh, but there is the horrid Bay to cross!' I hear some one exclaim.

Well, a century ago there was some excuse for a reluctance to face the terrors of the 'middle passage'—

the overland route was, of course, out of the question, except for armed men and millionaires!

When William Beckford—the author of *Vathek*—essayed to visit Portugal in 1787, the undertaking was a very serious one indeed. First of all, he was detained more than a week at Falmouth, waiting a fair wind, bored to death. 'What can a being of my turn do at Falmouth?' he exclaims pettishly. 'The Lord have mercy upon me! now, indeed, do I perform penance!'

The poor man was actually reduced to witnessing cock-fighting, though the 'cocks were unarmed, and had their spurs cut short.'

And twenty years later an officer, on his way to join the army in the Peninsula, was a whole month on passage from Spithead to Lisbon—three weeks tossing in the Bay! Still, the voyage had its *agréments*. 'Our passengers were continually quarrelling among themselves, and some of them had given and received so many challenges to mortal combat, that the number of duels to be fought when they got ashore was quite bewildering, and it would have been necessary that a diary of events had been kept by which to ascertain their order of precedence.'

How tame and commonplace, by comparison, must seem the experience of the present-day traveller! Why, dear me, more than fifty years ago we find the author of *The Crescent and the Cross* dogmatising in the airiest fashion about 'the much-calumniated Bay of Biscay, whose dangers are merely traditional, since the introduction of steam.'

'Merely traditional,' forsooth! But then, Elliot Warburton was inditing his journal amidst the pomp and splendour of an 'aboriginal' Peninsular and Oriental steamship, wherein, he tells us, was at work 'the convulsive energy of four hundred and fifty horse-power.' Think of that!—about the engine-power of a modern steam launch!

But the hero of a single voyage was ever opinionative; and the delightful confidence of assertion with which he is wont to lay down the law on all matters pertaining to the sea and its secrets, is well known. It was, therefore, quite in the natural order of things that this same charming *raconteur* should feel it his duty to 'bear willing testimony to the ability of the captain,' and doubtless this 'certificate of competency' from so distinguished a man of letters is still treasured up by the descendants of the 'old salt' who gained this much-sought-for distinction.

How unintentionally amusing great men are at times!

Even the overland route may now be accomplished in comfort. Though it is not an experience I would recommend, even with the pleasant accessories of kitchen and sleeping-berth provided by the 'sud-express'—express in name only, after passing the French frontier; and even this 'facility' runs but twice a week.

The sea route, as in Beckford's day, offers the 'line of least resistance,' and—provided the winds are not 'rude in Biscay's sleepless Bay,' as Byron sang—may be commended for comfort and celerity. For although it was the complaint of the sea-sick dominie that if 'Britannia rules the waves,' she cannot rule them straight —and, speaking with the recollection of some thirty crossings tolerably fresh in the mind, I am scarcely prepared to utter such a libel on my very old friend the Bay as to affirm that its dangers 'are merely traditional'—still, the voyage, in any one of the fine vessels that now run to the Peninsula, is a very insignificant affair indeed.

Take our own experiences. We left Southampton in one of the ships of the Royal Mail line, at 5 P.M. on a Friday —for steam, besides obliterating the terrors of the Bay, has annihilated the old superstition connected with sailing on a Friday, and played havoc with marine sentiment generally—and before dusk we were through the Needles and speeding down Channel.

As St. Alban's Head sank below the horizon, 'here I bade adieu to old England,' as Chaplain Teonge wrote in his quaint journal some two hundred years before, 'for no more English land was to be seen after that.'

Early next morning, 'wee enter upon the Bay of Biscaye, wher wee find the seas very smooth, contrary to our expectations'; and all Saturday rush through it at eighteen miles an hour, while 'the porpuses come tumbling in greate multitudes,' just as in Teonge's day. Finisterre was run past during the night. And here it is worth noting that the ship which bore Warburton, with its 'gigantic engine' and 'convulsive energy,' only struggled thus far on the 'fifth day'! By nine next morning (Sunday) we were entering the Bay of Vigo, one of the most beautiful harbours on the Atlantic seaboard, and soon after lay peacefully at anchor off the picturesque old town.

Embosomed amidst a tangle of lofty mountains whose slopes are besprinkled with hamlets, interspersed with gardens and corn-fields, vineyards and orange-groves, backed up with dark patches of pine-wood, the bay more nearly resembles some lovely inland lake than an arm of the fierce and fickle ocean; and, when viewed under such conditions as were vouchsafed to us, I know of no more lovely spot, and have often wondered why no poet has ever sung its praises.

Off the entrance a group of rocky islands lie, like watch-dogs, protecting the occupants of the bay from the furious onslaughts of the Atlantic rollers, which break on the coast with a fury that must be witnessed to be understood, fuming and fretting, during the winter gales, at the feet of these watch-dogs like wolves balked of their prey.

It was early in April, and yet the sun streamed down with a midsummer intensity which was the more noticeable after the cutting east winds we had parted with but forty-eight hours before, and of which we still bore in our persons a chilling reminder. One could hardly believe that so much genial warmth and loveliness existed within so short a steam of our native shores.

We seemed to have dropped into a veritable Eden on all sides. The glassy surface of the bay threw back the magnificent outline of mountains with startling realism, a line of golden strand just serving to indicate where land and sea blended into one harmonious whole. Towns and villages glistened brightly in the clear sunshine, while, gliding silently over the surface of the water, were numerous boats, crowded with country-folk in picturesque dresses, the white sails bellying out from time to time with 'cats' paws' of wind that stole in from the open sea.

Scarcely had the anchor touched bottom ere the vessel was encompassed with boats bearing tempting assortments of fruits — strawberries, cherries, loquats, oranges and lemons, interspersed with bouquets of bright flowers, well calculated to tempt visitors from cold northern lands. And, in a moment, the air resounded with discordant cries, as the owners of the luscious cargoes held aloft small baskets of fruit, shouting 'One-shilling-the-lot!' with full lung power.

Vigo Bay must ever be dear to Englishmen, seeing that it has been the scene of some fine feats of arms in days gone by.

One of the earliest visitors was the playful Drake, on one of his 'beard-singeing' expeditions, in June 1589: 'A verie pleasant, rich valley, but wee burnt it all, houses and corne, so as the country was spoyled seven or eight miles in length,' was the laconic entry of a diarist who accompanied the expedition. A certain Christ. Carleil who commanded a small squadron which looked in here some four years before this, seems to have dropped in for a nice prize or two. For, in a letter to Walsyngham, reporting the capture of some boats which had run for shelter to the head of the bay, he says: 'Amongst others, fell to my hands one wherein was laden a chest with the furniture of the high church of Vigo. All the copes and plate were in it, whereof one cross was as much as a man might carry, being very fine silver of excellent workmanship, and all gilt over double. The whole plate which was in the said chest, as well the crosses as other things, could not have cost less, or so little, as 500 marks.' No wonder Vigo church looks somewhat unfurnished at the present time!

Then, in later years, there fled in here that famous fleet of Spanish galleons with the treasures of the western world—of which every schoolboy has read—with Sir George Rooke close at their heels; and sooner than let their gold and their galleons fall into English hands, the Dons landed their treasure and made a bonfire of the ships.

It was always believed that in the hurry of the moment some of the gold and silver pieces had been left aboard the smouldering hulls. Be that as it may, I remember, when on a visit to Vigo many years ago, finding a company of French divers fishing in troubled waters for the long-sunken treasure. The only visible result of their labours, however, was a pile of broken china, of the old blue 'willow-pattern' brand. Years before this, the famous Ramsgate diving-bell was brought out for the same speculative purpose, and with equally barren results. But sunken treasure possesses as great a fascination for some minds as gold-mining.

Happily, all recollection of the sportive proceedings above mentioned have long ago faded from the memory of the inhabitants. Britons are no longer received here at the sword's point—nay, are gladly welcomed, especially since the Peninsular War days, when a combined force of Spaniards and Britons ejected the French 'liberators' from the old castle which is still seen capping the town.

Well, those were grand days for British sailors! It makes a naval officer's mouth water to think of all the pickings that fell to the share of a smart navy man in those days. It was the 'golden age' from a tar's point of view!

How sad it makes one to think of all these inspiring memories being a sealed book to roving Britons! For not one in a thousand of all who visit Vigo has ever heard of these naval exploits. It is surprising how cleverly our 'intellectual agriculturists' manage to secrete all knowledge of our glorious naval and military history from the youth of Britain! But it always will be so, as long as the dear old gentlemen who have the ordering of our minds believe that the exploits of the mythical heroes of antiquity—their murders and their abductions, contain deeper lessons than the lives and achievements of such unimportant persons as Drake and Marlborough, Nelson or Wellington; or that the siege of Troy is a more improving study than the storming of Badajoz; or that familiarity with the details of the Peloponnesian War is of more vital consequence to our future rulers and statesmen than some acquaintance with the several stages by which our own vast empire was built up. We laugh at the Chinese for worshipping their Classics: and yet in spite of Sydney Smith's satire on 'Too much Latin and Greek,' we train up thousands of our youths, every year, under the firm belief that any other sort of learning is vulgar. Knowledge, to be respectable, must be quite two thousand years old!

Meanwhile, the ship is swinging quietly at her anchor; and a halt of a few hours comes as a pleasant break in the monotony of a sea-voyage. It enables one to stretch one's legs by a run ashore; and in the present case to take a stroll through the quaint old town, of so many interesting associations, and peep into the 'high church' and the market, where are often displayed the famous 'Vigo plates,' so dear to the decorators of British homes.

A boat-load of wine, and another of emigrants for the Brazils, took ship here, and we quitted the bay as the sun, with a nice sense of decorum, retired behind an island to take that particular dip which poets and artists, regardless of the sanctity of the bath, have exhausted their vocabularies and colours in futile attempts to depict for us.

Deep shadows which had extended their lengths under shelter of the hills were now creeping up the mountain-sides, their purple tone throwing into brilliant contrast the glowing orange and rose tints of the summits, and imparting that mysterious charm to the face of Nature which she never displays under the crude illumination of a midday sun.

Once more the ship's head points south; and as we glide over the liquid mirror in full view of the 'wild Gallician shore,' one's thoughts turn involuntarily to the battered hulls resting fathoms deep off this inhospitable coast, and the thousands of poor victims to the Atlantic Juggernaut, whose bones lie scattered beneath this glassy surface. For there is no portion of the Peninsular seaboard that bears a worse reputation at Lloyd's than that lying between Capes Finisterre and St. Vincent. Our own naval annals tell of some appalling disasters hereabouts, while the *Wreck Register* affords sufficient proof that the dangers of this piece of coast-line are by no means 'traditional.'

Every one remained on deck while light lasted, examining the villages perched high up amongst the crags, and watching the exquisite effects of light and shade on the mountain-sides, whose slopes seemed to melt imperceptibly into the glassy sea. Then the moon rose, and soon all Nature 'lay wrapt in a pleasant trance.' And the morning and the evening were the second day.

Vianna, Oporto, the Burlings, Peniche, and many other familiar places, were run past during the night; and at daylight, 'to our greate joy, wee see the Rock of Lysbone,' or Cape Roca, as it is now more commonly called, with the lofty Cintra Mountains towering up behind, their topmost peaks hidden away in cloudland. Sunny Cascaes, where Drake lay with his fleet waiting to pick up Norris and fiery young Essex after their rebuff at Lisbon; bright Estoril, the summer resort of wealth and fashion; frowning St. Julian, and forlorn Bugio—that surf-lashed watch-dog that looks like a monitor moored off the Tagus mouth, and

THE ROCK OF LISBON AND CINTRA MOUNTAINS, FROM OFF CASCAES

UNIV. OF
CALIFORNIA

was once a 'wooden fort,' according to Teonge,—are all in turn left behind, and almost before the fact is realised we are entering the 'front-door of Europe'—the noble Tagus.

The voyage has occupied a little over two days and a half, with only one entire day at sea; and the water has been so smooth that an open boat might have accomplished the passage without discomfort. Surely that is not a journey to shrink from — especially amidst such surroundings, the comforts of a 'floating hotel'?

At about eight 'of the clock wee come to in the river Tagus, and just over the religious house, for wee must com no farther till wee have leave,' as Teonge quaintly puts it. In other words, we stop off Belem a few moments, for the health officer to board us, and grant *pratique*.

And here, I am glad to say, the similarity in our experiences ceased. For the navy chaplain tells us that, after being kept waiting two days at Belem, 'wee have command brought us to be gon speedily out of their haven, which wee cannot doe.' And after waiting two more days—Portuguese officials never hurry matters!—'at night cam the Leiutenant of the Castle, and the Prattick Master, with a message from the Prince Regent and the Chamber, to command us to be gon out of their port within twenty-four hours; or else wee must looke to be fyred out. And to affrite us, their Vice Admirall of 60 odd gunns coms down and anchors very neare to us; yet wee were resolved to stay rather then sink in the sea.' And stay they did, in spite of the threats of the 'Portingals,' for nearly a fortnight longer, 'resolveing to answer the Vice Admirall in the same coyne, in case that he fyre at us. Who knows what he may doe?'

Such was the spirit in which British seamen met 'commands to be gon' in the year 1676. Nowadays, foreigners can order us where they will, with no more dire consequences arising than questions being asked in Parliament.

How many pleasant memories does the sight of all the familiar spots around conjure up! For there was a time when these waters were haunted by the British Channel Fleet, and many enjoyable months were spent off Lisbon every year. Those were jolly times indeed! But lo! one morning our 'ancient ally' turned rusty—swore that her *amour propre* had been grievously wounded, and now—well, that is another story!

A noble river truly is the Tagus! What other capital is there that can boast of such an imposing approach as those twelve miles from St. Julian upwards? The northern shore looks like a continuous suburb—'a succession of villages tacked together,' as an old writer puts it; and in the early morning no more enchanting prospect can be conceived than the endless succession of castles and palaces, and lovely quintas, embowered in luxuriant gardens and orange groves, adorning the river-side.

The appearance of this noble city, when first it bursts into view, has been described so often that its aspect must seem familiar even to people who have never set eyes on it. By far the best description that I know of is that touched-in by an officer *en route* to join the army under Wellington, and as it exactly accords with the superb spectacle that met our gaze on the morning of arrival, I venture to reproduce it. 'On awakening next morning, and looking round me, the scene appeared one of enchantment. The world was basking in a blaze of golden light, such as I had never before witnessed. Lisbon sate, queen-like, enthroned upon her hills, surveying her beauty in the Tagus—calm and majestic, as if the earthquake which had hurled her to the dust had never slept below, or would never wake again.'

I believe there is only one other European capital that can compare with Lisbon in point of situation and splendour of appearance—Constantinople; and the resemblance seems to have struck other travellers besides myself. Certainly, when the morning mists are clinging to the shores, partly screening their beauties, and lending to the scene the charm of mystery that Turner loved so dearly, while far above, glistening in bright sunshine, the towers and palaces of the city rear their proud forms against the sky, Lisbon does seem like an enchanted city.

The Portuguese are proud of their metropolis, and justly so. They even believe there is no city like it; and, even in the old days, when it was 'a dunghill from end to end,' nothing could weaken their affection for dear, old, smelly Lisboa. Lisbon

'With all thy faults I love thee still!'

was the ruling passion. They even loved its faults as fervently as its perfections. Apropos to which an old writer quotes an amusing instance of what he calls 'Portuguese pride, veracity, and inveterate attachment to the offences of his own country.' A young Lisbon dandy, it seems, on being twitted with the filth and stench of Lisbon, replied that for his part, when he was in London, it was 'the absence of that filth, and the lack of the smells' that had been complained of, that had made his residence there so disagreeable and uncomfortable. How true was Southey's remark, that 'no passion makes a man a liar so easily as vanity'!

Those were the days when Lisbon enjoyed the reputation of being the most foul and disgusting capital in Christendom. '*Mais nous avons changées tout cela*,' is the boast of the modern Lisbonense: and with reason, for within a decade a wonderful change has been wrought in the place. The horrible sights and smells that once assailed visitors, and wrung from one the plaint that 'never was the promise of hope more cruelly disappointed than on the day that I entered Lisbon; dunghills are piled up to the very roofs of the houses, and the exhalations are so overpowering that I nearly sank under them': all this, I say, has vanished, and everything pertaining to the welfare of the town, and its attractions as a place of residence, has been brought up to a modern standard; and travelled people declare that, in the matter of cleanliness and freedom from smells, Lisbon compares more than favourably with most continental cities.

With evidences of progress abounding on all sides, there is every excuse for the present generation of Lisbonense being exceedingly well pleased with their city and with themselves, and they wrathfully resent any imputation of backwardness. A curious instance of the smug self-satisfaction that distinguishes this charming race was afforded during our progress up the Tagus. Amongst the passengers was a young Portuguese gentleman who had been spending the winter in Scotland—chiefly in Glasgow, poor fellow! He spoke English well, and had been so far infected with British ways as to have adopted a knickerbocker suit of startling pattern. He had been descanting on the attractions of his native city, dwelling especially on the marks of progress that greeted the eye, whereupon I ventured the remark—intending it as a compliment—that Lisbon must have greatly improved since I knew it, some five-and-twenty years ago. 'What would you have in a progressive country?' was the curt reply. He further informed us that he was going to 'take the waters,' for the benefit of his health; and here, again, most unwittingly, I trod on his corns, for, on asking him if he was going to Caldas da Rainha—the Harrogate of Portugal—he replied, with an air of offended dignity, 'Do you suppose those are the only mineral waters we have in Portugal?' He spoke of Brazil as 'the daughter of Portugal,' and confided to me that he thought the Glasgow people 'provincial, and narrow-minded'!

The pause off Belem, while the health officer examines the papers, enables the visitor to take stock of the first outward and visible sign of the spirit—in this case, the *evil* spirit—of progress which has entered into the Lisbon authorities, and which now thrusts itself into notice, in close proximity to that interesting link-with-the-past— Belem Castle. This little architectural gem, which marks the spot where Vasco da Gama embarked on his voyage for the discovery of India, on a projecting spit of sand about five miles below Lisbon, has been ruined artistically by the erection of huge gas-works, with the usual hideous accessories, exactly behind and abutting on to it! Never was a more wanton offence perpetrated against good taste in the name of 'progress'! A French authoress justly stigmatises it as a 'crime.'

But the 'Prattick Master' has gone ashore; the ship is heading for the anchorage off the Black Horse Square,

'And by the vision splendid
Is on its way attended';

and by nine we are at anchor, and a kind friend comes off to chaperone us to the Custom-house, and see us safely through the ordeal of search. For the roving Briton was not a *persona grata* with the Lisbon Customs' officials just at this moment, seeing that, but a few weeks before, a sturdy Briton who, with the morals of a smuggler, had inherited something of the spirit of the Elizabethan age, after having declared 'no dutiable articles,' was found to have laid in a stock of cigars for consumption during his travels—a piece of ill-luck which led to detention and other things; whereupon the Briton waxed wroth, threatened the officers with the displeasure of the British government, and even tried to frighten them by invoking the aid of the British fleet, behaving himself generally like an ill-tempered cad—a course of proceeding which has not greatly raised the veracity and importance of British travellers in the estimation of Customs' officials, or facilitated business.

Personally, I have always found Portuguese officials courteous and obliging, and by no means exacting in enforcing the 'right of search'; an experience which entirely accords with the character given them by a traveller of the last century, who wrote: 'We must declare, in justice to these officers [of Customs], that they performed their duty with so much politeness, that it carried more the appearance of a friendly visit than an official search.' And he adds, significantly, 'Those who have witnessed the visits of British Custom-house officers, upon similar occasions, will scarcely believe that so much urbanity exists amongst men of that class.'

It had happened that, but a short time before, the great Marquis of Pombal, on landing in England to take up his post as Ambassador, had been so rudely treated by the Customs jacks-in-office as to create in his mind an unfavourable impression of the English character which lasted him through life. It was this rough recep-

VIEW FROM THE PEDRA DO ALVIDRAR, NEAR CINTRA

UNIV. OF
CALIFORNIA

tion that is believed to have been at the root of the unfriendly attitude he ever after assumed towards the Oporto wine-trade, which has always been one of the most important British interests in Portugal. Even Customs' searchers may entertain angels unawares.

Landing at Lisbon is not an unmixed joy, and I would suggest that, when the 'progressives' of the municipal council can manage to spare a few moments from devising attractions for visitors, and building useless docks, they might provide something in the way of a landing-stage—say, a clean plank or two.

It would be an abuse of terms to speak of 'landing facilities' at the metropolis. The arrangements for disembarking travellers and their luggage at the Customhouse, or, indeed, anywhere, are a disgrace to a civilised country. The annoyance, moreover, of having to fight a passage through the boats and barges that block the steps, is intensified by the abominable stenches that assail the nose, for all the sewage of Lisbon seems to congregate at this particular spot, for the purpose of welcoming new arrivals.

The wise men who are so busily employed beautifying their city seem to forget that before travellers can admire it they must needs get there, and that visitors, on arrival at a presumably civilised spot, look for the ordinary conveniences of intercourse—such, for example, as are to be found at the most insignificant sea-ports in other lands. And I feel sure that a few pounds discreetly expended on a decent landing-place would well repay the trouble and expense.

And now we emerge into the magnificent Praca do Commercio—*Anglicé* Black Horse Square, Pombal's *chef d'œuvre*—the 'front-door' of Lisbon, and undoubtedly

B

one of the 'finest sites in Europe,' with its wide river frontage, and imposing archway leading to the heart of the city.

There was a time, within my own recollection, when visitors had to 'foot it' to their hotel, the luggage following on the backs of porters. Nowadays, comfortable landaus and broughams, with excellent horses, may be obtained in every part of the city. And how they travel! The driving of Jehu, the son of Nimshi, must have been a mere crawl to the headlong pace at which the Lisbon 'coachies' hurry their cattle up and down hill, and through the narrowest alleys, with but an inch to spare on either side. And yet, accidents are rare, for there never were surer-footed beasts than the horses that draw the *trens de aluguer* of the Lisbon streets. Would that carriages of equal comfort and cleanliness were amongst the common objects of the London streets!

Talking of fast driving, it has always been a puzzle to me why this nation of 'slow-coaches,' who pride themselves on never being in a hurry, and ordain it that their trains dawdle along in a manner that exasperates strangers, should insist on being driven at a break-neck speed the moment they find themselves behind a horse.

Having comfortably installed ourselves in a room overlooking the river at the quiet Braganza Hotel, we next essayed a tour of the city. But the heat was so intense that the streets resembled reverberating furnaces, and it was useless to think of attempting anything beyond a stroll along the shady side while the sun was up. Towards evening, however, our friend called with a carriage and took us for a delightful drive.

Twenty-five years had rolled by since I last set foot in Lisbon, and many pleasant surprises awaited me. In

those far-away times, even carriages were luxuries; so
that if you would peregrinate the town there was no
alternative but to trot off on 'shanks' mare.' The
conveniences of civilisation were conspicuous by their
absence: even the railway station was 'two miles from
anywhere,' in an out-of-the-way quarter of the city, and
the *caminho de ferro* only took you in one direction.
There were no 'facilities of travel' to the suburbs, and
other pleasant resorts around; while the streets of those
days were too suggestive of decaying matter, and corrupt
vestries, to invite loiterers. Lisbon was essentially a city
of slums. There were no large open spaces of fashionable resort, no boulevards, and but few gardens worthy
of the name, and those indifferently kept. The river
frontage was an abomination, presenting at low tide a
dismal waste of putrefying sewage, as offensive to the eye
as it was nauseous to the smell, and as useless as it was
disgraceful. And the comfort of passengers arriving or
leaving by ship was so completely ignored that there
was not a single spot where, at low water, it was possible
to set foot on the sacred soil of Portugal without risking
a plunge into the slimy mass that adorned the river-side.

What a change has come over the place since those
dark days! The demon of progress has broken loose
with a vengeance, and enterprise is writ large everywhere.
The city is now intersected by tramways. From the
Rocio and Praca do Commercio, the nerve-centres of
Lisbon, the lines radiate in all directions—wherever the
ground is level enough to admit of horse-traction—far into
the suburbs, and for miles along the river-side. And
the 'Americanos,' as the cars are called, are so well
patronised that the service has to be supplemented by
'road cars' and 'buses, and still there is a difficulty in

coping with the traffic. Some of the steepest ascents are climbed by lifts—'Ascenceurs.' For Lisbon is built on hills: 'Never did I behold such cursed ups-and-downs, such shelving descents and sudden rises, as occur at every step one takes in Lisbon,' wrote a visitor of the last century.

From the pretty little Praca de Camoens, with its trees and its kiosks, a rope tramway conveys one to the beautiful Estrella square, a mile away. And a most ingenious and difficult piece of engineering this is; for the road not only dips into the very deep valley that intervenes between the terminal points, but it has to traverse an intermediate hill, through a narrow street with some sharp curves. The entire service of cars—there are always four, in course of transit, on each line—is worked by a continuous wire rope, more than two miles long, the motive power being derived from an engine at the Estrella end. The friction must be enormous, especially on the intermediate curves and at the terminal points, where the cars run round a loop before commencing the return journey.

'Lisbon is the place in the world best calculated to make one cry out, "Hide me from day's garish eye," but where to hide is not so easy,' was the plaint of a visitor to this shadeless city in times past. The inhabitants were twitted with having a greater antipathy to verdure than Dr. Johnson, when he thundered forth his contemptuous anathema against 'green fields,' and those who 'babbled of them.' Of late years, however, much has been done to remove this reproach by tree-planting, which is going on in all parts of the city; and the foliage, besides affording shelter from 'day's garish eye,' relieves the otherwise monotonous aspect of the streets. The favourite tree for this purpose seems to be the 'Tree of Heaven' (*Ailantus glandulosa*), and, when pollarded, it forms a canopy so impenetrable as to defy the fiercest sunbeam.

The public gardens, too, have been greatly improved, extended, and multiplied of late, in furtherance of the policy inaugurated, in the first instance, by the Marquis of Pombal, who, his admirers say, was a great friend to the fair sex, and, as such, endeavoured to abolish many of the restraints under which they were most unjustly kept. With this object he laid out public walks and gardens, 'with a view to introduce a more general intercourse between the sexes,' and promote courtship and matrimony.

But Pombal was one of those great men whose ideas were far in advance of their time; and many of his schemes, including those for making flirtations easy, and thereby increasing the number of marriages, met with but a lukewarm support.

According to a contemporary, it was 'the jealousy of the men, and the causes or suspicions which gave rise to it,' that prevented the pleasant lounges provided by the Marquis from producing the social intercourse he had hoped for. And certainly, while the 'lords of creation' looked askance at any relaxation of the state of 'Asiatic seclusion' in which it pleased them to keep their female relatives, it was useless wasting money on 'cosy corners,' or anticipating the rapid adoption of the 'muffin' system in Portugal.

In reading books about old Portugal, nothing grieves one so much as the treatment meted out by 'fond parents' of the 'fidalgo' class to their daughters. In many parts of China, the young ladies of the family are still summarily disposed of in ponds. In Portugal it was the custom, up to within recent times, to throw them into convents. And I am not sure that the Chinese method was not the more humane of the two; for the Celestial mamma took the *première pas* in infancy, before the child had imbibed a taste for the vanities of this world, while the Lusitanian *mae*, after allowing her offspring to dip deeply into the treacle-pot of the present life, and become thoroughly alive to its attractions, suddenly, and without consulting the young lady's inclinations, encaged her, for the rest of her existence, in a dreary prison-house.

The Council of Trent sanctioned 'profession' at the age of fifteen, when, in priestly jargon, a young girl could become the 'spouse of Christ.' What cruel irony! Was there ever a daughter of Eve, born into this bright world, who at such an age would hesitate in her reply to the question, 'Is life worth living?'—'Yes! ten thousand times, yes!'

Now, these statements are not based on mere 'travellers' tales,' but on well-authenticated facts. A writer of the last century, when the system of incarceration was in full swing, describing a noted convent in the north of Portugal, tells us that all the best female blood of the province was there assembled. Owing to the poverty of the nobles, and their aversion to work, rather than bestow their daughters on any person they thought in the least inferior to them in birth, they had no resource —as they imagined—but to place them in this convent, 'to starve in character, without consulting their inclinations, or considering the physical and constitutional hardships to which they expose them.' But the strongest condemnation of the system comes from a Portuguese Secretary of State, and a Catholic, who declared the 'nunneries are prejudicial to the state,' because the women are 'forced there when their parents cannot afford to dower them suitably to their rank, lest they should marry according to their inclinations.' And this liberal-minded Catholic, with a view to mitigating the abuses occasioned by allowing females to make their vows at so early an age, recommended that no person should be allowed to profess before the age of twenty-five, 'that they may well consider the nature of the vows they take.' In many instances, the poor creatures took their portions along with them, a circumstance which of course offered additional inducement to their capture by the conventual recruiting-officers. So great, indeed, was the greed of the monastic authorities, that many of the convents admitted more nuns than were sanctioned by their statutes—sometimes to the extent of fifty per cent.

Still, as we know, 'stone walls do not a prison make, nor iron bars a cage'; and if one-quarter of the rumours that have drifted down to modern times are to be trusted, we may solace ourselves with the assurance that life in a convent was not necessarily the dull, insipid affair we are apt to assume, and that, in some instances, at any rate, there was a decided earthly element—something akin to friskiness—imparted to what it pleased the Church to call 'the higher life.' A certain nunnery at Odivellas, near Lisbon, for example, attained an altogether unsought-for notoriety in this respect, current report giving rise to endless conjectures concerning the manner of life of the fair inmates—'King John's recluses,' as they were called. This convent was famous for the pious retirement of 'that paragon of splendour and holiness,' King John the Fifth, the 'most magnificent of modern Solomons,' as he was styled, and who resembled his Jewish prototype in most things—except in his wit and wisdom. In this pleasant retirement the *grande monarque* whiled away many hours of a by no means ascetic life. 'Oh!' said an old priest, whose knowledge of matters conventual was both extensive and peculiar, 'of what avail is the finest cage without birds to enliven it? Had you but heard the celestial harmony of King John's recluses, you would never have been contented with the squalling of sopranos and the grumbling of bass-viols. The silver virgin tones I allude to, proceeding from the holy recess into which no other male mortal except the monarch was ever allowed to penetrate, had an effect I still remember with ecstasy, though at the distance of so many years.' Well might the divulger of these surprising revelations exclaim, 'Those were delightful days for the monarch and the fair companions of his devotions!'

The more one wanders amidst the mazes of Portuguese history, the more is one impressed with the long succession of Portuguese sovereigns whose lives afforded bright exceptions to the oft-quoted aphorism, that 'uneasy lies the head that wears a crown'—nay, rather, whose reigns seem to establish 'the divine right of kings to govern wrong.'

But we have wandered from our 'muttons.' Pombal's intention, in providing facilities of intercourse in the shape of gardens and promenades, was the promotion of marriages, and by this means to remove one of the great hindrances to the proper development of Portugal—its sparseness of population. That this was no imaginary evil is shown by some sensible remarks in a document drawn up by a high State official in 1740. He says: 'The blood of our country is drained at every vein. The principal, most excessive, and constant bleeding that Portugal suffers, is by the great number of convents of all orders of monks and nuns established all over the provinces, and in all the towns of this kingdom, multiplying the mouths that eat, but not the hands that labour, and who live at the cost of others.' And he justly remarks thereon: 'As you can easily know the exact number of monks and nuns, I will say that if only a third part of them were married, they might, in two ages, people a country as large as Portugal and her colonies.' No wonder Southey, who first gave publicity to these jottings, should have expressed 'astonishment at the boldness and liberality of the sentiments.' It required rather more than a hundred years to convert the Portuguese nation to the same way of thinking.

The lot of women, during the 'dark ages' of Portuguese history, was in many ways a lamentable one. Every writer of repute alludes to the state of 'Asiatic seclusion' in which the women of the better classes were kept by their benighted parents and jealous lords, a state of things suggestive of eastern lands, where the harem is still the mode, rather than of a civilised and Christian country. The British maid has much to be thankful for, when she compares her 'jolly good times' with the lot of her sisters in fair Lusitania, where 'keeping company' is anathema, and 'confidences exchanged' in secluded nooks would be relegated to 'the school for scandal.' Even nowadays, with 'progress' in the air, the sexes in Portugal are strangely gregarious. So much so that the frolicsome ways of our young men and maidens, with their water-parties and hansom-riding and general independence of the 'sheep dog,' would send any self-respecting Portuguese parent into a fit. For the Lusitanian Mrs. Grundy is a much more exacting old lady than is commonly supposed, and would assuredly turn crimson and uplift her hands in holy horror at the free-and-easy ways of the maids of merry England. But with the voice of the 'revolted daughter' crying in the land, and all the young men declaring she is very much in the right of it, it is useless trying to put the clock back. As long as our maidens abstain from walking about with pipes in their mouths, and spitting in public, there is no reason why they should not enjoy themselves to their hearts' content.

If the spirit of the great Marquis haunts the scene of his former labours, it may derive consolation for the opposition shown to him, while in the flesh, from the vast strides that have been made in the direction of realising his very particular and pet project for the promotion of marriages, by the creation of open spaces and gardens. The most noteworthy of these is the much admired Avenida da Liberdade, a fine boulevard, after the stereotyped continental pattern, extending from the Rocio nearly a mile and a half in a northerly direction, adorned with various sorts of trees, and with strips of ornamental gardens. The intention is, I believe, to extend it nearly a mile further, and to convert a bleak bit of undulating country into a park, with lakes—the whole to form a very pleasant resort. Even now, the completed portion is much affected of an evening by the beauty and fashion of the capital, who love to stare and be stared at as an improving way of killing time, the arch-enemy of 'smart' folk in all lands.

Some fairly good turn-outs, in the way of carriages '*faire l'avenue*,' as the Lisbon Guide-book terms it, '*et les bons cavaliers ne perdent pas une occasion de faire ressortir les qualités de leurs montures.*' The present rage of '*les bons cavaliers*' is to 'progress' sideways, on a prancing horse, whose speed in the desired direction may possibly attain to two miles an hour. One warm afternoon, the writer of these extravagances and his *compagnon de voyage* took it into their heads to '*faire l'avenue*,' and in a deserted part of the Avenida encountered a stout and florid gentleman on a strong and high-mettled horse performing the 'crab's march,' to the intense admiration of two equally stout gentlemen in attendance, a few paces behind. The spectacle was so engrossing and novel that I became perfectly oblivious to everything, and my companion had to dig me in the ribs with some violence, and shout, 'The King! the King!' repeatedly before I could collect my senses sufficiently to make a suitable obeisance and put on a decent expression of reverence. The fact is, I am so unused to 'crowned heads,' that the spectacle of one in a 'stove-pipe' hat, practising for a circus, quite unnerved me.

The completion of the Avenida da Liberdade has afforded a remarkable proof of the prescience of the great minister, the compilers of the *Guia Illustrada de Lisboa* declaring that the number of marriages in Lisbon has greatly increased since the inauguration of the said boulevard.

Another improvement I observed in the course of our drive is the Central Railway Station—a really handsome building, in the Moresque style, close to the Rocio and the chief 'nerve-centres' of the city, with a thoroughly up-to-date hotel attached, the said hotel having been furnished throughout, in sumptuous style, by a very famous London firm which needs no gratuitous advertising on my part. The old station was a couple of miles from anywhere, and the railway only led in one direction, whereas, from the 'Central,' one can go north, east, or west. And, quite recently, the Cascaes line has been brought up the river-side from Alcantara to the Caes de

Sodre, where there is a station, thus saving a circuitous route through the Alcantara valley. A trip to Cascaes—the Lisbon Margate—or to Estoril, the more modern and fashionable seaside resort, is now one of the pleasantest of afternoon excursions; and once the hot weather sets in, quite an exodus takes place to these bright watering-places.

Amongst the many ambitious schemes of the great Pombal, which never came off, was the reclamation of the foreshore. This has now been accomplished, though whether in the manner intended by the Marquis, I cannot pretend to say. The works have been in progress for many years; they extend from the Caes de Sodre to Belem, a distance of nearly five miles, and, when completed, will constitute one of the most ambitious and costly undertakings ever sanctioned by a small and debt-ridden country. The reclamation scheme comprises a vast system of docks and quays, designed on a scale that would have reflected credit on Liverpool or Antwerp, but which strikes the 'intelligent foreigner' as out of all proportion to the needs of Lisbon now, and for ever after. But the Portuguese are all for big things—whether the country can afford them or not. And the unfortunate part of the business is, that the great ocean liners, for whose accommodation the quays were designed, scornfully decline to make any use of them—the captains declaring them to be dangerous! Still, in justice to the dock authorities, I must admit that I have seen quite a number of river-boats, and even small coasters, landing firewood, and cabbages, all of which will in time—if the world lasts long enough—help to pay the interest on the millions of money that it has pleased the government of Portugal in its wisdom to pitch into the Tagus!

What an excellent chance was thrown away here! Had there been any one in authority endowed with even a glimmering of sense, or a perception of the 'eternal fitness of things,' would such a piece of foolishness have been sanctioned? Had the reclamation project been carried out in the spirit which characterised Pombal's measures for the improvement of the capital—with an eye to 'the greatest happiness of the greatest number'—the scheme would probably have taken the shape of an embankment forming the most superb boulevard in Europe—far, far surpassing, in extent and splendour, as well as in the variety and beauty of the prospects, our own Thames Embankment.

But, it is useless crying over spilt milk—and wasted millions. Nevertheless, the traveller who visits these works, prepared to bless, will surely come away with curses on the evil genius that has wrought the ruin of what was once 'the finest site in Europe.' From an æsthetic point of view the metropolis has been ruined; for, regarded as a scheme for improving and beautifying the city, the reclamation works can only be pronounced a ghastly failure. What Lisbon has accomplished, only too successfully, is to shut itself completely off from all enjoyment of the river. From the Caes de Sodre to Belem, the docks and railway not only block all access to the Tagus-side, but shut out the views of that noble river, thus ruining the fine Aterro de Boa Vista (*Anglicé*, 'embankment of beautiful prospect'!), the Belem Gasworks forming a fitting terminus to this sublime effort of national genius. After all, 'what would you have in a progressive country?' as my young Portuguese friend remarked.

I have often read, and heard it remarked, that the

Portuguese have no love of natural beauty—would not, in fact, stir a yard to gaze on a beautiful view; but I have always been inclined, heretofore, to class this statement with the generalisations which are said to be the 'peculiar vice' of travellers. The sad spectacle of the Tagus-side, however, affords a standing proof of the truth of this assertion.

Our drive extended far into the suburbs, to a place called Campo Pequeno, of many interesting associations, where one of the greatest surprises of all awaited me. This particular spot, as its name 'little field' implies, is, or rather was, a fine expanse of level ground, covered during the winter months with a pleasant surface of short turf, which, in the old Channel Fleet days, rendered it a favourite resort, not of fashion, but of cricketers. It was on the Campo Pequeno that the elevens of the several ships fought out their friendly contests for supremacy. Many were the exciting matches witnessed here, in those far-away times, and not always under the cloudless skies associated with fair Lusitania, but at times in torrential rain that sent us back like drowned rats, to become the butts of the Lisbonense. How many pleasant memories of days gone by, and of shipmates since scattered to the four winds of heaven—and others, alas! who have passed to the bourne from whence no return tickets are available, does the sight of this spot conjure up! What good times those were!—the merry lunches, and the rollicking drives home afterwards when we careered through the Lisbon slums, now usurped by the Avenida, puffed up with the pride of victory, or, perchance, in the chastened spirit that befits defeat, to the utter bewilderment of the populace, who are ever of opinion that *os Ingleses* are a little mad in their methods of 'recreating.' The dignified fidalgos of Portugal would as soon think of standing up to a 'legball,' or stopping a smart cut to the off, as they would of offering their sacred persons as targets for a 'scattergun'!

The Campo Pequeno is still *en evidence*. But what a change has come over the scene! A colossal bull-ring, 'circo tauromachico,' now usurps the favourite 'pitch'; while tram-cars run along the road where once the bullock-cart alone droned forth its melancholy dirge. It was quite time the Channel Fleet gave Lisbon the cold-shoulder on beholding its cricket-ground thus usurped.

The bull-ring is a structure of colossal proportions, in the Arabesque style, whose architectural beauties are duly emphasised in the Lisbon Guide-book. But the most remarkable thing about it is the fact of its paying its way—a distinction enjoyed by few *bona-fide* enterprises in Portugal at the present day.

It so happened that one of our party had never assisted at a bull-fight, and as the first performance of the season was announced to take place shortly, it occurred to us that so favourable an opportunity of improving the mind ought not to be let slip, and then and there we bespoke seats. Now, it is just possible that some reader who has never seen a Portuguese bull-fight may be fired with indignation at the idea of English people countenancing by their presence the brutalising, so-called sport of 'tauromachia.' Well, I admit that there was a time when the sport, as practised in fair Lusitania, was characterised by the same revolting cruelty that still appears to constitute its great charm in the eyes of that most Catholic and chivalrous nation across the border. But that was a century ago. Since those dark days the sport has been purged of all its disgusting and brutalising elements, and is now a mere frolic, in which much skill, infinite agility, and many mirth-provoking incidents are displayed, and it may safely be witnessed by a babe—or the most starched Mrs. Grundy; even Mrs. —— —— might sit it out, without the risk of a shock to her most pure and angelic sense of propriety. What more need be said?

That bull-fighting, as practised in Spain, is a bestial and debasing form of diversion, which no woman ought ever to disgrace her sex by witnessing, I am very ready to admit, for it must inevitably brutalise and harden all who find pleasure in the spectacle. And I believe there is much truth in the assertion that a cultivation of a taste for the sport, in early youth, is not unconnected with a certain inhumanity — indifference to human suffering, amounting to positive cruelty—which has characterised the dealings of Spanish officials with the unfortunate Cubans. 'Weylerism' has come to be synonymous with all that is brutal and unchivalrous in war, and will always be associated in men's minds with the deeds of a nation that still finds its chief diversion in witnessing the infliction of pain on helpless animals in the bull-ring. The fact that the Portuguese have been able to eliminate all the revolting and bestial elements, while preserving the 'sport' of bull-fighting, is very much to the nation's credit.

The spectacle we were treated to, under a cloudless sky of pearly blue, and in blazing sunshine, was as interesting as it was brilliant. The *coup d'œil* as we entered our box was striking in its novelty and grandeur, and was one which, if witnessed for the first time, could never afterwards be forgotten. Moreover, it was a gala performance, and the assemblage of beauty and fashion was in itself no slight attraction. And as the whole vast space was soon stocked to its utmost capacity, there must have been some twelve thousand people present on this occasion. All the world, in fact, was there except royalty. But the king was not the mode at the moment; for it is one of the advantages of the monarchical system that, if things go wrong, the blame of it all can be laid on the back of the sovereign: it is so easy to hang a person who can't defend himself.

While the preliminaries were being gone through, we amused ourselves by taking stock of the assembled multitude, and admiring the patience with which the spectators on the sunny side absorbed into their systems the stored-up heat from the stone seats, along with the original article straight from the source of light and warmth, which fairly beamed on its devotees. And we came away convinced that this little rehearsal—albeit of a few hours only—was a fitting preparation for the 'warming up' that awaited many of these poor mortals hereafter. It was surprising, though, with what hilarity they received this gentle admonition of the fate in store; but man was ever a reckless animal, and loth to benefit by the experience of others.

I won't weary the reader with a detailed account of the performance, for it has often been described before. I may remark, however, there was nothing to shock, much less to disgust, the most sensitive of natures. It was simply a display of uncommon dexterity and agility, the chief amusement centring itself in the efforts of certain bulls to jump the ring, and 'go for' the spectators, and in the attempts of the 'strong men' to 'take the bull by the horns'—an achievement which, when the bull was a beast of spirit, too often resulted in utter failure, the strong men being pitched most ignominiously over the animal's head on to the sandy floor of the arena, amidst the jeers and cheers of the multitude.

The only jarring notes that disturbed the harmony of the scene were the ironical yells which the vast audience gave vent to when Senhor Tauro proved 'one too many' for 'all the king's horses and all the king's men,' and, flatly refusing to be taken by the horns, made light of the pigmy efforts of the great hulking fellows who essayed the task, and now stood panting defiance, in the centre of the arena, as if inviting others to 'come on.' More than one of the 'beeves' succeeded in worsting his antagonists, and establishing such a wholesome 'funk,' that the doughty warriors refused to have any more intercourse with him: in which they showed a very wise discretion. But this pardonable solicitude for the integrity of their own anatomies excited the indignation of the audience to such a pitch—for at least one wounded warrior is regarded as a *sine qua non* of the entertainment—that, to avoid unpleasantness, 'o toiro' had to be hustled off the scene with ignominy, while the damaged 'strong men,'—who, to be sure, made the most of their contusions, were gently assisted into the wings.

Sometimes the bull, from an hereditary disposition to 'arbitration,' or an inclination for bed, vowed he had no stomach for the fight, and after displaying an angelic good humour under much provocation and insult, was howled home again; and there were many other humorous incidents which helped to beguile the time, and to keep the vast assemblage in excellent good humour.

There was something very pretty and pathetic, too, in the pastoral simplicity of the concluding scene of each act: when Tauro, having provided his modicum of sport—or otherwise—meekly surrendered himself to a bevy of domestic kine, and trotted off, in a thoroughly chastened spirit, to home and supper. And so the fight went on;

hour after hour, after the manner of all entertainments in this sunny land. And, as there seemed no signs of its ending, we withdrew; sought our carriage from the throng, and drove home, in the cool of a delicious evening.

Well, it was a sight worth seeing—one which no visitor would willingly forgo. It was a bull-fight conducted on humanitarian principles—a sight to be witnessed in no other land. Though, how it comes to pass that a few minutes' difference in longitude makes such a difference in the habits and tastes of the people, is a fact difficult of explanation.

Assuredly bull-fighting, as practised in Portugal, seems of all devices the one best calculated for killing time—the one commodity with which, in spite of prohibitive tariffs, this most ancient realm appears to be overstocked. And here let me bear willing testimony to the spirit of resignation in which natives of all ranks will sit, for hour after hour, in the brightest of sunshine, or in the stuffiest of atmospheres indoors, without manifesting the least sign of impatience, ennui, or even a desire for 'by-by.' In no country, indeed, is the art of killing time cultivated more assiduously, or with greater success, than in the land of Camoens.

The vast assemblage of people was alone worth going to see: a happy, good-tempered crowd, with none of the wild beast about it, which the sight of blood, albeit but the blood of a poor tortured horse, invariably evokes across the border. But somehow, we were not as favourably impressed with the 'beauty and fashion' of the metropolis as with the 'masses.' It is a curious fact, which has been observed by others, that the fair Lusitanians do not show to advantage in public. Perchance the Paris fashions, which are *de rigueur*, do not readily adapt themselves to the forms of what an old writer calls a 'fat, squabsical race': a people who, a generation ago, sat crossed-legged, and generally affected the manners and customs of the Orient, and who even now will never walk if they can drive, or exert themselves as long as others can be found to do it for them. It takes a generation or two to work off the effects of such a manner of life, and to develop the lithesome figures of gymnasts. The process has not even begun in Portugal!

There is an air of dowdiness, moreover, in the way the wardrobe is 'thrown on,' combined with a glaring deficiency in the colour-sense which always grates, and, at times, absolutely 'knocks one down'; while the national tendency to *embonpoint*, even in very early middle age, which the fashions of Paris so unpleasantly emphasise, would much more readily lend itself to easy, flowing drapery, which, like charity, covers a multitude of defects.

Of course I know there are brilliant exceptions to all this, though, alas! these never appear in public. But I have read about them in books; and I remember one author in particular, who has exhausted all his very considerable powers of 'puff,' and a most extensive vocabulary, in cataloguing the charms and graces of the fair ones of Portugal. To be sure, the writer had never been in Portugal—but that is immaterial; for it is not necessary in these enlightened days for an author, who aspires to light up the dark places of the earth with the torch of knowledge, to draw the fire of inspiration from an original source.

For my own part, too,—it may be mere prejudice, but— much as I admire hirsute appendages, I think it a mistake in women to push the 'sincerest form of flattery' to such lengths as to be visible a mile off; and I shall always be of opinion that the cheeks of the fair ones should not be too suggestive of the whitewash-brush. But all this is a mere question of taste; and perchance there are cases in which the fortunate recipients of favours conferred may welcome the presence of an antiseptic medium, or even the velvety 'pile' of an incipient moustache. Englishmen, curiously enough, prefer a clean cheek with a rosy bloom on it, and would selfishly keep the advantages of a hairy face all to themselves. So grinding a taskmaster is prejudice!

No very celebrated bull-fighter took part in the performance we assisted at. But the next occasion was to be a 'star' performance, to be graced by the presence of no less a person than Senhor Rafael Guerra—commonly known by the *nom de guerre* of Guerrita,—the most redoubtable bull-fighter in all Spain. Posters announcing this important fact were displayed everywhere; and great, it was declared, would be the company of sightseers. Guerrita enjoys the modest little income of £12,000 a year—more than a Prime Minister. But what Prime Minister was ever half so popular with the 'masses' and the 'classes' as the nation's darling, Guerrita, or whose appearance in public ever roused one-half the enthusiasm this most famous killer of kine evokes every time he appears? He never sports his sacred person in the arena under the moderate fee of £250; while the presents, and other little odds and ends, showered on him by admirers may amount to about a third more—a salary which would enable a man of parts to dispense many charities, commencing at home. Guerrita has taken part in as many as eighty bull-fights in a single season; and this hero of more than a thousand battles is said to be a fine, active fellow, albeit not of an intellectual cast of countenance. Still, a man who kills his century of bulls every season must be a person of varied accomplishments and refined tastes, and the world may still expect great things from him. It is strange that a nation which can produce such a noble fellow, and give him a competence, cannot govern an island without shooting half the populace every few years, and making the world cry, 'Shame!' The return of the number of bulls Guerrita has killed is not issued as a government document; but it is a comfort to think that, although the poor fellow is in no immediate want, when his present job comes to an end he can take up the trade of 'butchering.' His favourite theme, just now, is sitting on a chair facing the bull; and as 'beefy' delivers his charge, Guerrita skips nimbly aside, while the chair goes careering around the arena on horn-tip. This is said to be a most inspiriting sight, and as long as the exploit is performed to the satisfaction of the public, no Spaniard will care a fig for the loss of Cuba, or any other 'realisable asset.' Last of all, let it be recorded to the credit of this fine fellow, that he has never been known to 'strike' for a 'living wage,' or for a reduction of working hours, with a view to the cultivation of his mind.

A week or two may be passed very pleasantly in Lisbon by any one who enjoys the sights and sounds of a foreign town. Locomotion is rendered cheap and easy by the tram-lines—one of the pleasantest trips being by the river-side to a village a mile or so beyond Belem, the return fare for which is about fourpence. Or, if driving be preferred, the *trens de aluguers* will be found extremely comfortable, the drivers civil, and the charges moderate; and once you are off the cobble-stones of the streets, the roads around Lisbon are well kept and easy to run on. The churches, alas! are wofully deficient in attractions, both externally and internally, their 'style' of architecture having been compared to old-fashioned French clock-cases, such as were designed 'with many a scrawl and flourish to adorn the apartments of Madame de Pompadour.' For this 'taste' the Portuguese are indebted to Pombal, who, in his superior wisdom, ordered all churches constructed after the too-famous earthquake to be built like houses, 'that they might not spoil the uniformity of the streets.' By poking about in the older parts of the city many interesting 'bits' may be discovered which the earthquake overlooked, and some notion may thus be gained of what Lisbon was like before the 'demon of progress' broke loose; while, by way of contrast, and as an antidote to the sights and smells of Old Lisbon, a visit to the new market, close to the Rocio, may be recommended. Here, at any time up to about eleven o'clock—when every self-respecting housekeeper has done her marketing for the day—a series of delightful surprises awaits the traveller from northern lands. The first-fruits of the earth are already in their prime in the early days of April: great piles of the delicious Setubal oranges, not to have tasted which is to be unacquainted with one of the purest joys of this world; heaps of plump and ruby-coloured cherries, and baskets of red strawberries, luscious and toothsome, though lacking in the flavour of our own produce; and flowers of the brightest hues, which old women and maidens are deftly massing into bouquets of sizes and prices to suit all purchasers.

Even more picturesque, in some ways, is the fish-market, near the Caes de Sodre; though to see this at its best and busiest the visitor must trot down at an early hour—between six and seven,—when the handsome fishergirls are assembled in their hundreds selecting their stocks from the infinitely varied collection here displayed in all the wondrous forms and tints that distinguish the fish in these southern seas.

A pleasant feature of the Lisbon streets is the large number of handsome fountains. For nearly two centuries the capital has revelled in an abundant water-supply brought into the city by the famous Alcantara aqueduct, 'the most colossal edifice of its kind in Europe.' The 'water-mains' of a city are not usually enumerated along with the 'sights' which it behoves a conscientious traveller to gaze on; but here, at Lisbon, they form the exception, for not to have seen the Arcos dos Aguas Libres and the vast reservoir into which this noble 'main' pours its never-failing supplies, is to miss one of the finest sights of Lisbon. A passing glimpse of this fine aqueduct is obtained from the river, just above Belem; but to realise its splendid proportions you must not only obtain permission to walk across it, or, at any rate, as far as the centre, but you must pass under the central arch. Every traveller has been impressed with this splendid structure; and even now, with vast engineering achievements abounding in all parts of the world—works that throw this into insignificance—you cannot gaze up at the noble simplicity of the Alcantara aqueduct, rendered venerable by the one hundred and eighty odd years that have swept by since it first took shape, without a feeling of respect for the merry monarch who called it into being. It was one of the few useful works which John the Fifth bestowed on his country; was built in 1713; and, what is even more remarkable, escaped unscathed from the effects of the great earthquake. The Alcantara aqueduct is a work worthy of imperial Rome in her best days.

A mere enumeration of figures and statistics is not only wearisome, but a most ineffective way of helping the reader to grasp the dimensions of a structure. A simpler way is to compare it with some well-known edifice at home. Comparing the Arcos dos Aguas Libres with the Clifton Suspension Bridge, we find them about equal in height at the centre—about 240 feet. But it is in its length that the Lisbon aqueduct so greatly exceeds Brunel's fine work, measuring no less than 2463 feet, as compared with the 702 feet of the other.

Beckford was immensely struck with it, declaring, as he gazed up at the lofty central arch, that it was 'with a sensation of awe, as if the building was the performance of some immeasurable being, endued with gigantic strength, who might take a fancy to saunter about his works some morning, and in mere awkwardness crush one to atoms.'

The water, after crossing the Alcantara valley, is conveyed, chiefly underground, to the centre of the city, where it empties into a vast reservoir, contained in a noble hall, with windows to admit light, and provided with a promenade round the sides. The roof is cleverly vaulted, forming on top a fine open space where, to our surprise, we found a tennis-court marked out. It is a pleasant spot to come to of an evening and watch the sunset lights playing hide and seek with the shadows, as they steal out from their midday haunts and slowly overspread the city. Near here, on one of the arches, may be deciphered the inscription which a grateful people caused to be engraved in honour of their sovereign-benefactor, King John v., the author of the Aguas Libres.

A part of the original scheme—which dates back to the time of Emmanuel—was to bring the water down to the

Rocio, where a superb fountain was to be prepared for its reception. Unfortunately, the scheme never got beyond the paper stage; but the design comprised an allegorical figure of Lisbon, standing on a column, guarded by four elephants, from whose trunks were to issue a perennial stream of purest water. It is a pity Pombal didn't complete the project when he rebuilt Lisbon, but he was no artist.

Lisbon had gone a little mad at the time of our visit over the newly appointed Brazilian minister. There had been a tiff of several years' standing between the 'daughter of Portugal' and her starched old mother, which had been patched up through the intervention of Great Britain — a circumstance which has in no wise added to the popularity of the 'ancient ally.' However, the reconciliation was a *fait accompli*; Lisbon was determined to let bygones be bygones, and to make up, by the intensity of her well-simulated affection for her daughter's representative, for coldness in the past. Banquets and festa-performances were the order of the day; speeches and fine compliments were the stock-in-trade, and everywhere the new minister was received with *éclat*. Now as this distinguished person was lodging at the Braganza, pending the preparation of a palace, we saw and heard a great deal more of the love-making than is of interest to outsiders. There was one little incident, however, we would not have missed for worlds, as it gave us a delightful insight into the etiquette of court-life below stairs—a phase of existence to which we were strangers.

Descending, one fine morning, into the entrance-hall of the hotel, we discovered four gorgeously apparelled gentlemen, who might have been mistaken for bull-fighters decked out for the ring, seated in solemn state on a mere form. Feeling abashed at sight of so much splendour at this early hour, we sought out monsieur the proprietor for information, and found him all mystery and suppressed laughter; and it was only after infinite gesticulation, and pointing to the mouth, that we discovered our imposing friends to be royal flunkeys, from the palace of His Royal Highness Dom Carlos, come to receive their *pour-boires* from the Brazilian minister, after having done him the honour of attending on him when he arrived!

To visit Portugal without seeing the abbeys of Alcobaca and Batalha would be as inexcusable as to tour through England without seeing Canterbury and York Minster; for they are the 'Battle Abbeys' of Portugal, and, at the same time, by far the finest specimens of ecclesiastical architecture in the kingdom. Like all important ecclesiastical buildings in Portugal, these abbeys were built by sovereigns in fulfilment of vows, and as memorials of important events in the nation's history. Alcobaca, the most ancient of the two, was founded by D. Affonso Henriques in 1148, to commemorate the capture of Santarem from the Moors, and may be regarded as commemorating three great events of national history—viz. the origin of the Portuguese monarchy, the institution of the Bernadine order of monks, and the introduction of a new species of architecture into Portugal, called Modern Norman Gothic. The church of Alcobaca is not only one of the earliest specimens of this particular style of architecture in Europe, but is cited by Murphy—an architect who travelled in Portugal a hundred years ago—as 'perhaps the most magnificent of the early period in which it was founded.'

The royal monastery of Batalha is of later date. It was founded by D. Joao I., in commemoration of his glorious victory over the Spaniards at Aljubarrota in 1385, whereby Portugal won her independence: an exploit regarded by all true patriots as one of the grandest in their national annals. The glory of Batalha is its church; and—as the Portuguese are fond of reminding strangers— in the words of one of their greatest writers, 'Who has not seen Batalha does not know what is finest amongst the *chefs d'œuvres* of art in Portugal!' Murphy, whose opinion has been endorsed by all competent judges, says that as an example of Modern Norman Gothic the church 'may be justly considered one of the most perfect and beautiful specimens of that style existing.'

Batalha lies about seven miles north of Alcobaca, and seventy from Lisbon, on low ground, in a small and once remote village; and I should be inclined to compare it with Ely of a century ago: while Alcobaca stands in a town, and might be compared with our St. Albans. Neither are much affected by the Portuguese, who are by no means ardent apostles of the 'gadabout school.'

The construction of the Lisbon-Leiria railway of late years has brought these places within easy access. The traveller is thus no longer dependent on the primitive piece of carriage architecture known in this land as a diligence; and a choice of routes is offered, seeing that there is a railway station within five or six miles of either place. But the most pleasant and convenient way is to make the expedition by carriage from Caldas da Rainha, with the alternatives of driving on to Leiria, or returning direct to Caldas. Public conveyances run from the latter place daily during the season at convenient hours, and if the traveller is not fastidious, or averse to close stowage in a warm climate and fertile soil, why, of course, these supply an economical way of accomplishing the trip.

We decided on making Caldas our headquarters, to enable us to see something of this fashionable watering-place—the Harrogate, or rather Bath, of Portugal,—and from thence to make the round of the abbeys at our leisure. What, however, confirmed us in our choice was the assurance that the hotel at Caldas was about the best one out of Lisbon.

According to a Portuguese guide-book, Caldas da Rainha is not only 'an important city, but the most fashionable and most frequented thermal station, resorted to not only by natives, but by strangers from neighbouring countries.' It is situated in 'a smiling and picturesque plain,' and has the further advantage of being within easy reach of the sea, an arm of which, forming a pleasant lake, extends to within a couple of miles of the place.

Its mineral waters are extremely efficacious in certain complaints; and when the Cintra season is over—for Cintra has a season—the beauty and fashion of the capital, or such as can afford the extra dissipation, repair to Caldas to take the waters and enjoy life in their own simple way. But let us hear what the Portuguese say of the place. 'During the season,' says the book afore-quoted, 'life at Caldas is delicious. There is a constant succession of amusements, balls, picnics [even the Portuguese have to come to us for a title for this particular *divertimento*], excursions, bull-fights, concerts; everywhere animation': from which the stranger would infer that Caldas must be a continuous whirl of gaiety during the season.

As there is just the usual one train a day between Lisbon and Caldas, the knowledge of this saves much puzzling over time-tables. Moreover, as travelling is conducted in very leisurely fashion in this country, and as the line in question passes through some pretty scenery, there is no cause to regret the dilatory progress.

The Lisbon-Leiria line traverses a part of Portugal which ought to be classic soil in British eyes, for it was in this corner of Europe that the first act of the great drama of the Peninsular War was enacted, when the raw and inexperienced soldiers of Britain proved their superiority to the war-worn veterans of Republican France. It was here too that Sir Arthur Wellesley gave Napoleon's generals a foretaste of his genius.

To derive the full measure of enjoyment from travel in Portugal it is essential that the visitor be well posted up in his Napier. For there is scarcely a province but has been hallowed by the shedding of British blood in the noblest of causes—that of European freedom. Viewed in the light of knowledge derived from a careful study of the epoch in question, the whole country seems to wear a new aspect, and every part of it becomes invested with interest. The traveller, indeed, who comes to Portugal without some acquaintance with the leading incidents of the Peninsular War, comes but ill-equipped for his wanderings: for he will miss the intense pleasure derivable from the study, on the spot, of scenes associated with some of the most glorious achievements of British arms. And yet, for every thousand Englishmen who rush off to Rome and Athens, steeped to their finger-tips in classical lore, scarcely one finds his way to Portugal, or comes provided with the intellectual equipment necessary for an appreciation of its history or of its close association with British military exploits. Such is the fruit of our boasted education!

As the train jogs athwart this lovely land, one's thoughts naturally revert to the past. The very names of the stations seem to have a familiar ring about them, recalling some incident of the war: while even more interesting are the landmarks which greet the eye as the train emerges from the picturesque Pass of Mafra, which played so important a part in the great defensive system which came eventually to be known as the Lines of Torres Vedras.

From here onwards the interest of the landscape never flags. A run of a few miles brings us to Pero Negro, a village at the base of the lofty Soccorro mountain, where Lord Wellington fixed his headquarters while holding the Lines.

This curious mountain rises almost in the centre of the position, midway between the first and second series of redoubts, its summit commanding every part of the advanced works. A signal-station was established on the top, from whence, by means of subsidiary stations, messages could be transmitted simultaneously to every part of the Lines; and these signal-stations were worked by officers and seamen from the fleet.

Running through the Zibreira valley, we come next to Duas Portas, and thence on to Runa, at both of which points the advanced posts of the hostile armies were in touch during the time they faced each other; while away on the high ground to the left, nestling amidst vineyards and fruit orchards, lies Ribaldiera and other villages, wherein the British troops holding this portion of the Lines were quartered, the handiwork of these soldiers, consisting of redoubts on the higher ground at the back, being sharply contoured against the skyline.

As we draw up at Runa, a large building embosomed in delightful gardens and orange-groves attracts attention. This is a home for old and disabled soldiers—the Chelsea

Hospital of Portugal: truly a pleasant spot to end their lives in.

At this point the line strikes the river Zizandro, which formed the chief obstacle to the French advance during the winter of 1810; and following the line of river, the railway plunges into a series of narrow and picturesque defiles, emerging at last in a level valley of no great extent, wherein lies the world-renowned town of Torres Vedras. Though of no size or commercial importance, the place is famed in the annals of the war from having given its name to the whole gigantic system by which the invading French were stayed in their career.

On a hill with precipitous sides, springing from the centre of the town, stand the remains of a Moorish castle; and all around may be noticed vestiges of the works by means of which this important place, commanding the principal roads to Lisbon, was rendered impregnable to attack.

How many glorious memories crowd the mind at sight of these imposing monuments of British skill, energy, and determination! In the eyes of the writer, who had studied every detail of their origin and construction, these works possessed an absorbing interest as he now gazed on them for the first time, thus realising the desire of a lifetime.

The principal aim of the engineers here was to obstruct, by works of immense strength, the mouth of the pass from whence the roads to Lisbon debouched; and to this end, the summits of commanding hills on either side were crowned with great redoubts, whose embrasures frown down on the traveller as he speeds past.

From here on to Caldas, every feature of the landscape is associated with some incident in the brief though glorious campaign which ushered in the tremendous

ANCIENT AQUEDUCT OVER THE RIVER ZIZANDRO AT TORRES VEDRAS

UNIV. OF
CALIFORNIA

struggle of the next eight years. There, for instance, away to the left, about six miles off, lies the battlefield of Vimiera, where British troops gave the final *coup* to Junot's army, and brought about the evacuation of Portugal, under the much-criticised 'Convention of Cintra.'

Glorious as it proved to the British soldier, the battle of Vimiera afforded striking proof of the aphorism that 'too many cooks spoil the broth,' no less than three generals having succeeded to the command while the battle was in progress, the 'Sepoy general' being considered at that time, by the wiseacres at home, as incompetent to command a British army in the field. Well might the 'intelligent foreigner' speak of the British army as being composed of lions governed by asses!

Between the stations of Bombarral and S. Mamede we almost cross the scene of what was in many ways the most interesting battle of the war—that of Rolica, where for the first time British troops crossed bayonets with the veterans of France, and drove those redoubtable warriors from pillar to post.

British military reputation at that time had sunk to a very low ebb: even British officers scouted the idea of our 'raw and inexperienced' soldiers being able to face the victorious legions of France; while British generalship, under the withering influence of aristocratic favouritism, had become a byword. Lord North was heard to remark, on looking over the names of certain generals recommended for high command in the field, 'I know not what effect these names may have on the enemy, but I know they make me tremble!' And the feeling was widespread that Britain had none capable of opposing the skilled leaders of the Republic. But Wellington had not only the ability, but, what was rarer, the experience, besides ample self-confidence; and in speaking of the probability of his being opposed ere long to the French, he said, 'At any rate, I shan't be afraid of them.' He knew that continental troops were always half-beaten before ever they came into contact with the French—the terror inspired by the very name being sufficient. On the other hand, Wellington's knowledge of British soldiers had assured him that, if properly led—not by asses—they might be depended on not only to face but overthrow any troops in the world.

When at length our small army was landed in Portugal, people regarded it as a veritable forlorn hope, which would melt away or would be swallowed up by the war-worn veterans of the Republic. But British soldiers in face of the enemy have never been unnerved by the craven fears of their superiors; and many a time has the grit and stubborn determination of the private pulled his superior 'asses' by their ears out of a 'tight place.' Wellington's feelings we know: let us see the spirit in which the British soldier entered on this the first campaign of the war.

A private, recording his experiences of the battle of Vimiera, says: 'They came upon us crying and shouting to the very points of our bayonets—our awful silence and determined advance they could not stand. They put about and fled.' And he continues: 'How different the duty of the French officers from ours! They, stimulating the men by their example; the men, vociferating: each chafing each until they appear in a fury. After the first huzza, the English officers restraining their men, still as death—"Steady, lads, steady," is all you hear, and that in an undertone.' Or take the following: 'We kept them at bay, in spite of their cries and formidable looks. How different their appearance from ours! Their hats set round with feathers, their beards long and black, gave them a fierce look. Their stature was superior to ours, and most of us were young. We looked like boys, they like savages. But we had the right spirit in us. We foiled them in every attempt.'

Such was the spirit in which British soldiers faced the finest troops of Europe at the ever-to-be-remembered battle of Rolica. And such is the spirit in which they face the enemies of the empire at the present day in every quarter of the globe. Ninety years, with all their changes and teachings, have rolled by since that glorious 17th August 1808, and still dyspeptic politicians question the capacity of the British soldier for meeting his continental foe, and still the plaint about 'boy soldiers' echoes through the land. Meanness of spirit combined with the 'neurotic habit' bears fruit in the systematic disparagement of British soldiers; but it has ever been the 'asses' at headquarters who have brought disaster on our arms, though even the combined folly and cowardice of statesmen have never been able to destroy the fine fighting qualities of British soldiers.

The traveller must be dull-witted indeed who can pass through scenes hallowed by such inspiring associations without imbibing something of the spirit of the past, and feeling a glow of triumph at the thoughts of the glorious deeds accomplished here by British arms. And yet, in the introduction to the *Journal of a Soldier*, above quoted, the editor was not ashamed to give expression to the following disgraceful sentiments: 'It is to be hoped that this little work may be found useful in counteracting the pernicious influence of the generally received maxim that there is something peculiarly honourable in the profession of arms.' And this snivelling wretch was at that moment enjoying, in the quiet and comfort of his editorial sanctum, the fruit of all the suffering and loss of life endured by British troops during the eight years of continuous campaigning against that 'insatiable despot,' Napoleon. But such was ever the way in which a certain despicable school of 'politicians' display their gratitude to the men who fought and bled for them. And even now, alas! there are Englishmen—so-called—who need to be reminded of Ernest Renan's apothegm: 'The most fatal error is to believe that one saves one's country by calumniating those who founded it.'

During the years that have rolled by since the stirring times of the Peninsular War, Portugal has been too deeply engrossed in faction fights, economical crises, and in hatching revolutions, to trouble herself overmuch about the battlefields whereon the intrepid soldiers of an alien race worked out the country's salvation. Never did a nation show less gratitude to her deliverers than the Portuguese; and little do the present-day inhabitants of the land trouble themselves about the brave fellows who lie in spots unmarked and uncared for on the heights of Rolica and Vimiera, and whose graves recall to mind the noble lines of the Rev. Charles Wolfe:—

> 'We thought, as we hollowed his narrow bed,
>   And smoothed down his lonely pillow,
> That the foe and the stranger would tread o'er his head,
>   And we far away on the billow.
>
> Lightly they'll talk of the spirit that's gone,
>   And o'er his cold ashes upbraid him:
> But little he'll reck, if they let him sleep on
>   In the grave where a Briton has laid him.
>
> Slowly and sadly we laid him down,
>   From the field of his fame fresh and gory:
> We carved not a line, and we raised not a stone,
>   But we left him alone in his glory!'

And so the hours slip by, until in front the castle of Obydos—another ancient Moorish stronghold—is observed crowning the top of a conspicuous hill, with the remains of a many-arched aqueduct. We draw up at the Obydos station, under the shadow of its castle, and are struck with the perfect state of the walls.

A run of three miles brings us to Caldas da Rainha station, where we exchange the train for a comfortable carriage and pair, and drive through uninteresting rows of one-storied whitewashed houses to our hotel, where we engage a large, airy room looking across a vine-trellised garden towards a picturesque water-mill. The front of the hotel faces the Passeio da Copa—literally, Walk of the Cup—what we should call the public promenade; 'provided with a magnificent grove of trees, and one of the most popular resorts of the bathers,' according to a local guide-book.

The same immaculate authority says—'The town possesses fine streets and squares, with modern structures of handsome appearance'; but I regret to say we never discovered any of these embellishments, and moreover, thought the Passeio the most unattractive spot we ever gazed on. We could not get inside, for the gates were locked—so precious is it considered.

Portugal is a land flowing with—well, if not milk and honey, the most excellent mineral waters; and those of Caldas are amongst the best, and, owing possibly to their proximity to Lisbon, by far the most fashionable. The use of these waters dates back to very early times, one of the most important events in local history being the establishment of an hospital here for poor patients in 1485, by 'the virtuous queen' D. Leonor, wife of D. Joao II., who, in order to carry out this most charitable work, sold her jewels—an act of self-denial which none but women can appreciate the full significance of.

I won't trouble the reader with an analysis of the waters; these and other scientific data can be studied elsewhere; but should curiosity or a desire for health stimulate a wish to try the Caldas waters, I can only give a word of advice—don't come here in the 'season'!

Having settled into our room, and the day being young, we set off on a voyage of discovery. The road took us past the Passeio — carefully locked,—where beauty and fashion loaf about between meals, and listen to brass bands discoursing the soulless airs which are so popular in this land, and seem admirably suited to a people who eschew the violent exercise of any part of the body except the jaws. The town wore just the same 'sickly, unprepossessing aspect' that Beckford complained of a hundred years ago, and at this 'dead' season can hardly be commended as a lively place of abode. But since he drew his amusing picture of the 'famous stewing-place,' a change for the better in one respect has taken place, for it is now quite possible to move about without 'running your head against the voluminous wig of some medical professor, or hearing the formidable stump of his gold-headed cane.' In those days 'every third or fourth person you met was a quince-coloured apothecary, accoutred like a courtier on his march to the drawing-room, and carrying many a convenient little implement in a velvet bag as pompously as if he had been a Lord Chancellor.' But, as often happens in this mad world, the scientific equipment of these gaily-attired Galenists was hardly adequate to the responsibilities they had so lightly assumed. Dr. Ehrhart, a German physician of note who had accompanied Beckford, was nearly thrown into a fit by the spectacle of so much pompous ignorance in the treatment of patients. 'I found many of them,' exclaimed the irate medico, 'with galloping pulses, excited almost to frenzy by the injudicious use of these powerful waters, and others with scarcely any pulse at all. The last will be quiet enough ere long.' And commenting on the dreadful havoc these determined Galenists wrought, with their 'decoctions, and juleps, and spiced boluses, and conserve of mummy, and the devil knows what,' Dr. Ehrhart added: 'I expect a general gaol-delivery must speedily take place, and the souls of these victims of exploded quackery be soon released from their wretched bodies, rendered the worst of prisons by a set of confounded bunglers.'

Scarcely had we set foot in the bathing establishment ere a Portuguese gentleman accosted us in excellent English, and finding we were strangers, courteously offered his services as cicerone. No proposal could have been more agreeable; and, gladly accepting the guidance of our new acquaintance—who proved, as the sequel will show, a charming companion as well as a most accomplished and cultivated gentleman—we proceeded to make the round of the sights.

I am no connoisseur in stewing arrangements, though, with some superficial acquaintance with the baths at home, as well as at a famous German watering-place, I can confidently affirm that, if on a less pretentious scale, this particular establishment was in excellent order. Scrupulous cleanliness reigned throughout, and I am assured by experts that the entire system of cure here has been brought thoroughly up to date. The provision for poor patients, moreover, is ample, for the Portuguese are essentially a benevolent people, and dispense their charities with liberality if not always with discretion.

But baths are not the liveliest subjects of investigation;

and as we soon extracted all the fun to be derived from this particular source, our obliging friend suggested a visit to the famous Fabrica de Faiancas, where is produced the much-sought-after-by-English-people Caldas ware—those curious plates with crabs and lobsters and lizards and snakes that adorn the walls of English homes. It was explained to us *en route* that the factory had originated in a private venture, but, as happens to nearly every industrial concern in this country, had come to grief, and is now a Government concern. Seeing that this faience is the only 'art-product' in Portugal, its disappearance would be matter of regret, and under the circumstances the conversion of the establishment into a Government department is the best thing that could have happened.

Of course a host of inferior imitators have sprung up, for this particular ware is now the *spécialité* of the town, and factories are met with in all parts of it; but the productions of these hardly merit the appellation of 'art' ware. On the other hand, nothing but the very best specimens, both in regard to quality and design, leave the Government factory, and this is presided over by 'the eminent artist, Senhor Raphael Bordallo Pinheiro,' a native gentleman of rare genius—sculptor, modeller, and painter.

The show-rooms contained some really exquisite samples, admirable in design, colour, glaze, and execution, every article bearing the impress of the genius of the artist-manager. None but highly skilled workmen are employed here, and they are well paid. We watched with interest the various processes by which 'mother earth' is kneaded and shaped into the quaint and piquant designs for which the factory is celebrated. An object of special interest

at the moment was a model of the Torre de Belem—
Anglicé, Belem Castle—on which the highest skill of the
establishment was being applied with a view to producing
a worthy memento of a recent visit of the celebrated
English-hater, Madame Adam.

Senhor Pinheiro being well known to our cicerone, we
obtained admittance, as a mark of special favour, to his
sanctum sanctorum, where we were shown some admirably modelled groups, half life-size, representing scenes
from our Lord's Passion, intended, I believe, to replace
others which once occupied some chapels at Bussaco.
Every detail was worked out with the most scrupulous
care and accuracy, and these groups will constitute a
really noteworthy contribution to sacred art.

Senhor Bordallo Pinheiro is a man of wide accomplishments and high attainments, and we could not but share
our friend's regret that there was not a wider and more
appreciative field open to him for the exercise of his
remarkable talents. But Portugal affords very little scope
for artistic genius, and in this respect has made but little,
if any, advance during the last hundred years. Is it not
a little singular that a country so richly endowed by
Nature should never have produced an artist or musician
with any reputation outside of his own country? But so
it is. How differently is Spain situated in this respect!
The productions of the Spanish school draw students from
all parts of the world. But the man who goes to Portugal
in search of art, whether ancient or modern, might as well
look for gems at a pork-butcher's!

Murphy's strictures on the neglect of the fine arts in
Portugal in 1789 are just as applicable to the present
time. For although, even in those far-away times, Portugal had some artists 'not devoid of merit,' they were not

encouraged. And Murphy instances the case of a Senhor Glama, who had studied for several years in Italy, and who, 'had he the incitement to call forth the latent powers that were imprisoned within him, would do credit to any school in Europe.' And yet this artist assured Murphy that he could scarcely eke out a miserable pittance, though he painted everything that was offered him, 'from the sign-post to the apostle.'

Senhor Glama was employed by the Right Honourable William Burton Conyngham, when travelling in Portugal, to make drawings of antiquities, etc., and if these exist now, they must be valuable.

If one may be allowed to form an opinion from the paintings—I won't call them 'works of art'—that adorn the royal palaces of Portugal, and from the miserable daubs exposed for sale in the shop-windows of Lisbon, art in Portugal must have sunk to a very low ebb indeed, and there seems to be absolutely no demand for it. There are pictures hanging in some of the royal palaces at the present moment that would disgrace a third-rate British lodging-house—which is saying a great deal.

Both at Oporto and Lisbon I visited so-called 'art exhibitions'—collections of pictures got together by itinerant dealers. The results in both instances were absolutely beneath contempt. Why is this so? There must surely be some flaw in the national character to account for such a general deficiency in the art instinct?

It may seem presumptuous in a mere bird-of-passage expressing such sweeping opinions on the subject of Portuguese art, but the absence of all right feeling on the subject is so painfully evident throughout the country that one can't help noticing it—it knocks you down everywhere. Moreover, the conclusions I have arrived at—after, possibly, a very superficial study of the matter—are in accordance with the opinions of competent judges. Mr. Oswald Crawfurd,[1] than whom no better authority exists, and who to a wide acquaintance with the art of Portugal unites a cultivated and critical taste, writing on the subject, says: 'Their paintings are exceedingly poor, their decorative art worse, and their architecture an outrage.' It was not always so. 'A hundred years ago there were good art products in Portugal, two hundred years ago there were better, and three hundred years back far better works still were done in art.' And he goes on to describe the beautiful art-work produced long ago, especially in silk, pottery, and faience. The reader who is interested in the subject should study the entire chapter on Portuguese art.

The curious thing is that the 'leisured classes' are the least artistic. 'In Portugal,' observes Mr. Crawfurd, 'where the wealthier classes once loved art, they have now lost all sense of rightness therein. It is a puzzle why this should be so, but I will only note the fact that the Portuguese middle and upper classes are as much lost to all sense of propriety in art as we ourselves were in England fifty years ago.'

It would be impossible for any 'school' of painting, sculpture, or architecture to flourish under such discouraging conditions. The tawdry, the vulgar, is rampant. In fact, the national shortcomings in this direction are too glaring to escape notice. Offences against good taste rise up and strike you everywhere, and at all times and seasons, in Portugal, and, I am fain to confess, spoil much of the pleasure to be derived from travel in this pleasant

[1] Late H.B.M. Consul at Oporto; author of *Round the Calendar in Portugal*, and other works.

land. The horrible outrages against good taste that are met with in the haunts of 'beauty and fashion,' and in the best hotels, would never be tolerated for a moment amongst any people who were not entirely dead to all sense of the natural fitness of things artistic.

No doubt the unsettled state of the country during the last ninety years has much to answer for; but the fact remains, that in Portugal 'the wage-earning class is the most art-loving; it is the middle and upper classes that are conspicuously unæsthetic.'

Our obliging friend, Senhor D——, on hearing of our intention of visiting the royal monasteries of Batalha and Alcobaca, at once offered his services in the matter of hiring a carriage and arranging all the details of the expedition. 'You English,' he justly observed, 'would be charged nearly twice as much as a native of the country.' We accordingly left the arrangements in his hands, and on learning that he had never yet visited those grand national monuments, we persuaded him to accompany us.

To accomplish the trip in a day, it was necessary to rise with the lark. Accordingly, the carriage was ordered to be at the hotel door a little before six next morning, at which hour we embarked, and after calling for Senhor D—— at his own house, set off on our long expedition. The road was excellent, the carriage extremely comfortable, the horses and driver all that could be desired; and though the air was sharp—almost cutting—the morning was exquisite, and in such a climate, and amidst such scenery as our route led us, all seemed to promise an enjoyable outing.

It was in just such weather—in June too—one hundred years ago, that Beckford passed over the very same ground,

and on the same errand, on almost the same day, the 7th—
it was now the 6th; and what he wrote concerning the
delights of travelling in the climate of Portugal exactly
accorded with our own experiences: 'The heat was
moderate, the sky of a pale, tender blue, inexpressibly
serene and beautiful. To breathe the soft air of such a
climate is in itself no trifling luxury; it seemed to inspire
new life into every vein; and if to these gifts of nature the
blessing of a good government and the refinements of art
were added, more philosophy than I am master of would
be required not to murmur at the shortness of existence.'

Our road led through a pleasant country, diversified
and undulating, fertile and well cultivated, with peeps
ever and anon of distant mountains and the blue Atlantic,
and the air redolent of aromatic plants; and had the sun
been never so hot, its rays must have reached us pleasantly
tempered by their passage through the dense foliage of
fine trees that lined the road for miles.

We crossed a river, and began to ascend higher ground
interspersed with pine woods, and affording more extensive views to the eastward than we had before enjoyed.

A century ago the greater part of this particular tract
of country was clothed in pine forest; but the French
armies, in their devastating marches and countermarches
through Portugal, completed a work of destruction which
had been already begun, by cutting down the trees and
grubbing up the very roots for fuel.

We are now passing close to the spot where once stood
'one of the strangest scenes of fairyland ever conjured
up by the wildest fancy.' Picture, stretching as far as eye
can reach, a close bower of evergreens, myrtle, bay, and
ilex, with arches of box most sprucely clipped, opening
into squares containing rare and curious flowers; and in

the midst of each of the trim parterres a marble fountain enclosed within a richly gilt cage containing birds of every variety of size, song, and plumage: paroquets with pretty flesh-coloured beaks, and parrots of the largest species, all busily employed cracking and grinding filberts and walnuts; picture in the centre of the largest of these flower-carpeted spaces an immense circular fountain of variegated marble, enclosed by a gilt metal balustrade, on which are most solemnly perched a conclave of parrots and cockatoos, whose screechings at sight of an intruder alarm a multitude of smaller birds, which rise in clouds from every leaf and spray of the vaulted walls of verdure. 'At sight of this,' says Beckford, 'I ran off as if I had committed sacrilege, or feared being transformed by art-magic into a biped completely rigged out with beak, claws, and feathers.'

The effect of this uncanny scene, through the strange green light which pervaded the closely bowered alleys; the soft, perfumed, voluptuous atmosphere of 'this seemingly enchanted garden,' combined with the rustle of wings and the chirping and twittering on every side, was so completely bewildering and magical, that Beckford says, 'I almost doubted whether ever again I should be permitted to emerge into common life or common daylight.'

But the strangest sight of all was the sovereign mistress of this paradise, seated in the grand saloon of the establishment, which was far from presenting a palace-like appearance, being in height only one story. Her excellency was seated at its upper end in a high-backed wicker chair, stuck close to the wall. 'Seven or eight old hags of a most forbidding aspect, all in black, and all more sincerely bearded, I make no doubt, than the Countess Trifaldi's attendants, were ranged to the right and left on narrow benches, forming one of the ugliest displays of tapestry my eyes had ever encountered.'

The description of this paradise, and of the interview with the eccentric Senhora who ruled over the strange menagerie, fills several pages of Beckford's fascinating volume, and is well worth reading.

But

> 'Whither is fled the visionary gleam?
> Where is it now, the glory and the dream?'

Alas! not a vestige remains even to mark the site whereon this enchanted garden once stood. Within ten months of Beckford's visit the place was suffered to fall into ruin, and its feathered inhabitants were dispersed and destroyed upon the death of their mistress. The French troops, later on, in search of fuel and other things, gave the finishing stroke.

Other scenes soon crowd out the vision of that strange quinta, and any lingering regrets for the unrecoverable past give place to rejoicings that the road, at any rate, is not as it was in those far-away times, when 'there was no distinct track,' and the carriages fairly stuck fast and had to be pulled out by the combined efforts of 'forty well-clothed peasants,' under the supervision of a very efficient magistrate.

Here were we, rolling along in comfort, over roads as smooth and noiseless as the finest gravel-paths of an English garden.

The fat lands we were passing over once formed part of the magnificent heritage pertaining to the royal monastery of Alcobaca; and although it is to be feared the wealthy owners neglected their roads, and only provided 'ruinous bridges, unprotected by any parapet,' yet, as landlords, they were neither griping nor tyrannical; and the pleasant Arcadia Beckford has painted shows how much happiness, content, and outward prosperity was compatible with rottenness within. 'Here every object smiled,' he wrote. Every rood of land was employed to advantage, the Lombard system of irrigation being perfectly understood and practised. Every cottage, apparently the abode of industrious contentment, had its well-fenced garden richly embossed with gourds and melons, its abundant water-spout, its vine, its fig-tree, and its espalier of pomegranate. Such was the enticing scene that presented itself to Beckford's critical eye in 1796.

In reply to frequently repeated questions as to who taught them all this admirable system of cultivation, the invariable answer of the peasants was, 'Our indulgent masters and kind friends, the monks of the royal monastery.'

I repeated all this to Senhor D——, who fully confirmed the Englishman's high estimate of the monkish landlords; and he assured me that for such knowledge as the country people still possessed of viniculture, silk manufacture, and the management of their stock, they are indebted to the monks; and that since the suppression of the orders, evil days had befallen the land; that the peasantry are now taxed beyond endurance, agriculture has gone back rather than advanced, and the rural populace—the backbone of the country—are emigrating in thousands to the Brazils.

Beckford's subsequent remarks on the suppression of the monasteries are noteworthy. He writes: 'The revenue of the royal monastery of Alcobaca, at the time of my excursion to it, considerably exceeded £24,000, and the charities such wealth enabled the monks to dispense were most ample, and judiciously applied. Since those golden days of reciprocal goodwill and confidence between the landlord and tenant, the master and the servant, what cruel and arbitrary inroads have been made upon individual happiness! What almost obsolete oppressions have been revived under new-fangled, specious names! What a cold and withering change, in short, has been perpetrated by a well-organised system of spoliation, tricked out in the plausible garb of philosophic improvement and general utility!'

Over the admirable roads that now exist, and with excellent horses, the kilometres flew; and at 8.30 we drew up at the Gallinha Hotel at Alcobaca, ordered breakfast, and, while the preparations were in progress, set off to see the famous Mosteiro e egreja de Santa Maria de Alcobaca. A few steps brought us within view of its imposing front, which covers 620 feet of ground, and extends back a distance of some 750 feet. We tried to picture the impressive scene that met the gaze of the English traveller a hundred years ago, when the whole monastic community, four hundred strong, was drawn up in grand spiritual array before the monastery to bid the distinguished party welcome, while at their head stood the Lord Abbot in the splendid costume of High Almoner of Portugal. Alas, how far away it all seemed; and how much of the picturesqueness of life has gone out with the orders!

What a magnificent pile! dwarfing our Fountains and Glastonbury as the oak of four centuries dwarfs the sapling of yesterday. A native author, in speaking of the monastery, declares that 'its cloisters are cities, its sacristy a church, and the church a basilisk.'

The church occupies the central position, its west entrance forming the most attractive feature, and claiming attention first of all. On entering, to quote the words of

E

Murphy, 'one is struck with the grandeur of that general effect peculiar to the inside of Gothic churches, but very few possess that property to a higher degree than this.' The leading characteristics of the edifice, together with its merits and demerits, having been fully described by Murphy, and more recently by Kinsey, I shall simply confine myself to an account of such features as particularly attracted our attention.

The history of Alcobaca seems to resolve itself into three periods. First, we find the convent in the heyday of its career (1796), great, powerful, and wealthy—so wealthy indeed that the revenue derived from its vast domains is said to have rendered it one of the richest and most magnificent institutions of its kind, not only in Portugal but in Europe. The extent of the dominions over which the fathers owned sway may be gauged in some measure from the fact of its royal founder having endowed it with all the land and sea that could be seen from the summit of a mountain commanding a very extensive view.

Thirty years roll by, with all their changes—revolution, war, invasion, and desecration, the abbey shorn of much of its splendour, its revenues reduced, its monkish population brought down from four hundred to fifty, and now bearing on every feature of its life the clearly marked lines of age and the trials through which it has passed. Still it lives, though life is somewhat of a struggle; the attempt to keep up appearances, something of its ancient splendour, even on a diminished scale, entailing sore trials. Its days, though, are numbered; the time of departure of the orders is at hand; the stern decrees of fate are slowly developing in the womb of time, and even now the writing on the wall is discernible to those who have eyes to see—

the warnings are echoing through the cloisters loud enough for those who have ears to hear.

Seventy years more sweep over the royal monastery, bringing us to the present day. What momentous changes has the revolution of time brought in its train!—civil war, constitutional government, the power of the Church broken, the religious orders suppressed, monks and friars dispersed, Heaven knows where! their wealth appropriated to 'national purposes,' their vast domains 'restored to the country,' and, last step in the ruin and degradation of the once all-powerful monastic establishments, the seizure of the monasteries and their conversion to secular uses—this one a parliament-house, that a barrack, another government offices, and Alcobaca itself?—well, we shall see!

Of the three epochs the first is the most interesting, if not the most instructive; and so far as the monasteries of Alcobaca and Batalha are concerned, we are fortunate in the possession of such complete pictures of them in their golden prime as few other monasteries in Europe can boast of. Between 1789 and 1795 these establishments were visited, and their life carefully studied, by two intelligent and cultivated Englishmen, who have placed their impressions on record with a fulness of detail, not to say piquancy, that leaves little to be desired.

Of the two visitors, the architect Murphy—'that dull draughtsman,' as Beckford calls him—was the earliest; he spent three weeks here as a guest of the monks, studying the architecture and making careful drawings of the church and monastery for his patron, the Right Honourable William Burton Conyngham. During his residence he must have seen much of the inner life of the convent, though doubtless from a chivalrous feeling for the sacred character of his hosts he has left but a meagre account of his experiences in his *published* writings, though in his *unpublished* MS. he has been more explicit on the evils of monasticism.

Beckford came a few years later, under such powerful auspices and under such exceptional circumstances as have probably never been vouchsafed to any other Englishman. Moreover, being a cultivated man and an accomplished linguist, and combining a thorough command of the Portuguese language with an extensive acquaintance with native literature, Beckford was exceptionally favoured; and being endowed with high sensibility, and, as he himself says, 'not unapt, chameleon-like, to take the colour of what happens around, and to enter fully into the fashion of the place,' it may be supposed he was able to make good use of his opportunities. The result is one of the most fascinating pictures of monastic life that literature can produce. Even Lord Carnarvon, whose work on Portugal has been justly admired, speaks of 'Beckford's splendid account of this convent.'

To be sure, Beckford's stay here was brief, and it would be natural to surmise that a 'lightning sketch,' dashed off after so short a 'sitting,' would be of little value. But Beckford enjoyed quite unique opportunities of getting at the kernel of things, and as his book was not published until many years later, he had ample leisure in the meanwhile for digesting the information he had acquired during a long residence in Portugal.

Apart from its value as a portrait of a famous monastery in the days of its prime, no more fascinating story of travel was ever offered to the public. It has lost none of its freshness through age; and assuredly the traveller who visits Portugal without first reading Beckford's brilliant narrative loses half the pleasure of his trip.

And what makes the portrait all the more interesting is that we seem to be transported back to our own monastic period, and to be gazing into the cells, the cloisters, the refectory, and last—though by no means least in the scale of monkish economy—the kitchen, of our own Fountains, Glastonbury, or perchance St. Albans, when their abbots were a power in the land, and kings partook of their hospitality and made havoc of their cellars. The whole strange scene is conjured back into life once more. And what a scene it is! What wealth, and what regal splendour can be displayed when the abbot wishes to honour his guests! Truly might the monk of Alcobaca exclaim, as he smote his belly, 'My lot is fallen in a goodly heritage!' Whether the state of things depicted by Beckford and Murphy came within the intentions of the founders may be open to question: whether it was worth preserving must be left to the judgment of the reader.

A brilliant spectacle, truly, the abbey must have presented when tricked out in full dress! Who then could have helped falling under its spell? But the spectacle of so much wealth could not fail to excite envy even in those days. Murphy says that although of late years some of its privileges had been restrained, 'many people, however, are of opinion that it still possesses too many; they also think the revenue is too great, from an idea that wealth promotes feasting more than fasting and prayer. But during a residence here of nearly three weeks I could perceive no just grounds for such remarks; on the contrary, I found the greatest decorum and temperance, blended with hospitality and cheerfulness, prevail in every part.' And speaking of the manner in which the fathers dispensed the charities of the abbey, he says, 'hundreds of indigent people are constantly fed at their gates,' and their tenantry were apparently as comfortable as any in the kingdom. Comparing the attitude of the fathers with lay-landlords, he remarks: 'Those who declaim against their opulence would do well to inquire whether there be a nobleman or gentleman in Europe, possessed of a revenue equal to that of this monastery, who diffuses so many blessings among his fellow-beings as the fathers of Alcobaca.'

Murphy gives us a flattering picture, almost an ideal one, such as every good monk strove to realise. But is it a true one? Was Murphy sincere? Or was it a case of 'You tickle me, Toby, and I'll tickle you'? A visitor who had partaken of the hospitalities of the fathers for three weeks would be loth to 'look the gift-horse in the mouth'; he would naturally be to their faults a little blind, and make the most of their virtues.

Now, unfortunately for Murphy's reputation as a veracious historian, he has left two versions of his impressions. The published one we know; and although he was a Catholic, and therefore inclined to be towards the monkish failings very kind, he was not, it seems, an unqualified admirer of monastic life, seeing that in the unpublished portion of his journal he says, with special reference to Batalha, 'that the mass-friars have nothing to do but to eat and to drink, saunter about, or sleep. The prior is a plain, homely kind of man, distinguished from the rest only by a small black cap, and the privilege of wearing a dirty face. What a pity it is,' he continues, 'to see so many stout fellows leading a life of indolence and sloth that might be of service in cultivating the land, in feeding the poor, and enriching or defending their country!'

We seem to catch the echo here of certain sentiments expressed fifty years earlier by a liberal and enlightened

Secretary of State, who, albeit a Catholic, and well aware, as he himself says, that his opinions 'might appear violent,' and his antidote for the evils under which his country was suffering 'be thought poison,' declared, in a remarkable document which never saw light during his life, that 'this shall not prevent me from considering what means ought to be taken against the abuses which disgrace religion and ruin the kingdom.' The great evil was the number of convents 'of monks and nuns established over all the provinces, and in all the towns of this kingdom, multiplying the mouths that eat, but not the hands that labour, and living at the cost of those who, that they may support themselves and pay the tributes imposed on them, must plough and sow and reap what God has given them with the sweat of their brows. The natural indolence of the Portuguese increases the abuse: they can procure food by their profession, without the trouble of labouring for it, and without performing the duties of citizens.' And then he goes on to point out that men are the real mines of the State, that continually produce, yet never are exhausted. 'But what men are they?' he pertinently asks: 'men who cultivate the earth; men who labour that they may live and multiply, men who serve the Prince and the Republic by land and by sea in the offices of commerce.'

Reading between the lines of Beckford's sparkling narrative, we get glimpses of a fondness for soft living, a liking for the pleasures of the table, and of a pervading sense of boredom, which finds expression in theatricals—and other things which need not be mentioned here. Even Murphy has to admit that 'it is very remarkable that these people, avowedly assembled for the purposes of studying as well as praying, have not a library in their convent, unless that deserves the name of one which is not larger than a closet,[1] and scarcely contains as many books as there are pipes of wine in the cellar'; adding, with a touch of irony: 'We should not omit to notice the cellar, as it is one of the most valuable apartments belonging to the monastery.'

No library, but a big cellar! Here we have the monastic *motif* in a nutshell! There was not a 'Ha'penny Comic' or a 'Penny Dreadful' to relieve the tedium of the midnight vigil. Still, there was the kitchen: 'the most distinguished temple of gluttony in all Europe,' as Beckford caustically remarks of the wonderful apartment that was 'dedicated to culinary purposes' at Alcobaca, and of which he has given a quite inimitable picture.

Deeply significant, too, is the parting scene: 'Great were the lamentations in Alcobaca when the hour of our departure arrived—a voice of wailing scarcely equalled in Rama, when Rachael wept for her lost children. Had my Lord Abbot been the father of a dozen brats, he would sooner have spared the whole treasure than have lost the advice and exertions of a being he venerated above all others without any exception—a matchless cook. It was a cruel separation: the artist himself, who had a susceptible heart, as well as a hand gifted with the most exquisite sauce-making sensibilities, was far from being callous to the raptures of such a discriminating gourmand as the ruler of Alcobaca.' Delightfully naïve, too, was the *chef*'s excuse, on being rallied at the unwonted display of so much devotion at mass before setting out on the journey: 'Simon,' said Beckford, 'my Lord Abbot seems to have quite reconverted you; you are becoming astonishingly religious.' 'Ah, Monsieur, on le sera, à moins.

---

[1] The library described by subsequent visitors must have been a later creation.

Monseigneur rend la religion si aimable.' Monsieur Simon was not the first, nor the last, to fall under the spell of religion when made sufficiently pleasant. The effect of gorgeous apparel, coloured lights, sweet smells, and seductive music, in evoking the 'religious instinct' in some hearts is quite remarkable; though, to be sure, it would be difficult to quote precedent for such methods of conversion from the early Church.

And here, as the distinguished Englishman drives off, leaving my Lord Almoner standing on the grand terrace, 'with his eyes fixed on the pavement before the grand portal, immovable, and as if he had turned to stone,' the curtain drops on the drama of monastic life in the year 1795, and we are left to our own imaginings as to what went on during the intervening thirty years that elapsed before we are given another view of the interior.

From certain pretty broad hints dropped by Beckford, to say nothing of a certain private conference that took place just before his departure, and during which, in spite of closed doors, was heard 'a loud storm of indistinct but angry words approaching to a tempest, the exact import of which it is not in my power,' wrote Beckford, 'to reveal, supposing I had the inclination,' it would seem that even the royal monastery was not without its 'skeleton in the cupboard'—the one touch of human nature which makes the whole world kin, no matter what the garb which man in his pride and folly chooses to deck himself in.

From information imparted, 'though rather vaguely,' in after days, it would appear that the interview had reference to 'certain grotto-like communications between this sacred asylum [Alcobaca] and another not less monastic, though tenanted by the fairer portion of the holy communities—the daughters of prayer and penitence.'

The mention of which recalls certain 'unedifying frailties' into which the inmates of our own St. Albans were beguiled; reports of which, having reached even to Rome, shocked the tolerant worldliness of the much-enduring Pope, with the result that Cardinal Morton was ordered to visit the abbey and report; which said 'report' is to be seen in *Morton's Register* at Lambeth, and shows— as related by Froude in his *Annals of an English Abbey* —that the brethren of the abbey were living on terms of familiarity with the inmates of the dependent sisterhoods; that the adjoining Nunnery of Pray was a scandal to society, the prioress setting an example of indecorum which was too widely followed.

During the next thirty years the inmates of Alcobaca passed through the cleansing fire of suffering and deprivation, and emerged, let us hope, with chastened spirits— the royal monastery having been visited successively by French and English armies.

One would give a great deal to know all that took place on those interesting occasions, but the annals, so far as is known, are silent. It may be inferred, however, that even a friendly visitation of this sort would prove somewhat of a tax on the monastic resources—albeit with an income of £25,000; for, when French liberators threw themselves on the hospitalities of the fathers, there was not even the consolation of perchance entertaining angels unawares. The consequences would be worse even than John Lackland's visit to St. Edmundsbury, which proved so ruinous by 'tearing out the bowels of the convent (its larders, namely, and cellars) by living at rack and manger there.'

Hungry soldiers are not over scrupulous in their treatment of larders and hen-coops. But, at any rate, bare-faced plunder and wanton sacrilege is never tolerated in an English army on active service; and our soldiers, rough fellows as they were, seem to have mostly contented themselves with scribbling their names on the monastic plaster, intent on achieving immortality of some sort.

It was one of Napoleon's maxims that 'the country must support the war,' an injunction which the missionaries of the new religion of 'liberty, equality, and fraternity' were not slow to interpret in a manner agreeable to themselves. Assuredly no swarm of locusts ever swept a country cleaner than did the French armies who came to 'free' the Peninsula. Those 'disciplined brigands'—as Sir Walter Scott called them—had come to pillage, if not to stay, and pillage they did! And, not content with robbery, rape, and rapine, these ruffianly soldiers made a point of wantonly destroying every noble building that had afforded them shelter. Very sad to gaze on, even now, is the destruction wrought by the 'Philistine armies of France,' who seemed to take a savage delight in degrading to the utmost of their power those buildings consecrated to the purposes of religion.

Here, at Alcobaca, the traces of their vandalism are so palpable to the eye that 'those who run may read.' Commencing with the church, those 'enlightened barbarians,' as Lord Carnarvon calls them, set fire to the building, by which the arch of the roof between the choir and the nave was destroyed, and the two organs which formerly occupied positions on either side of the choir-screen were also burnt. Amongst the most interesting and beautiful memorials that the church contained were the splendid sepulchres of white marble, containing the remains of the romantic couple, Dom Pedro I. and the unfortunate Inez de Castro, whose tragic death forms one of the most romantic stories in the annals of Portuguese royalty. In a sacrilegious attempt to drag to light the imagined treasures of these tombs, the French destroyed some of the finest sepulchral carving by making large holes in various parts of the effigies which crown the tombs. They even dragged the royal pair from the vault where they lay: 'the countenances of the dead,' according to monkish tradition, 'wearing the expression they bore when alive.' Dona Inez was still lovely: 'her hair retained its auburn colour, and, unharmed by time,' was only injured by the remorseless hand that did not scruple to invade the dwellings of the dead. Her scattered locks were afterwards carefully collected by the monks and religiously preserved.

All the gold and silver utensils belonging to the service of the church were carried off and melted down by the French under Drouet, while the busts and relics of saints over the altar, together with the beautiful shrine-work in fine mosaic, were grievously damaged.

Amongst the literary treasures the monastery formerly possessed were a copy of Mickle's translation of the *Lusiad*, presented by Lady H. Frances O'Neill, 'in grateful acknowledgment of many and repeated attentions from the Illmos Rms Snres Religioszos de San Bernado em Alcobaca,' dated December 14th, 1791; a Glasgow Homer (1756), given by Lord Strathmore and Cavalheiro Pitt, after their first visit to the monastery in 1760; and lastly, a very fine edition of the *Iliad*, presented to the fathers by Mr. Canning, in acknowledgment of hospitalities received, in March 1816, and containing a Latin inscription in his own handwriting.

But the monastic orders were doomed: they had played their part in the economy of civilised life, and the fiat for their extinction was already taking shape. And yet, regardless of the writing on the wall, the fathers ate, and drank, and cracked the monastic joke, as if the foundations of their order were rooted in eternity, confident in their power of weathering the political storms of the future, as they had withstood the rougher seas of war that had surged around their domains in the past.

Lord Carnarvon, who visited Alcobaca in 1827, describing a supper he partook of here, wrote: 'This meal seemed to be their most jovial repast'—a succession of regular courses were served up, and afterwards wine and dessert were laid on the table. 'We sat long: old convent tales went round, legends of interposing angels were told, and anecdotes of friars long dead and gone excited peals of merriment.'

Eyes less blinded than theirs might have perceived the sword of Damocles hanging over them as they feasted; for even their guest, impressed, as he confessed himself to have been, with an 'awful sense of monastic grandeur,' could not shut out the solemn fact that those 'heaven-devoted structures' were already marked by the spoiler. 'Even then I felt their hours were numbered, and that the coming age would know them not.' The multitude, ever impressed with an overmastering sense of grandeur, never doubted the power of the orders to resist every attack; 'but the bolt,' added Lord Carnarvon, 'though still enveloped in the silent cloud, was rife for their destruction.'

A few more years and the bolt had fallen, and one more connecting-link with the past was severed. The story of the suppression of the orders in Portugal, though full of interest to the student of religion and of human progress, is too long to insert here. Suffice it to say that their wealth and magnificence bore within them the seeds of their destruction, by exciting the avarice of their enemies, and seducing their inmates from the path marked out by the pious founders. 'Religious luxury is an evil which requires to be checked,' wrote a far-sighted Portuguese Catholic a hundred years earlier. 'The orders are too rich. The Church ought seriously to consider that its wealth may one day be its destruction.' Prophetic words!

The blow fell with especial severity on the monastery of Alcobaca. Referring to the manner in which the decree was carried out, Lord Carnarvon, writing with a full knowledge of the facts, observes: 'The desecration of the convent of Alcobaca, one of the most magnificent monuments of the kingdom, was at once an insult to the religious feelings of the people, and disgraceful to the taste of the modern Portuguese.'

Sixty years have rolled by since then, and behold how altered is the aspect of the monastery! Externally, both convent and church present much the same appearance as of yore. But pass within, and all resemblance ends: the interior is now a mere wreck of its former self; the shell remains but the spirit has fled, and everywhere ruin, decay, and shameful neglect—emblematic of the nation whose property it is—stare one in the face. I hardly know which form of desecration excites the greater indignation—the destruction wrought by the French soldiers, or that of 'their imitators, the modern Portuguese.' Our friend Senhor D—— was pained and grieved at sight of so much vandalism, declaring that the thought of what the French had done to his country's most splendid national memorials 'made him hate them.' He even expressed regret that the edifices were not in English hands, for their better preservation. Suffice it to say that Alcobaca is now a cavalry barrack!

The edifice is kept water-tight, which is all that can be said; though, by a decree of D. Maria II., some years ago, the preservation of the whole as a national historical memorial was ordained. In a side-chapel is preserved an interesting memento of the victory of the Portuguese over the Castilian army at Aljubarrota, in the form of an immense bronze caldron which had been used for preparing the food for the Spanish soldiers, and was found on the field of battle.

We entered the sacristy, 'the gorgeous and glistening' apartment of Beckford's day, 'worthy of Versailles itself'; once adorned with furbelows of gilt bronze, 'flaunting over panels of jasper and porphyry.' Some copes and vestments were 'almost as ancient as the reign of Alfonzo Henrique, and others embroidered at Rome with gilt and pearls, by no means barbaric.' As no lynx-eyed lay-brother 'shadowed' us, we took a furtive glance into the drawers and cupboards, which concealed some particularly gorgeous vestments, but all in a state of moth, damp, and shameful neglect.

Then we wandered into the cloisters, where once stood a fountain, half hidden by the gnarled and crabbed branches of orange-trees, whose age was most venerable a hundred years ago, seeing that, according to monkish tradition, they were the first orange-trees imported into Portugal from China. But here again all was ruin and disorder.

We now placed ourselves under the guidance of a soldier—a civil and obliging lad, more intent, however, in impressing us with the economy of barrack life than in initiating us into the mysteries of a defunct monasticism. After being dragged round stables and barn-like quarters, we gently hinted that a sight of the old library—or even the kitchen—would be an agreeable relief. So off we set, mounting stairs and threading passages innumerable, and arriving at last at a truly noble apartment, which we were assured had been the library—it was now a barrack-room. The books—where were they? I remember reading in a work published some forty years ago, that the contents of the monastic libraries were then 'rotting in the collegiate vaults at Coimbra.' Let us hope that, under the influence of the renaissance spirit, of which we hear so much—and see so little—in Portugal, these literary treasures have been excavated and placed in a drier cupboard.

To visit Alcobaça without seeing its kitchen would be as bad as going to Rome without visiting St. Peter's; for there, in its golden days, all the learning, devotion, and industry of the convent was centred. 'Not an inch of it was unoccupied from morning to night,' wrote Murphy; the lay-brothers and their attendants, 'singing all the while as blithely as larks in a corn-field.' The results of so much research and industry would have been hard to beat, even in the culinary palace of Glastonbury in its palmy days, if Beckford's appetising accounts of the banquets dispensed here afford a just measure of its capabilities. To be sure, under such appreciative auspices as were then installed in this royal convent there was every inducement to a true artist to put forth his best endeavours. 'There,' said my Lord Abbot to his guests, pointing to the odds and ends of victuals displayed, 'we shall not starve! God's bounties are great; it is fit we should enjoy them.' And assuredly if gratitude, in the form of hearty appreciation of 'God's bounties' here on earth, meets with its reward hereafter, a most happy future awaited the holy fathers of Alcobaça.

And what a palatial chamber it is! measuring, says Murphy (who, being an architect, albeit a 'dull draughtsman,' may be depended on for his figures), near a hundred feet long by twenty-two wide, and sixty-three feet from the floor to the intrados of the vaults. The two most remarkable features of this temple are, first, the central fireplace, twenty-eight feet by eleven, with access on all sides, the fumes being carried off by a pyramidal chimney resting on cast-iron pillars: the other, a brisk rivulet of the clearest spring water running through the centre of the hall, and in and out of pierced wooden reservoirs, once stocked with the finest river fish. By an ingenious contrivance the stream could be made to overflow the pavement and carry off all impurities. Such was the interior of 'the most distinguished temple of gluttony in all Europe.'

The kitchen still exists, it is true, but

'Fallen from its high estate,
Deserted at its utmost need,
By those its former bounty fed.'

No rarities nor delicacies of past seasons and distant countries; nor strange messes from the Brazil, and others still stranger from China, 'dressed after the latest mode of Macao, by a Chinese lay-brother'—to such perfection was 'the art of dining' brought in those barbaric times! —no morsels such as these now leave the kitchen, for it is the barrack cook-house. Dinner preparations were going forward at the moment of our entry, and the food seemed wholesome and abundant, but oh, 'what a falling off was there!' Dirt and neglect had full sway; even the beautiful tiles that once encased the walls were tumbling off, and lay in a heap of shattered fragments in a corner. A passion for relics prompted an application to be allowed to carry away a small fragment; but the sacrilegious proposal was firmly though civilly refused, as was to be expected from the guardians of so religiously cherished a memorial of prehistoric gourmandising.

'Lead us to the garden!' we cried, in the hope that there, at any rate, might be found some lingering regard for order and appearances. 'The garden!' exclaimed our conductor in amazement, wondering what we meant. At length, after consulting with his elders, he led us to an open space in rear, where some yokels were being initiated into the mysteries of the goose-step. Some recently-made graves attracted our notice, and in the centre we observed the remains of what appeared to have been a pond or lake.

This, then, was all that remained of the lovely garden of former times—with its shady arbours, its cypresses cut into representations of men, 'some in the act of shooting, and others praying; some with long cues, and others with perukes.' The very rabbit-warren had been improved off the face of the earth: and yet it was one of the sights of Portugal, with its five or six thousand plump occupants!

It was with melancholy feelings and troubled thoughts that we retraced our steps to the hotel. Of a truth

'we had been
Moving about in worlds not realised.'

Breakfast over, we resumed our route to Batalha. The same excellent road carried us under shady trees and through pine woods, and a few miles run at a rattling pace brought us within sight of the village of Aljubarrota, which lent its name to the greatest victory in Portuguese annals.

Senhor D——, who had hitherto kept us amused and interested with his conversation, became silent and meditative, and after a long pause explained that we were passing over ground which, by reason of its glorious associations, appealed strongly to every true lover of his country. While respecting his feelings, and admiring his patriotism, we could not but contrast his attitude towards the past with the behaviour of my lords the Grand Priors of Aviz and San Vincente, on a similar occasion, just a hundred years ago. 'I tried to inspire my right reverend fellow-travellers with patriotic enthusiasm, and to engage them to cast a retrospective glance upon the days of Lusitanian glory,' says Beckford. But well-ordered lives of self-restraint had petrified their tastes in a spiritual mould. 'Times present, and a few flasks of most excellent wine, the produce of a neighbouring vineyard, engrossed their whole attention. *Muito bom—primoroso—excellente*, were the only words that escaped their most grateful lips.'

There, away to the right, on that very plain, was fought in 1385 the fierce battle which placed the diadem of Portugal on the brow of the glorious and intrepid bastard, Dom John I. And, under the guidance of our obliging cicerone we were enabled to distinguish, from the carriage, the several points in the landscape associated with the crises of the battle. There, away in the distance, amongst the blue mountains, was the very pass through which the Castilian army had entered Portugal; there, the ravine through which their cavalry was driven like a flock of frightened sheep; and there, towards the south, was the line the defeated and enraged King of Castile followed on his frenzied retreat to Santarem, when all was lost—including his tent, his chapel with all its priceless contents, not to mention the cooking-caldron afore-mentioned. 'The Constable hath informed me,' wrote the Archbishop of Braga to the Abbot of Alcobaca, in 'old Portuguese,' after the battle, 'that he saw the King of Castile at Santarem, who behaved as a madman, cursing his existence and tearing his beard. And in troth, my good friend,' he added, significantly enough, 'it is better he should do so to himself than to us: the man who thus plucks his own beard, would be much better pleased to do so unto others.'

The particular circumstance which invested this classic ground with additional lustre in our eyes, was the fact that in the battle Englishmen fought and bled in the cause of Portuguese independence. And it is a circumstance worth recording, that whenever Portugal has been threatened by Spain, she has turned to England for help. Dom John, aware how little chance Portugal alone would have in the struggle with Castile, sent post-haste to England for assistance, and in due course 500 of the famous English archers arrived to share in the glorious victory of Aljubarrota. 'The English archers,' says the historian, 'did yeoman service, and repeated the glories of Crecy and Poitiers'; and it was in commemoration of this great victory that John I. erected the magnificent convent of Batalha, which recalls in its name, 'battle,' our own Battle Abbey, erected on the field of Hastings.

The fifteen miles which separate the two convents were quickly accomplished; and as we sped through the woods, a glimpse of towers, and pinnacles, and fretted spires was vouchsafed to us, ever and anon, through the vistas of pine-stems. At length, in front and beneath, lay a quiet, solitary valley, from whence there arose in all its stately majesty, dwarfing by its size and magnificence every surrounding object, the glory of Portugal—the famed convent of Batalha.

Nothing could well present a more imposing appearance than this superb pile as it bursts suddenly into view at a bend of the road. Beckford, describing the effect created on him by this 'lofty, majestic basilica, surrounded by its glorious huddle of buildings,' says: 'I could hardly believe so considerable and striking a group of richly parapeted walls, roofs and towers, detached chapels and insulated spires, formed parts of one and the same edifice: in appearance it was not merely a church or a palace I was looking at, but some fair city of romance such as an imagination glowing with the fancies of Aristo might have pictured to itself under the influence of a dream.'

Driving up with a dash and a flourish to the western entrance, we exchanged the heat and glare which seemed to be concentrated on this particular spot most joyfully for the coolness and solemn grandeur of the interior.

The church of Batalha is the noblest specimen of ecclesiastical architecture in Portugal. And what invests it with a peculiar interest in English eyes, is the fact that it constitutes an imperishable record of the ancient alliance between England and Portugal, which was sealed by the Treaty of Windsor in 1386—the very year of the founding of the convent—and cemented by the marriage at Oporto, the following year, of the hero of Aljubarrota, John I., to our English Philipa, daughter of John of Gaunt by his first wife, Blanche of Lancaster. This union proved more momentous in its results than any that have been recorded in Portuguese history. The first-fruits were those glorious princes who ushered in the 'golden age' of Portugal, and whose names stand out so conspicuously in the history of the fifteenth century.

Batalha, therefore, may be held to symbolise three great events: (1) The victory of Aljubarrota, by which Portuguese independence was won by the aid of English soldiers, and the House of Aviz firmly established on the throne; (2) The Treaty of Windsor, by which the alliance between England and Portugal was inaugurated; and (3), The union of the old royal family of Portugal, in the person of the Great Bastard, with the blood of the English Plantagenets by marriage with Philipa of Lancaster.

The British traveller, unless indeed he be a mere scenery-gazer, must be stolid indeed if he can view this splendid pile without emotion, or traverse its aisles and chapels without being stirred by the recollection of its glorious memories.

Under the influence of feelings evoked by reading Beckford's affecting account of his visit to this glorious shrine, we at once sought out the chapel wherein repose the bodies of the noble couple who caused Batalha to assume form and substance. And as Beckford's book seems almost unknown to the present generation, I shall offer no apology for quoting the passage to which allusion has been made:—

'Mass was celebrated with no particular pomp, no glittering splendour: but the countenance and gestures of the officiating priests were characterised by a profound religious awe. The voices of the monks, clear but deep-toned, rose pealing through vast and echoing space. The chaunt was grave and simple, its austerity mitigated in some parts by the treble of very young choristers. These sweet and innocent sounds found their way to my heart; they recalled to my memory our own beautiful cathedral service, and—I wept! It was in this tone of mind, so well calculated to nourish solemn and melancholy impressions, that we visited the mausoleum where lie extended on their cold sepulchres the effigies of John the First and the generous-hearted, noble-minded Philipa: linked hand in hand in death as fondly as they were in life. This tomb is placed in the centre of the chapel. Under a row of arches on the right, fretted and pinnacled and crocketed in the best style of Gothic at its best period, lie, sleeping the last sleep, their justly renowned progeny. . . . All these princes, in whom the high bearing of their intrepid father, and the exemplary virtues and strong sense of their mother, the grand-daughter of our Edward the Third, were united, repose after their toils and sufferings in this secluded chapel, which looks indeed a place of rest and holy quietude: the light, equably diffused, forms as it were a tranquil atmosphere, such as might be imagined worthy to surround the predestined to happiness in a future world.

'I withdrew from the contemplation of these tombs with reluctance, every object in the chapel which contains them being so pure in taste, so harmonious in colour: every armorial device, every mottoed lambel, so tersely and correctly sculptured, associated also so closely with historical and English recollections—the garter, the leopards, the fleur-de-lis, "from haughty Gallia torn." The Plantagenet cast of the whole chamber conveyed home to my bosom a feeling so interesting, so congenial, that I could hardly persuade myself to move away.'

After Beckford's nervous language, how flat and commonplace does every other description seem!

The style of architecture has been called Modern Norman Gothic, the church being considered one of the most perfect and beautiful specimens of that style existing.[1] The interior is chiefly remarkable for a chaste and noble plainness, the grandeur and sublimity of the general effect being due to the correctness of the design. But one misses the solemnity of tone, the 'dim religious light,' that suffuses our English cathedrals through the many-tinted mosaics of their magnificent windows, the only colour here being derived from a few diamond-shaped

[1] A remarkable feature of the edifice is the entire absence of timber in its construction—even the roof is of stone.

panes of the crudest reds, yellows, and greens—modern insertions, and miserable substitutes for the beautiful glass which formerly adorned the windows.[1]

The magnificent west entrance, measuring 28 feet by 57, and embellished with upwards of one hundred figures in *alto-relievo*, is considered to be unrivalled by any other Gothic doorway in Europe. From here to the eastern extremity measures 416 feet, as compared with 513 feet, Canterbury, and 524 feet, York Minster.

The architect of this noble edifice is unknown; all that is certain is that D. John I., in his desire to build a monastery superior to any in Europe, invited from distant countries the most celebrated architects that were to be found. Certain portions of the edifice are believed to bear the impress of English skill, and it is not improbable— seeing that Gothic architecture at that time flourished in England—that some artists may have come over in the train of Philipa of Lancaster.

The chapter-house is a perfect square, measuring 64 feet each way, and being vaulted, without any central support, is regarded as a masterpiece of architecture. Beckford speaks of it as 'the most strikingly beautiful apartment' he ever beheld; and, in truth, the graceful arching roof overspreading the 'unembarrassed space' beneath, seems to be suspended by magic. Da Costa, the Portuguese historian, says that twice, when the centres were struck, the vaulting collapsed with dire results, but that success attended the third attempt, the centres being then struck by criminals under sentence of death.

[1] 'At about five o'clock in the evening, when the sun is opposite the great western window, the effect of its painted glass is most enchanting. The myriads of variegated rays which emanate from this beautiful window resemble so many beams of glory playing around them [the monks].'—MURPHY.

The unfinished mausoleum of D. Emmanuel, at the rear of the church, is considered the gem of the whole—'a veritable marvel of art.' And notwithstanding that it has stood open and exposed to weather since 1509, nearly four hundred years, it may be affirmed of its condition, as was said by Murphy a century ago, that 'it scarcely exhibits any traces of decay.' Strange to say, no plans were left for its completion, the intentions of the architect being unknown. In fact, in the opinion of men of taste, it would be impossible to finish the structure without spoiling the effect of the church as a whole. The chronicles relate that D. Emmanuel was so overjoyed with the discovery of India that he sent all the workmen employed at Batalha to construct the convent of Belem, founded by him in commemoration of the event.

The history of Batalha, during the last hundred years, runs on parallel lines with that of its sister at Alcobaca. At two important epochs of its life the curtain draws up for a brief while, displaying, as it were, before our eyes the daily life of the convent. First, when it was in the flood-tide of pride and power, confident in its strength, derived from the support of all who depended upon it, whether for their daily bread, for comfort and help in sickness, or for religious ministrations—the 'future all unknown'! And again, after it had passed through the bitter waters of French intrusion, desecration, and partial destruction.

For a picture of realistic force, drawn by a master hand while Batalha was in its prime, the reader must be referred to Beckford's inimitable sketch. Murphy's description is also worth reading.

From these we gather that the monastery of Santa Maria da Victoria was neither large nor wealthy. It was of the Dominican order, and contained, besides the usual dignitaries, but twenty-five mass-friars, four novices, and thirteen lay-brothers. The cook received 4800 reis a year, a sum equivalent to about one pound sterling of our money, which would rather imply a system of plain living in ill-accordance with the tastes of the Alcobaca fathers. The monks eat but twice in the twenty-four hours—at eleven and eight—the daily ration consisting of two small loaves, one pound and a quarter of meat, the same quantity of fish, besides soup, rice, wine, and fruit. 'In their mode of living,' wrote Murphy, after a residence here of thirteen weeks, 'there appears nothing to envy, but a great deal to admire and commend.'

The one disadvantage arising from habits of frugality and abstinence, such as were practised by the Batalha fathers, is the penalty Nature exacts for any chance over-indulgence. A curious illustration of this was afforded on the occasion of Beckford's visit, when, on the very evening of his arrival, the community was indulged with an enormous supper, and one of the monks who partook of it, though almost bent double with age, 'played his part in excellent style.' Animated by ample potations of the very best Aljubarrota that ever grew, and which, says our authority, 'we had taken the provident care to bring with us,' he exclaimed lustily, 'Well, this is as it should be—rare doings! such as have not been witnessed at Batalha since a certain progress that great king, John the Fifth, made more than half a century ago.' The remainder of this 'inspired oration' may be studied in Beckford's account; but the sequel was too entertaining to omit: 'So saying, he drained a huge silver goblet to the last drop, and falling back in his chair, was carried out, chair and all, weeping, puling, and worse than drivelling, with such maudlin tenderness that he actually marked his track with a flow of liquid sorrows.'

Even mass-friars, who, 'in every respect, consistently with the duties of their order, practised the virtuous precepts of their sacred religion,' were not, it seems, exempt from the one touch of nature. It is refreshing to be assured by that keen observer, Murphy, that he 'could not discern one drooping with the weight of years, or who had lost a tooth, or who had an eye dimmed with defluxion, though some of them had attained to the age of ninety and upwards.' And he proceeds to draw the following philosophic deductions: 'Such is the wise dispensation of Providence, that those men who have voluntarily secluded themselves from the mingled cares and enjoyments of the world, are compensated, even on this side of the grave, by a long and serene evening of old age, free from the infirmities, disappointments, and painful reflections which embitter the expiring days of the libertine and inconsiderate.'

But Murphy was an Irishman, and a bit of a wag. His private opinion has already been divulged. It is pleasant to hear that this same genial philosopher received, 'under the royal seal of the convent, a certificate of his good conduct during the three months he resided there.'[1] What could the poor fellow do, after this, but pass an act of oblivion over any little monkish frailties that had come under notice?

It was on the night of Beckford's arrival, after witnessing the monkish comedy afore-mentioned, that he became an unwilling spectator of a most weird scene. The de-

---

[1] Murphy's superb work, *Plans, Elevations, and Views of the Royal Monastery of Batalha* (published in 1793), is almost unknown to modern travellers, but should be studied by all who are interested in architecture.

scription of this incident forms one of the most impressive passages in his book. After the lapse of a hundred years it has lost none of its force; indeed, as you read on, the whole scene appears to rise up before you with startling realism, and induces a 'creepy' feeling which it is difficult to shake off. No wonder a man of Beckford's extreme sensibility should have been profoundly affected by the incident.

Studied in the light of after events, the appalling words 'Judgment! Judgment! Tremble at the anger of an offended God! Woe to Portugal! Woe! Woe!' which resounded through the still night air, echoing through the vast solitudes of the cloisters and gardens of Batalha,—as if the voice of a messenger from another world,—possessed a terrible significance. Who could possibly have foreseen the troubles in store for Portugal? The ever-widening perturbations of the French Revolution had scarcely reached to that remote corner of the Peninsula: one doubts if even the faintest echo of it had penetrated to the solitudes of Batalha. Another ten years were to elapse ere the wave of republicanism swept across the frontier.

It is the fate of prophets, in all ages, to be held in small esteem. But assuredly the utterer of those terrible words must have believed that the kingdom of Portugal was foredoomed to desolation, and its royal house to punishments worse than death. 'And, do you know, my lord stranger,' was the Prior's solemn comment to his guest, in allusion to the incident, 'there are moments of my existence when I firmly believe he speaks the words of prophetic truth.'

Alas, since that June night, 1795, how much has happened! The convent has passed through trials of which the holy fathers recked not at the time. The window from whence the tragic scene was viewed—nay, the very garden wherein it was enacted—may be sought for now in vain. But need I say that, as we wandered through the courts and cloisters of this superb edifice, the weird details of that midnight scene were constantly in our thoughts. Indeed, on beholding the desolation that was wrought within a few brief years of the deliverance of that awful message, no doubt can exist as to one of the fathers of Batalha having been endowed with the gift of prophecy. Verily, 'the arm of an avenging God' was stretched out!—the weight of impending judgment was 'most terrible.'

As Beckford rode off on his fleet Arab, leaving an open-mouthed swarm of friars and novices 'staring and wondering' at the velocity with which he was carried away, the convent and its monkish inhabitants melt away into the darkness of Egyptian night.

A period of thirty years elapses, and once more the curtain lifts from off Batalha. What destruction has been wrought in the interim! How many monkish hopes have been dashed to the ground! What fiery trials have the holy fathers been called on passively to endure! And as they surveyed with chastened feelings the desolation that surrounded them, the prophetic words of the holy man, uttered in the peaceful and prosperous times of old, must have echoed in their ears.

The shameful havoc wrought here by French soldiers may be thus summarised: The sacristy was turned into a kitchen—fires being kindled with the woodwork of the drawers, and the building was left in a ruinous state. All the little odds and ends, such as vestments, and the gold and silver chalices and candlesticks, were carried off by the light-fingered republicans. The founder's chapel was shamefully desecrated, the monuments and marble effigies being much mutilated, and the armorial shield which once decorated it broken in pieces, the fragments being mixed up together on the floor with broken stained glass from the windows and Gothic ornaments from the royal tombs. The body of King John II., formerly exposed to view in a small chapel, was dragged forth by the soldiers, who 'carried on war against the dead as well as against the living.'

The choir was turned into a stable, and it is believed that the circumstance of some of the tombs being hid by the hay and straw which was brought in may have preserved them from desecration; but in every direction the marks of French barbarity are discernible. The chapter-house was converted into a dormitory, and, to obtain additional room, the noble monuments of Alphonso V. and his grandson were broken in pieces and removed. Finally, the monastery was set fire to. 'A more sad scene of desolation cannot be imagined,' wrote a traveller. Such was the result of a visit from the 'Philistine armies of France.'

It is right that the real circumstances attending the French invasion should be remembered, in view of the ignorance that prevails on this subject, and especially having regard to the behaviour of a section of the Portuguese nobility when the country was writhing under the iron heel of Napoleon's lieutenants. Incredible as such base subserviency may seem, it is an historical fact that, while Junot was insulting the people of Lisbon, a deputation from that city, 'consisting of some of the principal noblemen of the country,' were cringing at the feet of Napoleon, at Bayonne, and presently issued an address to the Portuguese nation, in which they urged their fellow-countrymen to throw in their lot with the

French: 'for we have ourselves seen that the moment has arrived, in which he [Napoleon] has effected the happiness of his own country, and commenced that of ours.' And these sagacious patriots went on to say that 'his Majesty has no feeling of rancour . . . he occupies himself with nobler aims. He desires only to unite you with the other portions of Europe in his great continental system, of which we shall form the final link. He desires to emancipate you from those foreign [British?] influences to which you have been for so many years subject. The Emperor cannot permit an English colony on the Continent.' And the authors of the address concluded by calling on their countrymen to show their gratitude to the Emperor.

Amongst the signatories to this shameful document we find the names of the Marquis de Marialva, the Bishop of Coimbra, and the Grand Inquisitor. With such leaders, can one wonder at Portugal having sunk to the lowest depths of degradation?

On the suppression of the monasteries (1834), the edifice of Batalha was taken over by Government to be preserved henceforward as a national monument; and, unlike Alcobaca, is kept in excellent order and good repair. Much of the vandalism of the French has been repaired;—the majestic cloisters, with the marvellously-wrought tracery of their windows, happily escaped intact. A number of masons were employed on the restorations at the time of our visit, and the feeling of the country generally is in favour of encouraging the Government in its praiseworthy efforts to make Batalha worthy of its founder and the event it was raised up to commemorate. The refectory has been turned into a museum, wherein may be seen, amongst other relics, the sword and casque of

D. John I. It was in this building that the fathers entertained Lord Wellington and 125 British officers at dinner.

We got back to Alcobaca at six, and found an excellent repast awaiting us; and, leaving again, on our homeward journey, at a quarter to eight, had a most enjoyable drive in the moonlight, reaching our hotel at about half-past ten.

We had driven some fifty-five miles, the charge for which by agreement was 6000 reis—a formidable sum as far as figures go, but equivalent to about twenty-one shillings English, at the rate of exchange. The carriage and horses were excellent; and the driver, besides being a first-rate whip, was one of the finest specimens of manhood I ever saw. An insignificant tip put him in the highest good-humour; though my friend assured me that the bargain covered everything, and that this was an uncalled-for piece of generosity. Personally, I have carried away very pleasant recollections of native drivers. They have never even hinted at a *pour-boire*, and the small gratuity handed to them after a long excursion has always been accepted with gratitude.

CALDAS AGAIN.

The Grand Hotel Lisbonense is considered the best out of Lisbon. It boasts of *una vasta Sala de Jantar* (*Anglicé*, enormous dining-room), 'garden and shade,' and —oh! luxury of luxuries—' a post-box'! Yes, that is a fact!

In a pictorial advertisement in the *Official Railway Guide*, the hotel is shown upside down. I don't know whether this is a printer's joke, but it was typical of the state of things we found—the establishment being literally upside down, in consequence of structural alterations by which the *vasta sala* would double its holding capacity, and much additional space be added to the hotel. But this sort of enterprise was not without its drawbacks; for as the workpeople of Portugal begin to earn their 'living wage' with the sun, the *reveille*, in the form of a discord of noises, broke in on our slumbers at a most inconvenient hour.

Happily for us, the 'season' had not begun. The hotel was almost empty—there were only two other couples in residence; so, to oblige our insular prejudices, the dinner-hour was shifted from four to six. Whether the other *hospedes* were consulted in the matter, I cannot say; but as we all dined at the same snug little table in a corner of the *vasta sala*, and were all civility and kindness to each other, we presumed that no objections had been raised. Unfortunately, from ignorance of each other's language our mutual civilities were confined to signs and flourishes; but we meant a great deal more than we said; and when dinner had got well 'under weigh' our table companions made a pathetic attempt to win our hearts by producing a strange-looking yellow compound—a sort of curds—a *spécialité* of the university town of Coimbra, and compounded, as we afterwards learned, of raw eggs and sugar. It was not nice; but what could we do but shape our countenances into the nearest approach to an expression of pleasure we could achieve? with the result that the mixture was pressed on us, at intervals, during the rest of the repast.

The fare was excellent, the table liberal, and the cooking, as at all the best native hotels, in the French style.

One could not help trying to picture the *sala* in the season, with its two hundred feeders, all 'hard at it,' packed as close as herrings in a cask; every window and chink hermetically closed—for the Portuguese are particularly susceptible to chills when 'stowing their holds,' and the heat and fumes from the hot victuals making the room absolutely stifling. Heaven preserve me, and any of my dear friends, from being consigned to this form of 'everlasting punishment'!

The manager was all courtesy and anxiety to oblige, and we found the two young ladies of the house, his daughters, who mixed freely with the guests and graced the drawing-room with their presence of an evening, chatty and agreeable: they both spoke French, and one, who was an accomplished musician, often favoured us on the piano.

Our room, which was at the back, looked on to a pleasant garden, vine-trellised and shady, with a vista of pine-woods and hills beyond. A picturesque water-mill occupied the middle distance, whose merry clatter, in a subdued key, continued night and day. Great was our surprise, however, one damp, misty morning, to see steam rising from the mill-leet, and, on investigating the mystery, we found the mill to be worked by the warm mineral waters after they had washed the bodies of the patients.

A nightingale had taken up its abode amidst the vines, and rippled on in the peculiarly boisterous way affected by these little choristers. But there were two formidable competitors for supremacy in this empire of sweet sounds—a cricket and a frog! And all through the night, and sometimes far into the day, did this astonishing trio prolong the contest. When, however, it resolved itself into a question of staying-powers, the feathered one sailed away with flying colours, and won easily. But all three were 'up to time' next night, and every night after, so game were they, until we wished they would finish the contest elsewhere.

The Portuguese nightingale is a most pertinacious songster, to whom might aptly be applied Wordsworth's sonnet:—

> 'O Nightingale! thou surely art
> A creature of ebullient heart,
> . . . . .
> Thou sing'st as if the god of wine
> Had helped thee to a valentine:
> A song in mockery and despite
> Of shades and dews, and silent night.'

Caldas is much affected by the king, who finds in the quiet and solitude of the place opportunities for contemplation and the studies which are congenial to him, and which are lacking amidst the ceaseless round of dissipations of the Pena at Cintra. And yet there are malicious folk who assert that the king likes the gaiety of the place.

It was in the pine-woods around Caldas that the small British army, under Sir Arthur Wellesley, was encamped on the eve of the battle of Rolica, when, for the first time, the much-depreciated British soldiers and their doughty antagonists faced each other. First blood had been drawn the day before the battle, when some men of the 60th Regiment, in driving back a French outpost near Obydos, having got out of hand, were, in their turn, attacked and severely handled by a superior force of the enemy.

Obydos is about three miles from Caldas, and is worth a visit. Originally a Moorish castle of great strength, its massive walls have survived the wear and tear of ages in a surprising manner, and give one a good idea of the solidity of the old Arab architecture. The palace, or residence of the governor, though in ruins, contains some fine carving and a fireplace of regal proportions. A Roman aqueduct still supplies the town with water. There was much fighting round here in the times of the Moors; and during the Peninsular War the castle was occupied successively by French and English. The village seems literally to cling to the hillside in truly loving fashion: the quaint old houses, with their bright window-gardens, the narrow streets, and the sound of running water from the numerous fountains, carrying one back in fancy to Moorish times.

About half a mile from the town, on the Caldas road, stands a church of a very singular style of architecture—hexagonal in form, but with little to commend it in the way of internal decoration, the only noteworthy thing about it being the immense number of votive offerings from seafaring people contained therein, in the form of ships and boats, and seascapes in oil and water-colour. The latter display more imaginative power than is often apparent in the work of British marine painters, though somewhat deficient in technical skill. The collection was one of the most interesting I had ever seen, the works being full of realistic touches, and displaying every known phase of weather and sea, besides many that were strange to me; but when religious fervour guides the brush there is no controlling its vagaries.

After all, there is no need to go to Portugal for object-lessons in religious art gone mad. For do not our own church windows educate the young in the belief that the Apostles went a-fishing in purple and scarlet and flowing manes? We won't enter into the question of boats and oars and other marine details, for that would take us too far afield; but to any one of nautical instincts and

OBYDOS, FROM THE CALDAS ROAD

UNIV. OF
CALIFORNIA

training our church windows are fully as mirth-provocative as the achievements of the Obydos picture-painters; but *our* 'liars in paint' have invented the expression, 'conventionally treated,' to excuse their impudent fibs.

We had soon exhausted the attractions of Caldas, and came to the conclusion that a duller or more uninteresting spot we had never lighted on—though, to be sure, the local *Guide* assures its patrons that 'during the season life at Caldas is delicious'! May the Fates preserve us from an enforced sojourn at this famous stewing-place, in season or out of season! So, on the third day, we sought out the only train for Torres Vedras. To be strictly veracious, there is another, but a train which calls for you at one o'clock in the morning can hardly be classed amongst 'facilities'; it would seem to be intended for cats and night-prowlers. And though but twenty-five miles separate the two places, the journey occupies an hour and a half!

At Torres Vedras we were met by our kind and thoughtful friend, who had journeyed from Lisbon on purpose to see us settled into new and unknown quarters, and a short walk landed us at the 'Hotel Dos Cocos' (Cuckoo Hotel).

I must explain that our sole and particular object in coming to Torres Vedras was to examine those portions of the Lines that lie within easy reach; for it is not a place much affected by visitors—foreigners rarely stop here,—though attempts are being made by advertising to bring its thermal springs into notice as rivals of the fashionable Caldas. There are two springs, about a mile apart, one of which has been recently bought up by a company, who have built a small hotel for the use of patients, wherein are all the latest appliances in physical hydraulics, and cut paths on a bare and shadeless hillside for the poor penitents to disport themselves on,—though, to judge from appearances, some time will elapse before Torres becomes the resort of fashion, or even of the afflicted who can go elsewhere. Handbooks, crowded with those extraordinary hieroglyphics affected by chemists in their efforts to popularise research in the matter of mineral-water analysis, together with much valuable information on the subject of ailments and their cure, are presented to visitors, and I came away quite laden with this sort of light literature fully intent on enlightening the world on the subject of Portuguese thermal establishments; but the more I look into these dissertations, the more convinced I am that no British reader will care twopence about them.

As I have gone fully elsewhere into the results of our investigations around Torres Vedras,[1] I won't bother the reader here with details of earthworks, redoubts, scarps, or entrenchments, but confine my remarks to a general description of the place and its surroundings; for Torres is an interesting spot and worth a visit, apart from its association with one of the most glorious chapters of British military history. The town stands in a hollow, from whence valleys branch off in all directions, but it is of no great size or commercial importance, albeit of great antiquity, as implied by its old name, Turres Veteres, when under Roman domination.

The most striking feature of the place is the fine old Moorish castle on a hill which rises from the centre of the valley. But little remains of it now except the walls, the castle having met with rough usage in the wars. Tradition credits it with an underground passage to the river below, thus enabling the garrison to water their

---

[1] 'A Visit to the Lines of Torres Vedras,' with plans and views.—*Journal of the Royal United Service Institution* for 1897.

horses. Some vestiges of this were said to have existed early in the century.

If the visitor has artistic tastes he will find plenty of occupation for brush or pencil, the town abounding in quaint old bits, elaborately carved churches, and a grand fountain, which alone is worth coming here to see; picturesque streets and hanging gardens, glowing with bright carnations, scented geraniums, and bouganvillias; to say nothing of the delightful groupings of colour-schemes that meet the eye everywhere. Many of the better-class houses were once monastic property, which accounts for the beauty of their windows.

Most of the woods which surrounded the town in former times were cut down during the Napoleonic wars to afford a clear range for the guns; for war, alas! is no respecter of landscapes. And as one gazes down on the shadeless roads, the mind reverts to a passage in the engineer's report, on the eve of the arrival of Wellington's troops to take post here: 'The moment I knew of the army having commenced its retrograde movements, I commenced our final preparations, and we spared neither houses, gardens, vineyards, olive-trees, woods, nor private property of any description. The only blind to the fire of the works now standing is that beautiful avenue of old trees in the pass of Torres Vedras. The Juez de Fora and inhabitants pleaded to me so hard for the latest moment, lest they might be unnecessarily cut down, that I consented to defer it till the day before the troops march in; and as I have trustworthy men with axes in readiness on the spot, there is no doubt of their being felled in time.'

Some two centuries earlier, English soldiers traversed this same ground. It was on a May afternoon, in the year 1589, that Drake put ashore at Peniche Norris and his 12,000 Englishmen, intent on 'reprising' the 'Portingales' for their share in the Great Armada of the year before; and carrying along with them, as a sort of figurehead, the Pretender Dom Antonio, who looked forward to getting seated on the throne of Portugal. It happened that the Spaniards were cocks-of-the-walk in Lisbon just then, and a certain Pedro de Guzman, a gallant enough soldier in his way, set off from the capital with his Castilians to block the road; but a report reaching them that Drake had brought with him '900 great Irish dogs as fierce as lions,' and 'capable of eating up a world of folks,' the Castilians, having no mind to sample their teeth, fell back on Torres Vedras, so as to hold the road to Lisbon.

On the 19th May the English marched into Torres, while Guzman and his Spaniards marched out—somewhat hurriedly—towards Lisbon.

But the Britons had been 'spoiling' for a row ever since they put foot in Portugal, though Dom Guzman and his 'braves,' having no stomach for the fight, invariably made off at their approach. A chance offering at last, however, some companies of Spanish horse having been ordered to hang on the skirts of the advancing English, Captain Yorke, who commanded Norris's cavalry, determined to try their mettle, and sent a corporal with eight men, 'who rode through forty of the enemy,' whilst Yorke himself, 'with forty English horse, put to precipitous flight Alarcon's two hundred.'

And so the brave Britons passed on to Lisbon, where we must leave them, merely remarking *en passant* that Tommy Atkins was developing even thus early in history a dislike for foreign 'kickshaws'; for a Portuguese chronicler says the English soldiers 'found our food dry and tasteless, and hankered after their own fat meats and

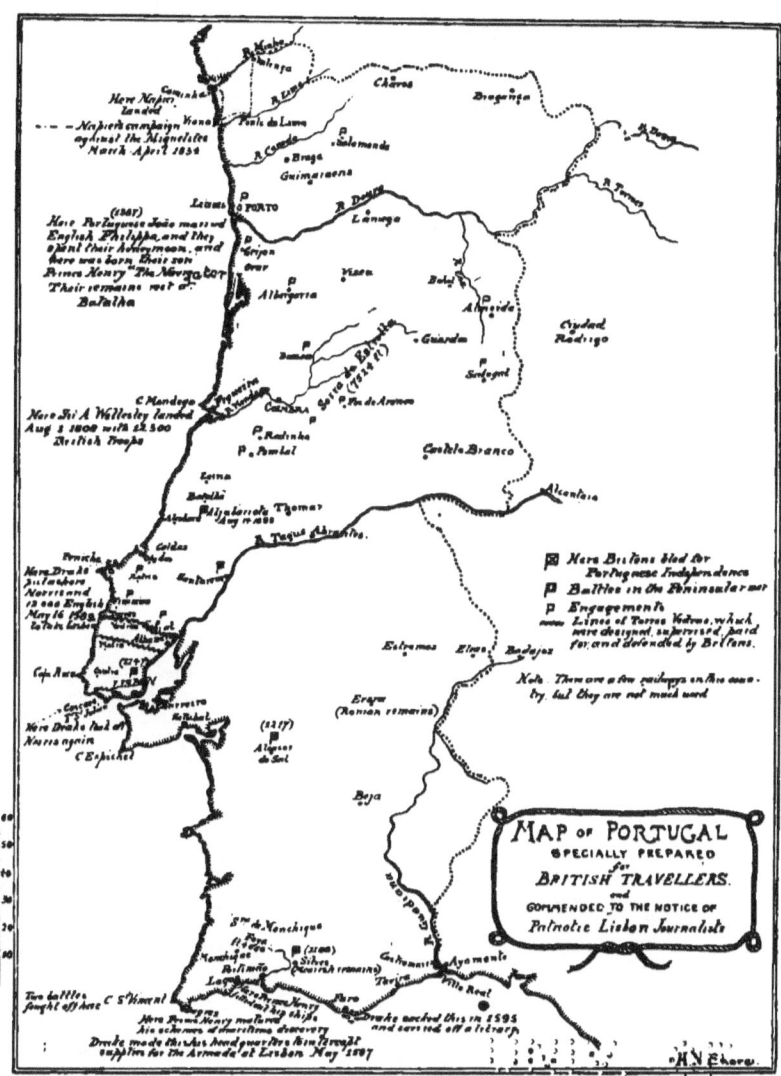

MAP OF PORTUGAL

birds, comparing our barrenness with the abundance of their own land.'

'There's no place like home!' was ever the cry of the roving Briton.

The morning after our arrival we took a long drive through the vine-clad valleys and olive-besprinkled hills that stand about Torres, and peeped into some of the well-tended vineyards from whose produce the wine which takes its name from the town is expressed, and which fortunately suited our palates to a nicety. The particular vintage that was dispensed at our hotel enjoyed an advantage over the Lisbon editions in being the 'expurgated' edition—'muito puro,' as the waiter kept impressing on us every time we imbibed it; in other words, the wine had not been 'doctored' to cover 'octroi dues.'

Returning from our excursion along the banks of the Sizandro, we paid a visit to the hospital for aged and infirm soldiers at Runa, the Chelsea Hospital of Portugal. In this picturesque spot, surrounded by extensive and tastefully laid out grounds, well stocked with fruit-bearing and other trees, bright with flowers, and with endless shady walks, there stands a large and well-ordered building, wherein thirty old soldiers who have served a specified number of years, without a mark against them, are supported in comfort, if not in affluence.

We were received here with the utmost courtesy and cordiality, conducted over every part of the establishment, invited to sample the provisions, cooked and uncooked, and shown the midday meal, which was being set out for the inmates, and looked tempting and palatable. Excellent soup, a savoury mess of meat, bread, a plate of loquats, and a glass of capital red wine, made up the dinner. The inmates seemed a fine body of men, were well cared for, and neatly clothed in an easy military dress, and looked as happy and as contented with their lot as one might expect in such delicious surroundings. Indeed, more than one of our party came away with the conviction that there were many worse endings to an active life than that of a Runa pensioner.

Little as the world hears of the achievements of the Portuguese soldier, at the present day, we ought never to forget what Portuguese troops accomplished in the Peninsular War, when fighting shoulder to shoulder with British soldiers, and led by British officers. Ignorance and indifference, and the studied discouragement of any kindly feelings towards their former deliverers by Portuguese officials, can never obliterate from our minds the recollection of the noble behaviour of our brave companions in arms—a companionship which dates back to 1147, when a body of English Crusaders bound for Palestine landed at Lisbon, and helped to drive the Moors from the castle of St. George. And on this account Englishmen must always feel an interest in the Portuguese army, and look with a kindly feeling on its old soldiers.

Our visit to Runa was mutually agreeable to all parties: and I think the old pensioners must have cherished pleasant recollections of it, for when we passed through Runa afterwards, any of those we had met and conversed with, who happened to be taking their walks abroad, would at once pull themselves up, give a military salute, and beam on us.

Our friend returned to Lisbon that evening, and we were thrown on our own resources in the matter of conversation, as no one here spoke a word of any language but Portuguese. We began now to reap the rich fruits of learning, the reward of many weary hours spent over

Portuguese conversation-books and grammars, and made amazing progress under the tuition of the chambermaid, and a fatherly waiter, to whose tender mercies we had been particularly consigned by our friend, and who nobly acquitted himself of his trust.

As this was the first country hotel we had stayed at, some account of the *ménage* may prove interesting. And let it be distinctly understood that such an hotel as I am about to describe corresponds with the places of entertainment we find at Cheltenham, Malvern, or Harrogate—not mere country 'pubs.'

Bare floors prevailed throughout the establishment, with the exception of the *sala de leitura,* or drawing-room; and this custom has obvious advantages in a warm climate, where Nature is prolific of animal life, and especially in view of the expectorating habits of the natives. The absence of woollen superfluities is much to be commended, too, in view of the conscientious scruples on the subject of carpet-beating so widely held by hotel proprietors, and which have been inherited from a remote ancestry.

Let me enforce this sermon by an illustration from real life.

While in pursuit of knowledge under difficulties, in an hotel that shall be nameless—I never insert unsolicited advertisements—curiosity prompted me to peep into a room from whence, for many hours, strange sounds had been disseminated through the house. There, looming indistinctly through a dense fog, composed of microbes of unnamed species and dust particles, I at length discerned female figures kneeling, not in a devotional attitude, but in a posture suited to carpet-scrubbing, and rubbing away for dear life with hard brushes on the woollen floor coverings, from whence ascended dense clouds of dust, to alight once more in due course, and in strict accordance with Newton's law of gravitation, on the carpet, with the exception of such stray particles as wandered forth into the wide world without, and floated down on the heads of passers-by. Taking advantage of a lull in the storm, which caused a temporary rift in the fog, I perceived the *raison d'être* of all this honest industry: the 'carpet' was an ingeniously contrived and put together species of mosaic-work, composed of many pieces and patterns, a sort of object-lesson in the making of Joseph's coats, kept in place by an infinity of big nails. Now, viewed simply as an example of 'piece-work,' there would be nothing outrageous in the assumption that such a job of carpet-laying would have taken even a hard working British mechanic, content with a bare 'living wage,' at least a week's steady work. Hence, some little prejudice against undoing such a masterpiece was excusable. After this, I have conscientiously abstained from carpeted bedrooms in Portugal.

The bare floors are always spotlessly clean; so clean, that, as a man-of-war's man says of his deck, 'you can eat your dinner off it.' Cocoanut or grass matting is often laid in the passages.

The equipment of the establishment is on a scale of Spartan, almost barbaric, simplicity. The bedroom 'furniture' consisting of an iron bedstead, sometimes provided with a spring mattress, but more often with the hardest and most unsympathetic of palliasses, built up of the straw and husks of Indian corn, which celebrate every movement of the body with a musical accompaniment. Pillows are of the same rest-repelling style of architecture. 'Nothing can be more uncomfortable to a stranger in Portugal than the beds,' wrote a lady nearly a hundred years ago; 'their extreme hardness really injures rather than rests the bones, especially those of a thin person.' In this I thoroughly concur, having accumulated but little superfluous fat during my rollings over the face of the globe. The bed-linen—or rather cotton —is dazzlingly white, and I am bound to confess we never detected any little 'skirmishers' galloping across country, nor even felt their presence, nor found marks of occupancy. A sort of 'cabin washstand' with a large plug-basin, a chair, and occasionally, I am bound to admit—as becomes the veracious historian—a table; and once—yes, once— a wardrobe! (but that was felt to be a mark of special distinction), complete the furniture.

How bare and comfortless! the reader will exclaim. Well, one gets used to it; and there is nothing like foreign travel for expanding the mind, and proving how little 'comfort' is really necessary. And really, in hot weather, a room such as I have described has a refreshingly cool and cleanly appearance.

The only part of the bedroom equipment we never became reconciled to was the blanket, which, being of cotton, is most unpleasantly heavy while affording little warmth.

Portuguese blankets would have exactly suited the impecunious individual who deluded his body into a belief in being warm, in the absence of suitable bed-clothes, by sleeping under a table, whose weight had all the effect of warmth.

Descending to the *sala de jantar*, there will be found a homeliness and absence of decoration suggestive of a Scotch kirk, while the table appointments would certainly be scorned from the banqueting-board of a village inn at home. The crockery and glass, in fact, remind one of those priceless gems of art 'given away with a pound of tea' by philanthropic dealers in breakfast beverages; and I was thankful to see, for the credit of my country, that her merchants had no share in the propagation of the villainous metal implements that figured under the heading of 'cutlery'; it was nearly all 'made in Germany,'—the 'universal provider' of cheap and nasty rubbish, as well as of great and beautiful things. The table 'linen' is the coarsest of cotton cloth, its surface often freckled with those quaint protuberances we are accustomed to associate with bed-quilts: perchance the table-cloths serve a double purpose!

The art instinct finds expression throughout Portugal, where table-decoration is concerned, in centre-pieces whereof the foundation is butter, and the superstructure toothpicks! True, I have seen flowers stuck in at haphazard into 'lodging-house' vases of the crudest design and colour; but this form of table-decoration is not so popular as the 'butter-and-toothpick design.' At a fashionable and deservedly esteemed hotel in Lisbon, the only form of table-decoration tolerated was a row of metal dish-covers. Flowers were anathema, so rigid were the proprietor's views of religion. It was here, too, we were privileged to view the ceremonial observed by the straitest sect of Lisbon fashionables in the consumption of strawberries. We had no idea, before witnessing the function, of the amount of dignity that could be thrown into the simple act of bolting those delicious berries. And as the performance was something in the nature of a revelation, I will explain the *modus operandi*. First strip the strawberries from their stalks, sprinkle thickly with sugar, take the plate in both hands, and, with a circular swinging motion, roll the berries about till the sugar is evenly distributed over their surface; replace the plate on the table, take a toothpick in the right hand—not the left, mind—and transfer the berries, as rapidly as is consistent with breathing, from the plate to your mouth, by impaling them successively on the point of the pick.

There is no implement of domestic economy to compare in point of general utility with the toothpick. It is really surprising the variety of uses to which it can be turned, while the deftness with which it is wielded by both sexes is quite remarkable. And, planted firmly between the lips, after eating, it is, I understand, provocative of those divine thoughts with which Portuguese writers are wont to enthrall the world.

José, the waiter, to whose care we had been committed, was a young man of regular ways and an inquiring mind, as I shall presently show. But first, I must explain that we had arranged to have our meals at more Christian-like hours than are in favour with the multitude, who make a big breakfast at 9.30, dine at 4.30, and wind up a well-spent day of consistent idleness with 'tea-water' and sweet biscuits at ten; whereas it suited our digestive ways and wandering habits to take early coffee in our room at eight, breakfast at twelve, and dinner at 6.30—an arrangement which enabled us to dispense with the ten o'clock tea-water, as well as the society of our fellow-lodgers.

On entering the *sala* at the appointed hours, José was invariably discovered in his shirt-sleeves; and after seating us, he proceeded to the corner of the room, where it is *de rigueur* to have a wash-stand and towel, soaped his paws, rinsed and dried them, tidied his hair, put on his white jacket, and then proceeded to serve the meal. By this demonstration we were enabled to satisfy ourselves of José's fitness for his duties at table. And then José was endowed with a fund of conversation and a flow of words, and we mutually improved our education by exchanging names of dishes: and no sooner had José mastered the English designation than he became so puffed up with the pride of learning, that he must needs go straight off to the kitchen and air his acquirements for the particular edification of the senhoras therein assembled. But that these flourishes of his were chiefly mirth-provocative, was evident from the merry peals of laughter that were wafted back to the *sala* along with the fumes of cooking. Apt pupil as José proved in many ways, there was one word that completely nonplussed him—bread; this he never could attain to. Everywhere in Portugal we found waiters and chambermaids courteous, good-tempered, and extremely obliging. In private families the domestics are on a more familiar footing with their employers than would be considered *en règle* in England; but no undue familiarity nor disrespect is intended, or conveyed, nor is there anything vulgar or offensive in this. To us, their ways appeared those of merry, unsophisticated children.

There were but half a dozen other guests in the hotel, all men, of solemn and studious cast of countenance, who, when not eating, spent their days, and much of the nights, in the *sala de leitura*, engrossed, as we presumed, in research. Subsequent peeps revealed these gentlemen seated round a card-table! What their particular mission in life may have been, I cannot pretend to say, but at Torres it appeared to consist in card-playing.

I forgot to mention that before our friend's departure for Lisbon we paid a call on the civil governor, a kindly and courteous gentleman, who, on the particular object of our visit having been explained, offered to facilitate our enterprise by placing the entire police force of the district at our disposal; he even offered to send his own orderly to escort us round the forts. Now, as we enter-

A STREET IN CINTRA

UNIV. OF
CALIFORNIA

tained a very particular aversion to State ceremonials, and had formed our plan of investigation on a much humbler scale than was compatible with a police escort, this addition to the programme did not at all meet with our approval; so merely thanking the governor for the honour he had done us, we promised to send for the orderly whenever we required his services. But as our locomotive ways would have been particularly distasteful to a Portuguese policeman—especially during the hours devoted, in well-regulated police-stations, to the *siesta*—we were careful not to trouble the senhor. Conversation having turned on the old war-days, the governor paid us the compliment of saying that Portugal was under great obligations to England; that, in fact, his nation owed its independence to the English alliance.

Excellent carriages and horses were on hire here, at a very cheap rate, and we had many pleasant drives about the neighbourhood. Amongst other places, we visited Sobral, a small town at the foot of the Monte Agraca, on the summit of which stands the most powerful fort on the Lines. It was here, in the last century, that 'a dignified churchman' tried to establish a silk factory, and finding a difficulty in keeping the workmen—who missed, in this secluded spot, the vices and amusements of a metropolis—the shrewd ecclesiastic not only provided his employés with a theatre, but with partners to share their joys and griefs, without the encumbrance of the marriage tie: a curious illustration of the doctrine of doing evil that good may come.

> "'Tis not in mortals to command success,
> But we'll do more, Sempronius, we'll deserve it!'

was the guiding principle of the good churchman's efforts to establish a silk industry at Sobral. But alas! how futile are all our endeavours to promote the happiness of others! Not a vestige remains of this example of clerical enterprise: a visitor to Sobral at the close of last century found nothing but ruins of 'the expensive buildings' that had been erected.

Our pleasantest excursion was to Mafra—about seventeen miles—by a route which is little known to strangers, though far preferable to the customary one from Cintra, which traverses a dreary, uninteresting bit of country. The drive from Torres, on the other hand, takes one through the beautiful and diversified mountain scenery in the pass of Mafra.

The road follows, the greater part of the way, the course of the old paved causeway between Lisbon and the north, vestiges of which are frequently met with *en route*. After ascending the Sierra de Chypre, and passing through the picturesque village of Gradil, the road dips into a deep gorge, perhaps a thousand feet below, where the river San Lorenzo—in summer a mere stream—is crossed, and from thence carried up a succession of gentle gradients, zig-zag fashion, by an admirable bit of engineering, to the summit of the pass, where there are grand views of some fine scenery. The old paved road, in its hurry to reach its destination, ran straight up the face of the mountain, just outside the high wall enclosing the Tapada, or royal park of Mafra, which covers a wide extent of country, and affords good sport for the royal sportsmen.

I shall resist the temptation to launch out in praise of the glories and wonders of the combined convent, palace, and church, commonly called the 'Escurial of Portugal,' at Mafra, for the very excellent reason that it has been described and re-described by every traveller who has visited it. Suffice it to say, the pious founder was consumed with a desire to build a big thing—to 'go one better' than his neighbours the Spaniards—and he built a very big thing indeed; though, whether it was wanted, or whether his country was one whit the better for it, John v. was not the man to trouble his head. The reader who is fond of studying statistics by way of mental relaxation, will find every detail relating to its length, breadth, height and depth, the number of windows and doors, and the length of the rooms, the books in the library, and even the number of soldiers that can manœuvre on the roof, set forth with the dry humour that pertains to this sort of knowledge, in sundry guide-books and manuals of travel.

The story of its origin is of some little interest as illustrative of the principles underlying most royal enterprises in Portugal. Mafra was built by that 'paragon of splendour and holiness,' Dom Joao v., in fulfilment of a vow; but whether the vow was made by him or his wife, Maria Anna of Austria, seems uncertain. Authorities differ on the point, as well as regards the nature of the vow. The commonly accepted version is that the vow was made conditional on the birth of an heir to the throne, which auspicious event was brought about by the intercession of that obliging saint who has done so much for Portugal—S. Antonio. A binding clause of the contract was that the convent was to be built on the site of the poorest religious house in Portugal, which was eventually discovered at Mafra. The site having been thus fixed, John v. set to work to build what was intended to be not only the most magnificent temple in Portugal, but to eclipse, if possible, the glories of the Spanish Escurial by the splendour and magnificence of this new venture. There was no cramping question of cost, seeing that, as a despotic sovereign, he could dip his hand into the national money-bags to any extent: and he dipped as kings love to dip when no account has to be rendered. Portugal furnished the materials—stone, marbles, and jasper, and it was said that 25,000 workmen were employed on the building for thirteen years. Indeed, it is more than hinted by a writer of the last century that the only use King John ever made of his soldiers was to dig and carry the stones to build 'a magnificent church and convent for three hundred idlers at Mafra.'

The internal decorations were carried out on the most costly and lavish scale: Europe was ransacked for sculptors and artists; while an additional army of 20,000 workmen were employed for more than a year on the preparations for the consecration. The entire edifice was designed, and its erection superintended, by a German mechanic—a goldsmith by profession, who, Murphy declares, 'had neither the mind to conceive, nor the hand to execute, a design for a glebe-house, much less a basilica and royal palace.'

The cost of this royal folly was simply appalling. It has been estimated as high as five million pounds sterling —enough to have furnished the kingdom with a very respectable fleet!—but as Dom Joao never deigned to submit the accounts to the public audit, the actual sum will never be known. It has been asserted, moreover, that the vestments and altar decorations, which were specially manufactured at Lyons, of the richest silk and with the most sumptuous embroideries, almost equalled in cost that of the edifice itself; while the chimes of bells located in the two towers—fifty-seven bells in each—were made at Liège, at a cost of over 4,000,000 francs.

Such is the Escurial of Portugal—the *chef d'œuvre* of

that 'most magnificent of modern Solomons,' Dom Joao v., of whom it is recorded that he 'surrendered himself to a corrupt nobility, an intriguing and artful priesthood, and women of bad character.' In fact, the resemblance between the two Solomons was by no means confined to the building of a temple; for John v.

> 'wide as his command,
> Scattered his Maker's image through the land.'

Without going into details, it may be remarked that the interest this pious monarch manifested in the fair occupants of a celebrated nunnery near Lisbon almost developed into a scandal. John v., however, was not the only 'staunch churchman' whose *laches* have been winked at as long as he 'paid up': though whether the building of the temple of Mafra has been counted unto him for righteousness' sake will never be known while the present world lasts.

'Mafra,' caustically remarks Kinsey, 'might be supposed to commemorate the triumph of folly, bigotry, and the inquisition.' King John installed here three hundred monks, and it was to this religious house the monarch was wont to go into 'retreat,' with a few special lay favourites, and encourage theatrical entertainments, at which actors, orchestra, and audience were all monks: a precedent which was soon followed by other religious houses, if one may judge by the performance at Alcobaca so felicitously described by Beckford.

Never was a faithful son of the Church rated higher for his moral lapses than was this paragon of splendour and holiness, John v.; and never was nation mulcted more heavily for the sins of its monarchs than poor Portugal: for, of course, it was with the money that his subjects had earned with the sweat of their brows that pious King John 'squared' the Church. And with the public chest to draw on he sinned right royally. In fact, Portugal has probably never recovered from the squandering of the national resources that went on in the reign of King John. It has even been affirmed that there was not five hundred pounds in the treasury when he decided to die.

Of course the Pope—as befitted the representative of the Almighty on earth—felt it incumbent on him to reward so much devotion; and in return for John's 'services to the Church' he conferred on him the title of 'Most Faithful,' which has ever since been borne by the kings of Portugal. The end of this staunch churchman was in keeping with his life: 'Having lived like a sultan in the enjoyment of his favourite pleasure,' says a writer of the last century, 'he had both time, and all the means of conversion and reconciliation with Heaven which disingenuous and flattering priests could afford him, to die like a saint (1750); so that his subjects said of him, "He lived and died exactly as he could have wished."' Verily, the parable about the camel and the needle's eye could never have applied to the kings of Portugal!

And now there arose a minister in the land who cared for none of the things which had amused John v.; nay, who hated Jesuits and churchmen, and proceeded to lay his hand heavily on their rights, their privileges, and their property, and soon scented out the abuses of the royal monastic dovecot at Mafra. This minister was Pombal, the aim of whose life was to root out the 'monastic vermin' who depopulated and ruined Portugal. And of all the religious orders, Pombal regarded the mendicants as the most mischievous. Accordingly, the three hundred Franciscans who vegetated at Mafra were sent about their business, and the monastery handed over to the regular canons of St. Austin, who, as they lived upon their own revenues, were less likely to bleed and impoverish all around them.

The wheel of time in its revolution brought the Franciscans their revenge; for, after the death of King Joseph, who had been content to leave the reins of government in the firm grip of his able and strong-willed minister, Pombal—the Richelieu of Portugal, as he has been called—there was a 'general post': Pombal's power collapsed, and great was the fall thereof; and within a few years 'an imbecile and superstitious Queen' re-installed the Franciscans at Mafra, and revived all their privileges.

The manner in which this restoration was brought about sheds so striking a light on monarchic government in Portugal, that it is worth recording; the more so, as guide-books are diplomatically silent on these matters—on anything, in fact, which throws a side-light on monarchical rule in the land of Camoens.

The facts are briefly these: When the Prince of Brazil married, his confessor, who was a Franciscan, and naturally keen for the restoration of his order to their convent and their rights, told him he would never have a child unless the Franciscans were reinstated at Mafra. 'The Prince had faith, the mendicants had Mafra, S. Francisco had pity, and the Princess had a child.' Amongst the names conferred on this 'young hopeful' at his christening was that of a saint, the selection of which was a source of continual perplexity to the courtiers. At length, the question having been put direct to the Prince, he informed his puzzled *entourage* that the name was selected because it was on that particular saint's· day he took it into his royal head to have a son!

Again the wheel of time brought a change in the

fortunes of the dwellers at royal Mafra—to wit, the arrival of the French, whose artistic sense was strongly excited by the spectacle of so much splendour; with the result that these 'liberators of the oppressed' are said not only to have fallen in love with the church vestments, but to have annexed some of the best by way of mementoes of their visit here. However, to their credit be it recorded, they left the library intact, and the convent uninjured—a few smart vestments could very well be spared.

Again the wheel turns, and behold, a British cavalry brigade takes up its quarters here—the greater part of the 16th Light Dragoons being put up in the stables and cloisters of the convent. Then the tide of war rolled onward: the soldiers departed, and once again Mafra is left to solitude and the Franciscans.

Years roll by, and once more, in 1827, the convent is occupied by British troops during the Miguelite troubles and the threatened intervention of Spain, the officer commanding, General Sir Richard Blakeney, having rooms in the palace. It is pleasant to read that the conduct of the troops was excellent: 'The occasional ejectment of an old shoe from a window into a neglected garden appeared to constitute the maximum of British aggression,' wrote a visitor to Mafra. In fact, this 'British occupation,' like many another, left nothing but agreeable memories behind: 'It was gratifying to hear the praise everywhere lavished on our troops,' wrote the same visitor, 'even by persons the most opposed to the principles which brought them to the country.'

It was reserved for men of Portuguese blood to deal the 'knock-down' blow at Mafra; the worst foes the religious orders ever had were those of their own household.

For years the abuses of the monastic system had been crying aloud. But no reform was to be hoped for from within the orders themselves, the entire monkish army having for long shown itself intent only on guarding 'the stuff,' and using the whole power and influence of 'the Church' in support of a race of imbecile and despotic monarchs, who, in return for these faithful services, upheld the rights and privileges of the orders. 'You tickle me, and I'll tickle you, Toby!' In 1834 the blow fell, an edict having been passed for disestablishing the monasteries and convents throughout Portugal: and who shall say the punishment was not deserved? Mafra ceased henceforth to be a resort for the idle and the profligate; the edifice was converted to national uses, and now provides accommodation for a military college, an asylum for the sons of soldiers, the civil court of the district, and a practical school for the infantry of the army. The only part of the vast establishment which still retains something of its former splendour is the church, which is a marvel of decorative work and costly marbles.

As the present-day visitor wanders through the dreary chambers of royal Mafra, let him ponder over the circumstances of its origin. Some little familiarity with the facts, thus briefly summarised, will not, it is believed, diminish in any way the interest with which he gazes on it.

Having seen enough of Mafra to satisfy ourselves that it was an 'established fact,' and not a myth, as a sceptical churchman once affirmed of the Great Wall of China, we made a futile effort to get some light refreshment at the local 'hotel.' But it was the hour of dinner, about half-past four, and at this solemn hour it is useless to ask for anything in the way of 'light' refreshment at Portuguese inns, as I have more than once discovered, to my grief and very grave inconvenience. Dine—you may, but refresh yourself in any other form—never! So we adjourned to a small wine-shop, where we got the requisite sustenance.

I remember reading, in an old book of travels, that one of the good effects of the British occupation of Mafra in 1827 was the establishment of an inn, which, in point of comfort and cleanliness, vied with the inns of old England. Alas! many changes have passed over Mafra since those far-away times. The only inn that now opens its portals to travellers is referred to in a native guide-book under the qualifying term of 'passable'!

The town cemetery at Torres Vedras, with church attached, stands on an eminence near the hotel once occupied by a fort. Observing one evening a funeral *en route* to the church, we followed it in with a view to observing the ceremonials, concerning which some queer stories had reached us. From the circumstance of there being hardly a dozen people assembled to render the last honours, the funeral was evidently that of a very poor person—a fact which, in the opinion of those present, seemed to be considered as sufficient apology for some very strange proceedings.

On entering we found the priest at the head of the coffin, and attended by an acolyte, reading the services for the dead, the 'mourners' laughing and chatting aloud in the most free-and-easy way conceivable. Evidently death had no terrors for them; nor was the priest, I regret to say, visibly oppressed with a sense of the solemnity of the occasion: on the contrary, he was performing his part, not only with shocking irreverence, but in a manner altogether too suggestive of a job that was regarded and paid for as 'piece-work.'

A procession was presently formed for the cemetery, the coffin being hurried along anyhow and deposited in the grave, over which 'their sort of ceremonies' were gone through with more expedition than reverence. The priest, his share of the performance being completed, without more ado tucked up his petticoats and scrambled over the wall, with the acolyte at his heels, who, to save trouble, dragged censer and other instruments of office clattering over the stones, as if they were so much old metal, amidst the laughter—I had almost said, jeers—of the spectators.

The 'religious' ceremony over, the lid of the coffin was removed, and the occupant well peppered with quicklime, and earth bundled in on top. We agreed that it was the most unedifying spectacle we had ever beheld—

> 'Rattle his bones over the stones !
> It's only a pauper, whom nobody owns.'

Having exhausted the attractions of this stuffy, shadeless spot, we determined to return to Lisbon. Our departure from the hotel was the occasion of a touching display of affection on the part of the chambermaid, who, throwing herself on my wife's neck, kissed her affectionately, which seemed to imply a very friendly disposition towards a 'British occupation.' The performance was repeated at other country hotels; and I often thought this 'stamp of approval' ought to have been extended to the paymaster of the party. But it was never even proffered!

The train was timed at about 8 P.M., but it is necessary, when travelling with luggage, to be at the station quite half an hour before the time, seeing that the process of weighing and calculating the sum chargeable engrosses the attention of the entire station staff. On entering the station we were dismayed to find it in possession of a seething and odoriferous crowd of country-folk. To get even within sight of the booking-office was out of the question, and as the ceremony of issuing tickets is regarded as a State function in Portugal, not to be slurred over or hurried in any way, and as it involves a good deal of arithmetic, the prospect of getting a ticket that night seemed utterly hopeless. Fortunately the faithful José had accompanied us, and, grasping the situation at a glance, he nobly offered to rush into the *mêlée* on our behalf. To hand him the money was the work of a second, and forthwith he plunged in, and for twenty minutes was lost to view. At length, after we had quite given him up, expecting to hear nothing more till a claim for the loss of an affectionate and devoted son was put in by sorrowing parents, José emerged—a limp, a hot, and utterly bedraggled person—the perspiration streaming from his honest face, waving the tickets triumphantly. 'Twas nobly dared, and nobly won!

I must explain that the cause of this unwonted bustle was the S. Antonio fêtes at Lisbon, which were to be celebrated with unusual *éclat*—the year 1895 being the quincentenary of the saint's departure from this world. Reports of wonderful goings-on had been spread abroad, and country cousins were flocking into Lisbon from all parts, intent on having a good time of it.

The train was three-quarters of an hour late when, to the usual accompaniment of bell-ringing, horn-blowing, and whistling, it drew into the station; and as it was already packed as close as average humanity cares to be packed, we wondered where the Torres contingent was to be cornered, especially as the ticket-office was still besieged by a clamorous multitude, rendered the more importunate by the almost certain prospect of missing the only train that night. And here let me do the presiding genius of the ticket-office the justice to observe that nothing could exceed the slow and dignified decorum with which he dispensed the passes for the State Railway of Portugal; oblivious to all clamour and the imprecations that irreverent rustics were hurling at him, he calmly went his own way.

Fortunately, the first-class compartments were empty; and having ensconced ourselves therein, we watched the frantic efforts of about a hundred people to find standing-room in an already overcrowded train. Owing to the gallantry of the guard, no attempt was made to storm our castle; but just as the train was about to start, an elderly peasant who had strayed from his flock, espying the empty space within, and blissfully ignorant of any distinction of classes, promptly seized the chance and ensconced himself in a corner with his impedimenta, consisting of the usual patchwork bag and a monstrous blue-cotton umbrella, under which, doubtless, it was the old gentleman's intention to camp out in the open spaces of the metropolis. When he had fairly realised the comfort of his surroundings, his honest and really handsome countenance absolutely beamed with delight. But alas for the vanity of human hopes! the train drew up again, just without the station precincts, and an unfeeling official bundled the old man out most unceremoniously, umbrella, patchwork bag, and all.

As every one of the fourteen stations between Torres and Lisbon presented the same scene of struggling humanity, the allotted time of two and three-quarter hours for the forty miles was stretched to an additional hour and a half;

and the clocks were striking the midnight hour when we drew into the Lisbon station, and caught sight of our friend, who had been waiting for us ever since ten o'clock.

Here the scene of confusion beggared all description; for even on the rare occasion of an excursion, bringing up its hundreds of exhausted voyageurs with their impedimenta, all anxious to get to home and mother, none of the ceremonial observed on the State Railways of Portugal is dispensed with, or even in the least curtailed. The usual military guard was drawn up at the one exit to receive and do the honours of the station to the State guests; and as the State's solicitude for the welfare of its charges extends to the contents of every single package and camping-out umbrella, the 'reception' at the journey's end was as long and tedious as State functions ever are.

Such are some of the inducements to travelling in functionary-ridden Portugal—*pour encourager les autres!* The turmoil of that night I shall never forget. In fact, had not our friend brought a Portuguese factotum who understood the foibles of officialdom, and who commenced by grossly insulting the sergeant of the guard, and followed up the attack by 'riding the high horse' all over the place, I verily believe we should never have got clear.

All this confusion, delay, and annoyance came of the absurd system of octroi, under which every single article of food or commerce that enters Lisbon is chargeable with a tax. Thus it comes about that every road leading into Lisbon is blockaded; a cordon of armed men encircles the city, and on the arrival of a train the passengers, as they emerge from the platform—congratulating themselves on a speedy deliverance from worry,—are confronted with a phalanx of armed men, not to do them honour, but to search their bags! I must do these octroi warriors the justice to admit that they perform their disagreeable duties with courtesy and forbearance, and if you are frank with them the contents of your boxes are not rummaged inconsiderately. The hands of the searchers, moreover, are always encased in clean white cotton gloves—a precaution which might be adopted with advantage in more advanced lands.

Of course, methods such as these could never exist in countries where railways are looked on and treated as means of facilitating travel. Picture the consequences at Waterloo or Liverpool Street of attempting to enforce such a system on the evening of a Bank holiday! It is 'unthinkable'! Dear me! why, barriers, searchers, and the whole absurd army of octroi officials would be swept bodily into space!

There are some things in which Portugal, albeit a 'progressive' country, is still many centuries behind the rest of the world. And I am very far from affirming that the octroi system is not one of those remnants of mediæval times that could very well be dispensed with. It opens the door to a shameful amount of bribery and corruption amongst an army of subordinate and poorly paid officials, and puts a huge premium on smuggling. 'Were you not surprised?' said the Prince of Brazil to Beckford one hundred years ago, 'were you not shocked, at finding us so many centuries behind the rest of Europe?' There are many surprises of this sort in store for the traveller in Portugal at the present time.

As we dashed out of the station in one of those delightful carriages-and-pairs which fulfil the functions of the London 'growler,' we found the whole city *en fête*: the beautiful Rocio a blaze of light, snakes of gas-jets encircling the central column, and thousands of Japanese paper lanterns festooned around, forming delightful discords of colour. The avenues connecting the Rocio with the Praca do Commercio were all glowing with light, while pretty devices carried over the streets broke the monotony of the long line of lamps on either side. We seemed to have entered fairyland, and, in spite of much weariness of the flesh, the temptation to make a detour before turning homewards was irresistible on such a lovely night and amidst such enchanting scenes.

THE SAN ANTONIO FÊTES

The history of Mafra gave us an insight into the motives underlying royal enterprise in the matter of church-building in times past. And in the same way the story of the S. Antonio celebrations affords an interesting illustration of Papal methods at the present day.

The cult of S. Antonio is a very old one at Lisbon; and seeing that the saint was born there, and that he still holds the honorary appointment of Patron Saint, the cult is likely to last. Each centenary as it comes round is welcomed by all good churchmen, whose enthusiasm finds vent in special services, fêtes, feastings, and fireworks, all of which result in a temporary accession of clerical influence, followed by the inevitable lassitude and falling away on the part of the saint's admirers after the cup of jollity has been drained to the dregs.

It happened that the year 1895 was the quincentenary of the saint's death; and seeing that the power and influence of the Pope's party in Portugal are not what they were one hundred years ago—have, in fact, sadly declined since the army of idlers who encumbered the land and filled up the convents were turned out to grass, and their extinction as a 'religious body' ordained—the grave and reverend seigneurs who manage the Pope's affairs in this corner of Europe discerned, with the perspicuity which distinguishes the old gentleman's agents all the world over, a fine chance for resuscitating in some measure their influence amongst the 'masses and the classes.' Accordingly, the word went forth from head-quarters that it was to be a 'record' centenary. The Church put forth all its strength and resources. Money flowed in, and great was the company of preachers.

Now, as S. Antonio is a Portuguese saint of the first holiness, his glorification would naturally redound to the honour and glory of Portugal, and as the Portuguese are a profoundly patriotic people—they are even said to suffer from an excess of patriotism—anything tending to magnify their country in the eyes of the world, and to create a fictitious idea of their own importance in the scheme of the universe, would be likely to find adherents.

To affirm that the bump of self-importance is abnormally developed amongst the Portuguese would perhaps be rather too bold an assertion in the field of phrenology, in view of what is known of other races; but that the nation has every reason to be satisfied with its past, and to look forward complacently to the future, may be proved from the old writers, who boldly assert, by irrefragable proofs taken from Holy Writ, that before the end of time the Portuguese nation is to conquer and swallow up all the others.

The Powers of Europe need not, however, be alarmed at this; because, as was remarked by a commentator in the last century, 'this positive prophecy may serve as a comfortable reflection to those who do not wish for a speedy

I

dissolution of the present system of things, for, according to every human appearance at present, no nation in Europe is at so great a distance from being in a condition to fulfil such a prediction.' The suggestion of a 'record' centenary caught on. The Court threw the whole weight of its influence into the scale; Government followed suit, and all Lisbon went mad. Money flowed liked water, or perhaps it would be more correct to say that bills were incurred as if there was to be no reckoning up before the last trump; and the city was turned upside down, the principal thoroughfares displaying a glowing mass of colour—banners and wreaths, and silks and satins by day, and a coruscating galaxy of light by night.

Lisbon having set its mind on doing something big, it was natural for the inhabitants to suppose that the rest of the world would be palpitating with excitement and anticipation, all eagerness to take part in the good things provided. A vast influx of visitors was anticipated, equalling, if not exceeding, that which flocked to the Paris Exhibition—for was not the motive of these ecclesiastical high jinks such as must needs appeal to the sympathies of all peoples?—though where the visitors were to be accommodated, no one cared to inquire. But that all the 'world and his wife' would come, no one for a moment doubted, for no one cared to ask why people should travel to the extremest corner of Europe to gaze at fireworks and join in the cult of S. Antonio.

The celebrations began on the 12th of June—the day of our return to Lisbon,—and were to be spun out over an entire month. Every day witnessed an increase in the area over which the decorations were displayed, and every night some new feature was introduced in the scheme of illuminations; the grand climax being reached on the last night of the fêtes, when Black Horse Square blossomed out into a sort of fancy fair or carnival of all classes, ending up with such a display of fireworks as had never before been witnessed in Lisbon.

Certainly the decoration committee deserved credit, seeing that the results of their labours and cogitations were deservedly admired. Lisbon became 'a thing of beauty,' if it was not to remain 'a joy for ever'! And wherever the eye turned it was met by avenues of Venetian masts, vistas of banners, triumphal arches, and lavish floral decorations, gracefully disposed draperies, with miles of Chinese lanterns, and labyrinthian arrangements of gas-pipes for illuminating purposes.

Never in the history of civilised peoples was such an ado made about nothing—or, shall we say, about such a very unimportant anniversary? The 'intelligent foreigner' might have supposed the nation to be *en fête* over an event of the profoundest national importance—Trafalgar Day, for example, or its equivalent in Portuguese annals! No one would have believed that all this fuss was because a baby was born seven hundred years ago, who, after his death, was given the honourable appointment of patron saint, with contingent emoluments. And the stranger's astonishment would have been even greater had he been told that all these high jinks under exalted patronage were being enacted for the purpose of resuscitating the Church's waning influence in Portugal, and enticing back stray sheep into the Papal fold.

The 'opposition'—that is, the Republican press—took the matter very much *au sérieux*, at first, and poured out the vials of its wrath freely on all concerned in what it was pleased to call 'these disgraceful celebrations.' The most influential and outspoken of these journals declared that 'the festival of the centenary of S. Antonio, and the unqualified language used at the Catholic Congress, were an imprudent and impudent provocation which awoke in the hearts of all liberals a lively sentiment of detestation, which was latent amongst the mass of the populace, against the Jesuits, the monks, and the religious reaction.'

The programme comprised ecclesiastical processions with banners and relics, in which all the supporters of the Church participated, backed up with an imposing display of municipal guards and the whole available military force of the metropolis; or, as the Republican organ expressed it: 'The creatures of the Court and Government obtained recognition of the seventh centenary of the Portuguese Franciscan who died at Padua, in order to arrange a grand review of the forces of reaction.'

The festivities were protracted over an entire month, but long before the time had run its dreary length of enforced merry-making the public had heartily sickened of the whole thing, while the Republican press busied itself in turning it all into ridicule. Meanwhile, the world beyond Portugal remained coldly indifferent to the record centenary, had other business to attend to. Hence the organisers of the fêtes reckoned without their host, the influx of visitors being waited for in vain. Portugal, truth to tell, is too far removed from the 'centres of effort,' at the present day, to draw people for religious fêtes and firework displays; and so, when all was over, the shopkeepers and others who had been inveigled into heavy expense had the dreary consolation of feeling that they had honoured the patron saint, and encouraged 'the forces of reaction'!

The ostentatious display of military force during these

celebrations was interpreted by the 'progressives' as a direct challenge, and it certainly filled up the vials of their wrath. Nevertheless, the only *contretemps* that marred the outward harmony of the centenary occurred on the last day of the fêtes, when, as the Republican organ above mentioned reported, 'On June 30th, the directors of the Jesuitical reaction sallied forth in a procession through the streets, in the midst of an enormous municipal force, but even thus it was impossible to avoid the procession being broken up.'

The 'breaking up' came about in this wise. There had been dark rumours floating about of Nihilist or Republican plots to disturb the solemnity of the occasion; and the Church party, as a result of over-excitement, excess of jollification, much processioning, and prolonged tension of feeling, having been worked up into a highly nervous state, it needed but a spark to generate an explosion or bring about a collapse. The spark was administered on the occasion of the 'grand review of the forces of reaction,' on the 30th June, when, as the procession was passing the most densely crowded part of the route, an enterprising fellow discharged a handful of papers from a window into the very centre of the demonstrators, and as the sheets fell fluttering down a most startling change came over the spirit of the scene. The effect, indeed, was electrical. The clericals, mistaking the innocent sheets for Nihilist manifestoes, or bombs—albeit, I believe, no more dangerous to life and property than advertisements usually are—were seized with childish panic, and, forgetful of the solemnity of the occasion, to say nothing of the protecting power of S. Antonio, whose arm would surely have been stretched forth to shield his protégés from harm, they threw dignity and self-respect to the winds, and scattered in all directions, their example being followed by the guards and military —priests, churchmen, banners, emblems of the faith and relics, soldiers and civilians being all mixed up in a general *sauve qui peut*. Never was the passage from the sublime to the ludicrous more quickly bridged. It was lamentable; it was disgraceful.

However, beyond a goodly list of personal injuries received in the stampede—an elderly Englishmen being nearly killed—there was little harm done. But the episode was not lost on the Republicans, who seized on the fiasco as a telling text for their next day's discourses.

Such, briefly, were the celebrations on the occasion of the seventh centenary of the patron saint of Lisbon. And if the organisers hoped to rehabilitate the Church as a power in the land by such means, they must have experienced a chilling disappointment. *Mais, que voulez-vous?* To our cold northern temperament the whole thing seemed inexpressibly childish: though, to be sure, it was not the first time, in the history of the Papal Church, that an attempt was made to gather the wandering sheep back to its bosom by means of flags, feastings, and fireworks. The secret history of the movement, the sources from whence were derived the sinews of war, to say nothing of the accounts, have yet to be disclosed.

The one touch of humour imparted to the affair was the invitation to the European Powers to send their ships to add *éclat* to the festivities—an invitation that was coldly ignored by all but the 'ancient ally,' England, who sent a solitary cruiser, whose fine display of rockets and electric light lent additional brilliance to the scene float. Thus did Great Britain lend its support to what the opposition press declared to be 'an imprudent and impudent provocation,' on the part of the 'forces of reaction,' which, with 'the support of the public authorities, was offered to the Portuguese people.' The fleets of all the Catholic Powers were conspicuous by their absence. Protestant and tolerant England alone swallowed the bait.

The sequel was as singular as it was totally unexpected. Exactly a month later, all Lisbon was engaged in priest-baiting. Rumours having been spread abroad concerning the supposed kidnapping of children by the Jesuits, one of those fierce and unreasoning panics which sometimes take possession of an ignorant people seized the populace of Lisbon, and for the greater part of a day the city was the scene of the wildest confusion. Outrages were committed on the persons of all who bore the smallest resemblance to a priest, the populace being only too glad of an excuse for venting their rage on a despised and detested class. The long pent-up feelings of the ignorant people immediately found vent, with the result that every man with a close-shaven face, or whose clothes bespoke the ecclesiastical cut, was flying for dear life. Schools were broken into, shops invaded, and even the tramcars stopped and their occupants thrust forth, in the eagerness of the priest-baiters to discover their quarry. Ovens and other odd places were utilised as havens of refuge from an infuriated rabble; and but for the intervention of the police, many of the unfortunate objects of popular fury, laymen as well as priests, would have been done to death.

Towards night the passions of the mob cooled down; their superfluous energies having been turned into the more prosaic but less harmful pursuit of bread-winning, and once more the city resumed its wonted aspect. But the affair was sprung so suddenly on the authorities—the panic having spread like wildfire through city and suburbs—that at first it seemed like the premonitory sputterings of a revolution, and the Government was really alarmed.

It was certainly a disgraceful spectacle that Lisbon presented to the civilised world on the 30th July 1895. And what a commentary on the celebrations of the month before! It was all brought about by the dissemination of what are believed to have been baseless reports concerning the kidnapping of children by Jesuit priests. 'Some enemy hath done this evil thing!' might well be the exclamation of the Church party. It was a poor result to point to, for all the lavish display of the centenary. For surely if folly and fireworks could rehabilitate a decaying system, the organisers of the fêtes had every reason to look for better fruits!

The Republican press was quick to seize on the humour of the situation, and to point the moral. 'The Consequences of a Provocation' was the startling heading, in large type, of a scathing article in the most influential journal next morning. 'It was truly significant what took place yesterday, in Lisbon,' the article ran :—

'If after the incidents that occurred exactly a month ago, in connection with the procession of S. Antonio, doubts were any longer permissible concerning the opinions and sentiments of the people of Lisbon with regard to the administration of Jesuitism, the strange and violent proceedings which took place yesterday, in different quarters of the city, ought to make clear to the most obtuse understanding the true significance of the causes. The indescribably grotesque incidents of the 30th June convinced all who reflect that the religious question is alone quite sufficient to raise a tempest. What took place yesterday proved this. Public opinion was excessively irritated with the Jesuitical festivities of June, and with the brutally irritating assertions which certain bishops, Senhor ———, and other orators launched forth from the tribune of S. Vincent, where they made an apology for institutions and principles incompatible with the democratic doctrines and the spirit of this century. With these irritants acting on the liberal elements, any cause or incident was enough to lead to an explosion of popular fury and to produce disastrous consequences. And this provocation resulted in the deeds of yesterday, which were in contrast to the usual disposition and extreme tolerance of our nation. The people, however, were not content with the ridiculous failure of the procession of 30th of June. Observing that the Jesuits and the Court continued to labour to get possession of the education of the young, and knowing that every moment religious institutions were being multiplied, in which girls suffered bad treatment, and were cut off from the love of their parents, and observing that every day the authorities made fresh concessions of State buildings to the founders of *bona-fide* convents, which are not allowed to exist in Portugal, and seeing that the Court and the Government were at the service of Jesuitism,—knowing all this, the masses of the populace felt increased irritation on each occasion, and this irritation resulted in violence such as was witnessed yesterday. The responsibility for all this rests with those who provoked it with their abuses. They invoked the religious question, which in Portugal seemed dead. They sought to hand over the instruction of the young to the Jesuits and the other religious sects subordinated to them, and behold the consequences of their improper proceedings! They provoked a tempest. The Portuguese people wish no ill to the innocent priests; but they detest the Jesuits with their monstrous morality, which is capable of the greatest outrages. It was on this account that a violent temper was observable yesterday. Would to God this highly significant fact might serve as a lesson to all! If the governors and directors of Jesuitism insist on forcing their reactionary schemes on our attention, it is not strange that they should produce the gravest consequences.'

Such tall talk is apt to provoke a smile in countries where Jesuits have ceased to be taken *au sérieux*. And it is easy to pooh-pooh this violent tirade against the 'forces of reaction' as the mere 'hare-brained chatter of irresponsible frivolity'; but clerical supremacy is much too recent an affair in Portugal for the people to forget it, or what it stands for, and assuredly no well-wisher of the country would desire to see this power restored.

The condition of things that prevailed when clerical influence was supreme, and the grossest abuses abounded, is, as the above-quoted writer says, 'opposed to the spirit of this century,' and too fresh in the memory of the people to admit of an attempt being made to re-establish it without raising a tempest of evil passions. But the Jesuits forget nothing and learn nothing; and, in the Peninsula at any rate, are ever wakeful and ready to take advantage of the chapter of accidents for gathering up something of their lost power.

The sentiments embodied in the above article may be held to represent the views of a numerous and influential party in Portugal, whose opinions can no longer be ignored by those who navigate the ship of State, without incurring risks which all sane pilots would desire to avoid. The Republican party is already a power in the land; and although its bark is supposed to be worse than its bite, it may at last be driven to use its teeth in self-defence.

To know something of the principles underlying the conduct of opponents is essential if we would gauge the measure of their competency for government, or forecast the future that awaits the country under their guidance. The key-note of the Republican policy is anti-clericalism, the party's action being inspired by the sentiments embodied in the celebrated phrase coined by Gambetta: '*Le cléricalisme, voilà l'ennemi!*' If the party is united indeed on any policy, it is in a determination not to allow the Church to 'rule the roost' again in Portugal. Though whether the Republicans have any satisfactory substitute for the 'authority of the Church,' any sound principles of government that would make it worth people's while to rally round, support, and fight for—a centripetal force, rather than a centrifugal one—remains to be shown. A nation can't be expected to throw a monarchy overboard for the sake of a 'philosophical ideal.'

The most significant feature of this movement is the fact of antagonism to the Church having sprung up in a close Roman Catholic preserve, wherein Protestantism is unknown. 'The spirit of the century' has manifested itself in a land—well, if not given over to idolatry, as some writers have affirmed, a country wherein clericalism has dominated every department of public and private life, and was, until recently, supreme in the State; wherein the Inquisition existed as late as a hundred years ago; and wherein the most corrupt, degraded, and despotic form of monarchy was upheld and encouraged by the Church, till nation and monarchy literally fell to pieces from their own inherent rottenness. The wave of reaction against clerical domination which swept over France and Italy, after passing over Spain struck the shores of Portugal. Spain remains the last stronghold of clerical domination in its worst form. And what is the condition of Spain at the present moment? Why, the very angels must weep and veil their faces at the spectacle of national decadence therein presented!

The question is, Will Portugal succeed in keeping off this 'Old Man of the "See"'? Every one knows that a nation's extremity is the Jesuit's opportunity. The followers of Loyola will stick at nothing. At present they are lying quiet, biding their time. But the 'review of the forces of reaction' at the S. Antonio celebrations, and the doctrines enunciated on that occasion, show that the Jesuit snake in Portugal is merely scotched, not killed, and only waiting its chance to lift its hateful head and gather up its lost power.

Even the anti-clerical government of France is being drawn into the 'bosom of the Church,' which, like some huge octopus, stretches its tentacles into every cranny of the social organism, and draws sustenance from its very vices. Romanists cannot exist without a Pope; and no self-respecting 'Head of the Church' will tolerate anything short of absolute subjection, the most degrading and servile surrendering of self, on the part of his subjects. 'Man cannot serve two masters,' and the 'Head of the Church' only knows of one, himself; and if the Pope does not at present enforce servitude in its strictest sense, this remissness is not owing to any spirit of tolerance, but merely to policy—'the time will come!' In France, Madame la République has become the humble servant of the Church. 'At present there is nothing more to lose, not even honour!' exclaimed the French paper the *Radical*, recently: 'there is no Republic any more, neither are there Republicans. There are neither men nor women, but only Jesuits!' What is happening in France will doubtless follow later on in Portugal. The Church's view of the matter, was concisely put by the *Revue du Clergé Français*, in Paris: 'The Church possesses the right to govern not only individuals and families, but also peoples. In other words, the State is not independent of the Church: the State is obliged to accept the Catholic religion, to profess and to defend it. By divine right, the Pope, as supreme Head of the Church, has power to enact mandates with obligatory force for princes.' This is frank, at any rate.[1]

[1] See a remarkable article in *The Contemporary Review* for March 1898, entitled 'The Demoralisation of France.'

Now, His Holiness Pope Benedict XIV. having conferred on that 'paragon of splendour,' Dom Joao V., the title of 'Most Faithful,' in consideration of his sins and his 'backsheesh,' and seeing that the distinction descends, along with the regalia and other emoluments, to the reigning sovereigns of Portugal, it would ill become a mere king to kick against the pricks of Papal authority. The present monarch therefore finds himself 'twixt the devil and the deep sea! What his private opinions may be on the subject of Papal infallibility, or as to the right of the Head of the Church to thrust his infallible finger into every pie, it would be presumptuous in a mere outsider to guess at even. But that the recognition of the Church as a power in the land gives mortal offence to the Republicans, is well known. Though, unless he would forfeit the title of 'Most Faithful,' what is the poor king to do? The question resolves itself into the old tug-of-war between the devil and the baker!

During the S. Antonio celebrations, the king and his ministers were charged with seeking to re-establish clerical domination, the extravagant displays which attended the fêtes, under the ostentatious approval of Court and Government, causing the utmost indignation amongst the 'progressives.' One or two extracts from the opposition press will afford an insight into the thoughts that are troubling the Republican breast at the present moment.

Said the *Correio de Manha* ('The Morning Post'): 'Without doubt the improvidence of certain governments has encouraged the increase of the Jesuit sect amongst us, contrary to the express laws of the realm, which have never been revoked.' Other journals were more explicit: 'The Jesuitical reaction has been scandalously favoured by the authorities, and, owing to their protection, Jesuitism thrives and multiplies its means of action.' Or again: 'The Government, and with the Government the Court, have with this affront to the laws of the country and the national sentiment, impudently and infamously protected the sect of the Jesuits, as well as the dark deeds of fanaticism to which it is addicted.' The situation was thus summed up by another paper: 'There is not the least doubt of this, that the monarchy exposes itself to ruin. Abandoned by the regular clergy, it throws itself into the arms of the Jesuit, and makes common cause with him, a course which is inimical to liberty and civilisation. This is why the people turn against the Jesuits and against the monarchy.'

In their desire to drive home the Republican text by illustrations of the inestimable blessings that flow from a Republican form of government, the organs of the party are not always happy in their choice of examples. For instance, I was amused, on one occasion, to peruse an extremely eulogistic account of the Transvaal, the prosperous condition of which was cited as proving the advantages a small country derives from the purity and enlightenment that invariably flow from a Republican source! Any stick, though, is thought good enough to beat 'a rotten old monarchy' with!

The attitude which the king and his ministers ought to adopt with respect to the clerical party was tersely summed up in the leading Republican paper, in its issue of July 31st 1895, the morning after the riot:—

'DEATH TO THE JESUITS!

'Irritated by the continued provocations of the Jesuits and the reactionaries, and excited by the rumours which were persistently circulated concerning the kidnapping of children by the sinister crows of —— [a nickname for the Jesuits], the people broke out yesterday everywhere, and gave chase to the assassins of the Society of Jesus. It was a coincidence that yesterday was exactly a month since the celebrated procession of the centenary, and the eve of the festival of S. Ignacius de Loyola, the founder of the Jesuit sect, which the Church celebrates to-day. . . . The urgent duty is incumbent on the Government to expel from the country the Jesuit sects, which have provoked the utmost indignation by their procedure, dividing the Portuguese family, and raising anew the religious question, which every one had agreed to leave alone. It is impossible to tolerate once more the Jesuits. The people of Lisbon showed this yesterday in the strongest manner, proving themselves absolutely inimical to that rabble of fanatics which swears war to the death against progress and liberty.'[1]

Crowns are resting somewhat precariously on more than one European head at the present moment, and, it must be confessed, there is much in the existing state of Portugal to cause uneasiness on the part of its well-wishers. As the latest writer on Portugal has remarked: 'There is no concealing the fact that Charles I. will have to show the greatest political wisdom if he is to weather the storms now besetting the position of Portugal, and to save the Portuguese monarchy.'

TO SETUBAL

The most extensive view from the Lisbon heights is that across the Tagus to the Arrabida Mountains, a bold range occupying the southern portion of the Peninsula, and ending abruptly at Cape Espichel. The eastern extremity forms the craggy rock on which Palmella Castle is perched so conspicuously, and beneath which, in a

[1] The translation of this and the preceding extracts from the Lisbon papers helped to while away many an hour of enforced imprisonment in native hotels.

beautiful valley extending to the shore, is esconced the town of Setubal, corrupted by the English into St. Ubes, now connected with Lisbon by rail. Westward of this happy valley, along the southern slopes of the Arrabida range, lies some of the most exquisite scenery, on a pocket scale, in Southern Portugal; and yet, strange to say, this little district, almost within sight of Lisbon, is practically a *terra incognita* to natives and strangers alike!

Now, as there was a week to while away before the arrival of the homeward-bound steamer, and as we had seen most of the places around Lisbon, our host proposed a visit to Setubal for the purpose of exploring some ancient remains on an island, and taking the Palmella mountain on our way back. As this proposal exactly accorded with our roving disposition, we embarked that very evening at the Praca do Commercio, in the steamer for Barriero, the terminus of the southern railway system, on the south bank of the Tagus, and which has now taken the place of Aldea Gallega in the economy of travel. 'Charming weather for crossing to Aldea Gallega,' wrote Beckford a hundred years ago, just before setting off on his journey to Spain from the Lisbon stairs, 'where the old Marquis of Marialva's scalera was waiting, with eight-and-twenty rowers in their bright scarlet accoutrements.' But then it took him two hours to make the crossing, which we, with less state but more expedition, accomplished in thirty-five minutes, and without having to satisfy the 'mute clamour' of eight-and-twenty 'salaried beggars' for backsheesh—to say nothing of the coxswain!

A bee-line from Barreiro to Setubal would measure about twelve miles; but the railway has to make a detour round the Palmella mountain, and covers rather more than sixteen. 'We left Aldea Gallega, and ploughed through deep furrows of sand at the sober rate of two and a half miles an hour. On both sides of the heavy road the eye ranges uninterruptedly, except by the stems of starveling pines, through a boundless extent of barren country, overgrown with stunted ilex and gum-cistus.' What a change has come over the face of this particular bit of landscape since then! Nowadays the 'barren' desert has given place to great stretches of market-gardens, wherein vast quantities of fruit and vegetables are raised for the Lisbon markets, and agreeably diversified with orchards and vineyards.

And yet I can remember, when, as a youngster, just nine-and-twenty years ago, one lovely spring morning I and a brother-mid footed the whole twelve miles to Setubal, there was just such a tract of country as Beckford describes. How we ever pulled through those dreary miles of sand and pine-trees, under a burning sun, I never shall understand. The experiment certainly evoked feelings of the liveliest sympathy for the Israelites; and though no friendly manna descended on us, and no Moses handy with his rod appeared to fetch water from the rock, we stuck to our bee-line, and duly 'eventuated' into Setubal; from whence we returned, as every one but a British midshipman would have *gone*, by train.

Twilight was falling when we drew up at Setubal station; and as the information supplied to us as to hotel accommodation was somewhat contradictory, we set off on a voyage of investigation. Of the two hotels, one was found to be full; so it was 'Hobson's choice,' and we took up our abode at a house kept by an aged Frenchwoman—a bare and poverty-stricken establishment from the 'hotel' point of view, whose internal economy left much to be

K

desired. But seeing that madame was far in advance of the period of life which even ladies admit to be the 'middle age,' and had long divorced herself from the spirit of enterprise—*que voulez-vous?*

Still the cooking was good, and the old lady all geniality and anxiety to oblige. The beds!—well, suffice it to say, they nobly sustained the national reputation for 'uncompromising firmness' in their intercourse with strangers; though I must admit that our occupation of them was undisturbed by the importunities of rivals, and that not even a daylight investigation revealed any 'light cavalry.'

Having selected our rooms—to be quite accurate, there was no choice—we sallied forth and made a tour of the town. A strict regard to veracity compels me to declare that Setubal is a deadly dull, unattractive little place. Nature has performed her part in excellent style, but 'Art' has done nothing to help along the old lady. The usual Praça, with a few scrubby palm-trees, and the indispensable bandstand, decked out in garish colours, adorn the sea-front; but the only feature of the place which forces itself into notice, and that in a most objectionable manner, is a stream which meanders through the town, and on this particular occasion loaded the evening air with its disgusting perfume. Some day, perchance, a dawning sense of decency will prompt the inhabitants to cover up the town sewer!

As a nation, the Portuguese are remarkable for their courtesy. We were totally unprepared, however, for the salutations which greeted our progress through Setubal; and our self-esteem rose in proportion to the frequency of these agreeable marks of respect, all of which were most conscientiously acknowledged with befitting condescension. Great was our consternation when it dawned on us that all this hat-lifting was in response to our coachman, whose circle of acquaintances was both extensive and select, and whose whole time was taken up in lifting his hat to passing 'familiars.' It was certainly a little embarrassing.

Now, seeing that the hour of *table d'hôte* was 4.30, and that our hostess had neither the means nor the intention of preparing a second repast, we were recommended to try 'pot luck' at an adjacent eating-house, which enjoyed a reputation for good cookery; and here, sure enough, we got a substantial and well-cooked meal, the culinary operations being transacted within a few feet of the table, to which the food was transferred 'piping hot.' This 'noted house' was located in a side-street of slummy and uninviting aspect; and as the doors were kept wide open, and the arrival of *os Ingleses* had apparently been extensively advertised amongst the juvenile part of the inhabitants, there was no lack of audience. To be sure, we thought the young ladies were a trifle forward, seeing that, nothing daunted by the fierceness of visage we at first assumed, the *donzellas* marched boldly up to the table and demanded 'contributions in aid'; while the boys, with the diffidence and modesty which invariably distinguishes the male sex, hung back. Now, as we made a point of gratifying native curiosity whenever it could be done, with due regard to the conventionalities—and really, after so much touring, we felt we owed the Portuguese a debt of gratitude for giving us the run of their country, and for all the attention they had shown to us at custom-houses and other 'state-aided' establishments for the encouragement of travel—we made no attempts to repel the advances of these forward young women. So, after sampling the several courses, the contents of our plates were duly transferred to their pinafores. The proprietor, who was perfectly oblivious to these little irregularities, seemed to take them as quite in the ordinary course of business, and never even ventured to raise a blush on the rather soiled cheeks of the pert *dònzellas* by closing the door in their faces. It was delightful dispensing our charities in this informal manner—without cost to ourselves; and many an agreeable little memento of our visit did these enterprising young ladies carry away. Let us hope that many a hungry waif was fed from the crumbs that fell from our banquet that night.

Considering what a squalid little hole it was, the excellence of the dinner was remarkable. The wine, too, was delicious; and the oranges at dessert were the very largest and best I had ever tasted. But the Setubal oranges are famed throughout the Peninsula. The Portuguese declare the whole world produces no better fruit; and really, I am more than half inclined to indorse that pious opinion; for in the course of my wanderings over the face of the waters, and contact with many shores, I have never come across any fruit to compare with them, unless it be certain oranges I once tasted in the island of St. Michael's. Alas! I am told that disease has played havoc with the St. Michael's fruit-trees, nearly all of which have been grubbed up, and the delicious *spécialité* once associated with the name of the immaculate saint is no more.

We retired late to bed, and extracted as much pleasure as was to be expected from the act of supererogation comprised in rolling about for hours on the unsympathetic planes that did duty for beds. Further reflection has convinced me that it must be the identical 'hotel' that Southey put up at just a century ago, and concerning which he wrote—'There is an hotel here kept by an Irishman; I had expected a good house, and was completely disappointed. We procured a *ground-floor* apartment there, *two stories above the street*, in which two little bed-closets stood.' I should say the Irishman's stock-in-trade has done duty ever since!

Now, as I said, the particular goal of our pilgrimage was some ancient remains of considerable interest to archæologists, on a spit of land opposite to Setubal. To reach this it is necessary to take a boat for a village called Troja, corrupted by the English into Troy, and, in consequence, to my certain knowledge, believed by many of my countrymen to be the ancient and famed city of Troy. The city which once stood here, and of which I believe scarcely a vestige remains, was called Cetobriga, and from time to time Roman coins are still unearthed, or rather unsanded, here. A Corinthian pillar, which was excavated in the last century, was erected in the square of Setubal, 'scraped, and then ornamented with a crucifix!' I entirely forgot to ascertain what 'scheme of decorative treatment' now prevails thereon. From certain inscriptions, it has been conjectured that Cetobriga was occupied successively by Romans and Phœnicians. That the Romans, at any rate, made excellent use of this pleasant corner of Portugal there is no doubt, seeing that the little town of Alcacer do Sal, near Setubal, was the 'fashionable summer resort' of the wealthy Romans from Beja, Evora, and other parts of South Portugal, during the bathing season. What attractions the modern town of Alcacer do Sal possess I know not, but the name is suggestive of its whilom masters, the Moors, and scarcely a town in Portugal can boast of more interesting historical associations. It was only after repeated attempts that the Portuguese succeeded in wresting the place from the Moors, who seized it again within a few years. And when, at length, the final expulsion of those warriors was determined on, the arrival of a party of English crusaders at Lisbon was too good a chance to be let slip, and the Bishop of Lisbon easily persuaded them to throw in their lot with the Portuguese, who were about to attack the common enemy. Accordingly, under their own leaders, the Earls of Wight and Holland, the Englishmen advanced to lay siege to the city of Alcacer do Sal.

While thus honourably employed, a huge army of forty thousand infantry and fifteen thousand cavalry, under certain redoubtable *walis*, advanced to the relief of the besieged. The two armies met and fought in September 1217; the Mohammedans were driven from the field; the Cross was once more triumphant; and it is said that the Knights Templar chased the Moors for three days and nights. At any rate, Alcacer do Sal surrendered, and its gallant defender, Abu Abdalla, 'in admiration of the valour of the Christians, consented to be baptized.'

Here was a 'feather in the cap' of the small body of Britons who helped to clear Portugal of the Moors! And when, in years to come, a Briton wanders within sight of Alcacer do Sal, let him salute the brave English crusaders who, within sight of its walls, put to flight the army of the aliens, and nobly sustained the fighting reputation of Old England's sons.

We were loth to turn from the goal that was beckoning us across the intervening expanse of water; but rain was falling steadily, and although we sallied forth as far as the edge of the tide, the rain was too persistent to be ignored. So, regretfully countermanding the boat, we sought refuge in a crockery shop, where for two hours we beguiled the time, and vastly astonished the proprietor by the variety and extent of our purchases.

I must explain that ever since landing in Portugal we had cast covetous eyes on the native delf-ware, which litters the poorer sort of china-shops. We had even planned a field-day amongst these for the purpose of carrying off a consignment to England. The chance had come at last, and we made the most of it. Fortunately, the proprietor was not overburdened with business on this particular forenoon, and directly he had recovered from his first surprise, and convinced himself we were not fooling him, he entered into the spirit of our enterprise. Every hole and cranny of his rambling establishment was rummaged; and not content with articles within easy reach, we clamoured for a ladder, and, perched on its topmost rung, I unearthed plates and basins from the accumulated dust of centuries, handing them down to the partner of my travels—a rabid china-maniac,—who sorted the wheat from the tares, and laid out the most promising specimens for final selection. At last there was no more standing-room—the superficies covered amounting to a great many square yards; whereupon we gravely announced our intention of buying the lot. An hour earlier, the good man would probably have turned us out of his shop as demented people, but now nothing surprised him; he even showed symptoms of pleasure, though, to be sure, I thought I detected, in a corner of his 'business eye,' a twinkle of scepticism at such an unlooked-for stroke of good-luck befalling him. I won't weary the reader with the details of our investment. Suffice it to say the collection comprised plates— in which John the Baptist's head would have looked small,—bowls, soup-tureens, teapots, jugs, barbers' basins, and mugs. Many of these homely articles must have been 'shopkeepers' for years, the present fashions inclining towards hideous, commonplace china of native manufacture, imprinted with some of the very crudest patterns and colours that were ever turned out of a British factory at the worst period—which is saying a great deal.

At an early stage of our investigation, the worthy shopman, mistaking us for people of 'taste,' if lacking in intelligence, had taken us aside to a case in which his very particular treasures were stocked, and lifting the cover, produced some china of British make, from which he proceeded to extract that musical ring peculiar to good china when tapped with the finger-nail, and watched the effect on us. Bitter was the worthy man's disappointment when we turned away in disgust and rushed back to his twopenny-ha'penny delf-ware.

The third member of our party had been acting the useful part of looker-on, and when he interpreted our decision to take the lot, the merchant, on recovering his breath, asked if there was going to be an exhibition in England!

The making up of the account proved rather a tax on the worthy merchant's arithmetic. Still, it was accomplished; and how much do you think the bill amounted to, reader? Rather under one pound sterling! And that included packing it all—fifty or sixty pieces—in a strong case fit to stand the journey home! It was the cheapest bargain we ever made in the crockery line, and probably the best morning's work our friend the merchant had done for a very long time.

As good-luck would have it, an English steamer, bound to London, was in the harbour. The shipping-agent was known to our friend, and in a very short time the whole affair had been satisfactorily arranged—the skipper promising to take extra care of the consignment while *en route* to Old England. The sequel? Well, although we did not exactly cast our bread in the form of pottery upon the waters, it nevertheless returned to us after many days. In plain English, the case turned up at home in due course; and when its precious contents were excavated from the straw—in fear and trembling, I must confess—and laid out in order, counted, and compared with our list, the truth gradually dawned on us that not a single item had been either broken or even chipped. And this result, looking to the extremely brittle nature of the ware, was very much to the credit of the packer, whom I complimented by letter, written in my best Portuguese!

Time forbade a visit to the Arrabida Mountain or the Convent of Nossa Senhora da Arrabida, a circumstance we all very much regretted, after reading Southey's delightful account of the locality. 'Never did I behold scenery so wild and so sublime as the mountain of the Arrabida presented,' he wrote enthusiastically, after his visit in 1796.

The English associations of the monastery, moreover, are eminently calculated to draw the traveller thither. For, if monastic traditions lie not—and, to be sure, no one could 'draw the long-bow' with better effect at a pinch than the brethren of the cowl,—the convent owes its origin to a miraculous image that belonged to the chaplain of an English ship which had been preserved from shipwreck off this very coast. It seems that the image, having fled to the shore during the storm—rather a base act of desertion,—was afterwards snugly ensconced on the spot where it was found by the devout mariners, who, with the ingenuity that distinguishes the British tar, 'rigged up' a little temple here, and voted their shipmate, Mr. Haldebrant, the owner of this skittish piece of wood, into the post of chaplain-in-charge.

It is a fascinating legend, and I shall ever regret not having paid my respects to Nossa Senhora da Arrabida, of British origin, and possibly manufacture!—Or was it 'made in Germany? We shall never know.'

Looking to the associations of Nossa Senhora, it was only meet and proper that a proportion of the accommodation in the convent, that afterwards arose here, should be reserved for monks of British origin; and when Southey looked in, sure enough there was an English hermit *in situ*: he had abused his trust as an agent at Lisbon, and 'chose this way of life'!

That the inhabitants of Setubal are capable of better things than the casual visitor might imagine from the *dolce far niente* air which pervades the 'second-best port in Portugal,' is shown by the flourishing state of the sardine industry. There are several factories for tinning the fish; and I was informed that previous to the passing of the Merchandise Marks Act, which compels imports to carry the name of the place of origin, the Setubal sardines were largely imported as French, and being of equally good quality and flavour, were eaten with avidity. Their Portuguese origin having become known has since created a prejudice against them.

At the time of the Miguelite troubles, Captain Napier, the 'Fighting Charley' of Baltic renown, who was admiral of the Constitutionalist Fleet of Portugal, succeeded in galvanising a little life into the lethargic inhabitants of Setubal, and by his personal exertions and foresight, prevented this important harbour from falling into Miguelite hands. 'He seemed to possess the power of ubiquity,' wrote a contemporary; and pouncing down here one fine day, this gallant sailor, with his bustling ways, got the forts put in order and the guns remounted, 'under his personal inspection,' and left a garrison of British marines, enlisted into the Portuguese service, to keep watch and ward over the town. There is no manner of doubt that Napier saved the Constitutional cause in Portugal. And yet, amidst all the grand monuments to 'Liberty,' and the heroes of the Constitutional war, you may search in vain for any statue to Charles Napier, the very recollection of whom has quite slipped out of the national conscience. But, 'twas ever thus with the countrymen of Camoens!

With all their indolence and apparent lethargy of temperament, the Setubalese, like their countrymen in general, are very devils incarnate when roused. 'Scratch a southerner and you find a tiger,' is particularly applicable to the inhabitants of the Peninsula; and if any one is inclined to doubt their capacity for acting the rôle of the wild beast, let him study Lord Carnarvon's account of a visit to Setubal when the Miguelite troubles were at their worst. Describing a meeting of Miguelite adherents, he says: 'The popular enthusiasm was at its height, and characterised by such extreme ferocity that I could not behold it without awe, or hear the deadly imprecations heaped upon the Constitutionalists without feeling that a terrible hour of vengeance was at hand. I have mingled much in revolutionary scenes, but never before, or since, have I seen the human face distorted by such a variety of horrible passions—passions cradled in fanaticism, nursed in silence and gloom, but now roused to madness, and ready to break down every barrier opposed to their gratification.'

The whole of this particular chapter is a fine piece of word-painting, and is well worth reading.

At the time of our visit Setubal was as calm and smiling as a summer sea, and it was difficult to realise such stormy possibilities lying latent as those so graphically depicted by the writer I have quoted.

Shortly after midday the rain ceased, the sky turned blue, and soon the sun shone with all its wonted brilliancy, and we determined to visit Palmella.

The turreted crags on which this famous castle is perched seem almost to overhang Setubal, and yet there is a drive of nearly six miles before commencing the ascent; but the intervening country is so lovely that you almost regret the speed at which this pleasant oasis is traversed. For the first mile you pass through the luxuriant groves from whence are derived the famed oranges of Setubal; but as the season was nearly over, the golden crops were not as conspicuous as would have been the case a fortnight earlier. Still, the scent of lemon-blossom pervaded the air, and wild-flowers, ferns, and creepers, and the common bramble climbing over the hedges—which are allowed to grow freely here—forcibly recalled the lanes of Devon and Cornwall. Vegetation was still at its loveliest; the bright green tinge, which changes to a duller olive as the summer advances, being still in evidence.

The road is carried by a gentle incline up the south side of the mountain, and passing under the 'beetling crags' whereon rests the castle, it winds round to the village of Palmella, on the western slope, at which point we quitted the carriage and climbed the remaining few hundred yards to the summit.

The old castle—of Moorish origin—covers a great extent of ground, and was evidently regarded as a post of the highest importance, and made correspondingly strong, and provided with ample storage for water and corn, as well as stabling for cavalry. Government has now taken this interesting relic of Moorish times under its paternal wing, not, however, before all the most valuable remains had been pilfered and carted away by relic-hunters. For example, the interior walls of the mosque were once encrusted with beautiful embossed tiles, but only a few damaged fragments in inaccessible places now remain, the ground beneath being littered with morsels from which we proceeded to select a few of the least damaged. Our cicerone—an old army pensioner in Government employ—noticing this act of vandalism, gesticulated wildly, while from the fierce cast of countenance he assumed we pictured ourselves being consigned to a dungeon for breach of rules. But C—— quieted our alarm by assuring us that the guide was only explaining that if we would wait a moment he would get us some much finer specimens from another apartment. And as this courteous and most obliging employé proceeded to strip the walls for our benefit, he condescendingly explained that before Government took possession, the gentry living around were wont to carry away the tiles, and other odds and ends, by the cart-load. We brought away these little tokens of official esteem with joy in our hearts, and they now excite the admiration of friends. But we always found Portuguese officials pleasant to do with.

The view from this exalted post is indeed grand. 'The prospect is the most beautiful I ever beheld,' wrote Southey. And the atmosphere being singularly clear, after the rain, we now beheld Lisbon standing forth across the shining expanse of river from her many-hilled throne in all her regal splendour, while to the south, ensconced amidst orange-groves, lay sleepy Setubal—a veritable slumbering volcano.

A pleasant run down, through a country entirely abandoned to fruit culture: orchards of immense extent spreading over the landscape on all sides, wherein peaches, apricots, cherries, figs, apples, and almonds were all struggling in promiscuous fashion for supremacy, and we found ourselves at the Palmella station with an hour to while away before the *comboio* for Lisbon was due.

SPRING THE SECOND

TO NORTH PORTUGAL

'You must not think of leaving Portugal without visiting the north. For all the finest scenery is in that part; in fact, you can form no idea of what beautiful scenery exists in Portugal without going there.'

Such was the injunction of a friend.

Our appetite for travel in the north had already been whetted by reading Lord Carnarvon's pleasant narrative, in which he says: 'The exquisite beauty of the country baffles all description. I had now traversed the Entre Minho twice, and during my second journey through the country was still more impressed with a sense of its surpassing loveliness. All that is most graceful in cultivated scenery, all that is most striking in the wild landscape, have combined to render this little district a fairyland.'

After this we felt that we must see the north; but how to get there? Oporto is not one of the ports of call of the 'Royal Mail Company,' though an 'extra' boat is occasionally despatched there in connection with the emigration to Brazil, of which lucrative traffic the Company takes a large share, and is, I believe, 'first favourite,' by reason of the liberal treatment accorded the emigrants on board their ships.

It so happened that one of the 'extra' boats was

advertised to start at the time we wished; and although these vessels do not lay themselves out for saloon passengers—in fact, only convey them on the understanding that they are willing to accept such accommodation and 'table' as offers on board—we decided to risk the uncertainty, and had no reason to regret our decision.

Besides ourselves there was but one other passenger, and it was a unique experience having the run of a 6000-ton ship with an empty saloon, and rows of vacant cabins—all the first-class accommodation remaining intact.

We crossed the bay in brilliant sunshine and smooth water; and at an early hour on the third morning, awoke to find ourselves in the harbour of Leixoes.

The great 'bar' to the development of Oporto was placed by Nature at the Douro mouth in times past, and no human agency has hitherto succeeded in removing it. The bar is one of the worst known to seafaring folk, and during a continuance of westerly gales the rollers tumble in here with a majestic force and savage fury that can be but faintly realised without witnessing the sight, thus effectually sealing the river to all intercourse. And when the Douro is in full flood—and few rivers change their mood more rapidly or with more disastrous effects—traffic on the river is suspended, vessels are dragged forcibly from their moorings and carried away, to be ingulfed in the seething caldron of raging waters on the bar.

For this reason Oporto is by no means an ideal haven. And in times past there was a delightful uncertainty about sailing and arriving, with the result that the state of the bar, like the weather at home, was a never-failing topic of conversation.

From specially prepared Photographs

Railway Bridge across the Douro at the spot where Wellington's celebrated feat of arms was accomplished

The Great Hospital   Tower of the Clerigos used by Soult as a lookout-place

The principal street

SPRING THE SECOND

Since those days the spirit of enterprise has been abroad, and a great artificial harbour has been constructed at vast expense about six miles to the northward, wherein large ships may lie in safety, if not always in comfort.

Leixoes (pronounced Ley-shewings), the new port, is enclosed by two immense breakwaters; but the design has been objected to on account of the harbour being open to the quarter from whence the worst gales blow home, so that, at times, a very nasty sea rolls in. And then, alas! like most ambitious schemes in this distressful country, the original plan, which included dredging the harbour, has never been carried out, so that the anchorage space is limited. The facilities, too, for landing passengers and goods are still in the embryonic stage—we were put ashore on the beach! But a fatality clogs every enterprise in Portugal.

Thanks to a 'friend in need,' who was well known to the Customs officials, our detention here was neither long nor tedious; and we could not but compare our experience with that of a visitor of last century, who arrived at an unfortunate moment, for such was the force of the current—the Douro being in flood—that his ship was kept waiting in the river for three days before receiving the customary visits. And when at length communication was established, the health-officer sent his deputy. 'This illegitimate son of Esculapius,' says our author, 'commanded every person on board to appear on deck, whilst he surveyed them from the opposite shore at a distance of about two hundred yards; and indeed I could not help surveying him from head to foot, for so curious a figure in the medical line never struck my sight before. His dress was rather convenient than otherwise: it consisted of a red cap, a blue jacket somewhat lacerated at the elbows, etc. Having considered a few moments, he took a pinch of snuff, then, nodding his head, pronounced a few words to this effect—'"I certify that ye are all in good health."'

A railway connects Leixoes with Oporto—or rather will do so when the line is extended to the landing-place—and a steam-tramway has its terminus close by. But 6 A.M. was too early to expect these 'conveniences' to begin running, so we got a carriage and drove the intervening eight miles.

The country lay basking in bright sunshine, the scent of flowers was wafted to us from gardens whose brilliant occupants attracted the eye on every side, and if even commonplace scenery is refreshing after the monotony of a sea-voyage, how much more so is a beautiful country, with the sights and sounds of a foreign land?

We took up our abode at the Grande Hotel do Porto—*Hotel de primeira ordem, o mais importante e mais bem situado da cidade*, as the prospectus runs, and which, unlike most prospectuses, we found accurate in every respect. The table was liberal, the cooking excellent, the bedrooms all that could be desired, and the manager courteous and obliging; suffice it to say he is a native of Switzerland, the country *par excellence* of good hotels and polite managers.

Heavy thunder-showers and a biting wind—the proverbial April weather of Old England—kept us indoors for the rest of the day; but towards evening the reflection of a glorious sunset in the sky above attracted us to the lofty and rather gracefully-proportioned iron bridge that spans the Douro, and from whence, at eventide, the finest views of town and river may be obtained with a minimum of effort.

The spectacle presented here embraces almost every point of interest in

> 'That proud port half-circled by the wave,
> Which Portugalia to the nation gave,'

as Camoens sang, in allusion to the pleasant tradition which assigns the origin of the word Portugal to a small town which stood in ancient times on the left bank of the Douro, near its mouth, and was called Gale, from whence came Portus Gale, or the harbour of Gale, and from whence the transition to Portugal was easy and natural.

As we strolled across the bridge, gazing on the panorama that gradually unfolded itself in a succession of lovely pictures as the eye followed the windings of the river, the accuracy of a German traveller's description of the place a century ago much impressed us: 'When the traveller suddenly beholds a large city, with innumerable churches and towers, on the side of a steep mountain, between rocks that seem torn asunder, surrounded by rude mountains, adorned with gardens, churches, and other edifices, interspersed with pine-woods, and looks down on a fine and rapid stream covered with ships, amid scenes of human activity, that occupy a spot designed by Nature for the haunts of the wild beasts, he is at once astonished and delighted with the prospect.'

From an artistic point of view Oporto enjoys a decided pre-eminence over the more stately capital of the south. Lisbon, it has been justly said, 'strikes at a distance by its great extent and magnificence; Oporto surprises by its elevated situation.'

In other respects, the contrast between the two capitals is no less striking. Lisbon has been described as gracious, courteous, queen-like — Oporto as merry and pleasant.

There is a bustle and animation about the latter town which befits a great commercial emporium. And, notwithstanding its long intercourse with strangers, the place still bears the stamp of individuality more palpably than the cosmopolitan metropolis of the south. Besides which, more bright colour will be found in the dresses of the people here, more jewellery is worn by the lower classes, and the inhabitants generally are distinguished by a finer physique, with features more closely approximating to our ideas of good looks, than is the case at Lisbon.

The Portuense, as the dwellers in the northern city style themselves, have yet another source of self-congratulation, in that they have preserved the purity of their blood from intermarriage with the coloured races, who, in the days of Portuguese world-wide dominion, were imported in thousands to cultivate the then neglected farms of the Alemtejo and other districts. Here, in the north alone, is to be found, at the present day, the Portuguese *de puro sangue*, as also what remains of the energy and spirit of enterprise which contributed in times past to the making of the little kingdom.

The difference between the two capitals impresses itself so forcibly on visitors, that the exclamation of a foreign diplomatist, on visiting Oporto for the first time, rises almost involuntarily to the lips: 'This is another race of men altogether; these are the Portuguese I have read of in history.'

There is no need to bother the reader with a detailed description of a city which has been frequented by Britons these three centuries past. Any one who is fond of statistics will find lists of churches, and other 'objects of local interest' which it behoves the traveller to visit, set forth in handbooks of travel.

Still, to be in a position to rightly appreciate a place of such great antiquity and of so many historical associations, one must know something of its history. It is a mere waste of time arriving, say, in the morning, and, as I have seen people do, take a hurried drive round the town and suburbs, and then take the night-train to somewhere else, and imagine that you have seen Oporto.

Opinions differ about 'sight-seeing'; though for my part I must confess a dislike to rushing from sight to sight, with book in one hand and watch in the other, intent only on getting the greatest possible number of visits into the briefest space of time. For this is a sort of athletics which only induces disgust—the inevitable sequel to satiety,—leaving the mind oppressed with the particular form of intellectual indigestion known as 'brain-fag.'

Far preferable is the leisurely stroll, regardless of time or method, until you find yourself in complete sympathy with your surroundings. For, be it observed, this grand old city has charms which can only be appreciated by those who are imbued with a respect for its past, and feel interested in its associations. A gifted authoress has justly remarked: 'Despite all the charms lent to it by Nature, the place must be wanting in real interest if it has no human associations, no ancient legend, to give a pathos to rippling river and woodland glade.'

Strolling about Oporto in such a frame of mind, the visitor slowly falls under the spell of the place; and the truth begins to dawn on him that there is a great deal more to see and understand in this *terra classica de liberdade e d'industria* than is dreamed of in the philosophy of the harum-scarum tourist intent only on record-breaking.

A WEDDING AND ITS CONSEQUENCES

On the 2nd of February 1387, there was celebrated in the city of Oporto, with the splendour befitting so interesting an event, a marriage which was destined to prove of deeper importance to the little kingdom of Portugal than any other recorded in her history. This was the union of King John I. (afterwards called 'the Great') with an English lady, Philippa, daughter of John of Gaunt by his first wife, Blanche of Lancaster, and granddaughter of our own Edward III.

This importation of English blood into the royal line of Portugal was fraught with consequences of a very far-reaching nature. For from the marriage there issued a race of princes of strong character, lofty ambitions, and noble aims, under whose guidance Portugal attained to the zenith of power and influence, springing almost at once from a position of poverty and obscurity into the forefront of nations.

During the next hundred years the foundation was laid of those over-seas possessions from whence the Portuguese derived so much glory and profit—if destined ultimately to prove their ruin! For it was during those years, and as a direct consequence of the studies, researches, and profound enthusiasm in the cause of maritime exploration of one of the sons born of the marriage, that there ensued those wonderful discoveries which, besides enriching Portugal, paved the way for that ever-increasing intercourse between the nations of the East and the West.

The name of Prince Henry, 'the Navigator,' will ever hold a prominent place on the roll of the world's greatest men, for it was he who stimulated the activity and enterprise of Portuguese seamen until their efforts were rewarded by the achievement of one of the grandest exploits recorded in history — the discovery of a route to India round the Cape of Good Hope; and from this there resulted, in the course of time, and through a series of circumstances as little foreseen as the discovery of India itself, the great Indian Empire of which Britons are now so proud.

From the marriage, then, of John I. with our English Philippa, five centuries ago, there ensued the discovery of India, and, indirectly, the brightest jewel in Queen Victoria's crown — that splendid heritage, the Indian Empire.

The quaint old town of Oporto must therefore ever be chiefly associated in our eyes with the alliance of the two monarchies, and with the strange sequence of events that arose therefrom ; and also as being the birthplace of a prince to whom Britons owe a deep debt of obligation— Prince Henry, 'the Navigator.'

The immediate effect of the marriage was to put the seal to the Anglo-Portuguese Alliance, which had been officially proclaimed the year before by the signing of the Treaty of Windsor (May 9, 1386), under which the kingdoms of Portugal and England were declared to be united henceforth -in the closest bonds of friendship. This alliance has lasted, ' off and on,' to the present day. For the tiffs that subsequently arose were brought about by the arrogant pretensions of Spain, rather than by any deeply-rooted feeling of animosity against Portugal. Spaniards and 'Portingals' were apt to be lumped together as one and the same people when it came to fighting; and the hard knocks the poor Portuguese received were chiefly owing to the inability of British seamen to discriminate between the inhabitants of the two kingdoms. Moreover,

Portugal, being under the domination of Spain at the time, was forced to share her troubles.

In 1662, another marriage between the royal lines of England and Portugal—that of Charles II. with Catherine of Braganza, daughter of the King of Portugal—was the means of reviving the ancient alliance.[1] And forty years later the bond was drawn still closer by the much-maligned-by-Portuguese Methuen Treaty (1703), which proved of the greatest advantage to both countries, but especially to Portugal, and her northern metropolis, Oporto.

For nearly two hundred years now, the closest tie of commercial intercourse has bound together Great Britain and Portugal, and in no part of the little peninsular kingdom have the results of this connection proved more beneficial than in the city on the Douro—the Liverpool of Portugal.

[1] It may be well to remind readers of a fact which has slipped out of recollection, namely, that Catherine of Braganza brought to England as her dowry, £300,000 in cash, the island of Bombay, and the city of Tangier. But the only person who then seems to have set much value on the East Indian island was the Portuguese governor, who for four years refused to give it up. To Englishmen it was a *terra incognita*—its future all unknown. Who could have foreseen that it would become the mightiest commercial city in the east? The only thing about Bombay that now reminds us of its origin is the name, compounded of the two Protuguese words, Bom Bahia—Good Bay.

The history of Tangier supplies a striking commentary on the narrow-minded spirit of 'little Englandism,' which dominated the House of Commons in the reign of Charles II. The story may be thus briefly stated:—

Tangier, already a strong fortress, within a few years after coming into English hands was rendered impregnable. A mole was built which ran 600 yards seawards, the masonry of which was so well executed as to resemble the solid rock, the castle was enlarged and repaired, new walls were built to the city, which was greatly improved and practically reconstructed, and many improvements were carried out in the harbour. All these works were initiated by private enterprise at enormous cost, but funds failing, the Government took matters in hand, and 'the whole was finished in such a manner that it might be said to vie with the works of the Romans themselves.'

Eighteen years later, Tangier was besieged by the King of Morocco,

What Oporto would have been in default of this connection may easily be conceived by any one acquainted with the country and the character of its inhabitants. And though it may gratify the *amour propre* of the modern Portuguese to close their eyes to the most palpable facts—and assuredly the inhabitants of Fair Lusitania have no false modesty in asserting their country's importance—there can be no doubt but that the prosperity and wealth of Oporto has been brought about in great measure by the enterprise and industry of British merchants in times past—to say nothing of the very obvious advantages arising from commercial intercourse with Britain at the present day.

The true state of things that arose out of the Methuen Treaty has been thus described by Mr. Morse Stephens: 'The close connection thus formed went deeper than mere

and King Charles applied to Parliament for the means of defending it, recommending its preservation and pointing out its importance to our commerce in the Mediterranean, and reminding the Houses of the fact that two millions had been expended on the place since it came into the country's possession. In reply, the House of Commons expressed their disapproval of the management of the garrison, which 'they suspected to be no better than a nursery for a Popish army'; and announced their determination not to vote supplies until satisfactory explanations were furnished by his Majesty. Upon this the king determined to abandon the place, after destroying the fortifications which had been so laboriously raised at vast expense. This disastrous measure was carried into effect in 1683 by Lord Dartmouth, who, acting under instructions, blew up the works, and destroyed the harbour by throwing into it the rubbish of the mole, and, after embarking the garrison, abandoned this important place to the Moors. The destruction of the mole and defences occupied six months, for the stone-work had been so solidly cemented that holes had to be drilled in it, and the stones destroyed piecemeal.

One circumstance attending the demolition deserves notice. King Charles directed a large number of new-coined crown-pieces to be buried in the ruins, that if, through the vicissitudes of fortune, this place should ever again be restored, some memorial might be found of its having once belonged to England.

With so little wisdom were the affairs of the kingdom managed in those far-off times!

commerce: it established a friendly relationship which was of infinite advantage to the smaller nation. At Oporto a large colony of English wine-merchants and shippers carried on business operations, which doubled the prosperity of the beautiful city on the Douro. The steady influx of English capital increased the wealth of Portugal, and the vineyards of the Entre-Minho-e-Douro became proverbial for their prosperous and industrious peasantry; while, on the other hand, the importation of English goods gave means of comfort and luxury to the Portuguese people which distinguished them in the eyes of all travellers of the past century from the Spaniards and Italians.'

A German who visited Oporto a hundred years ago was so struck with the effects of this intercourse that he wrote: 'We seem almost to have quitted Portugal, and to be suddenly transported to England—so regular, so light and neat, are all the buildings.'

Travellers in the early part of the present century were very fond of tracing the influence of English ideas and customs on the habits of the people. The meal-hours of the upper classes, the introduction of such 'home-comforts' as fireplaces, and the fine china which often graced Portuguese dinner-tables, were all traceable to the old-standing connection with England. 'Even the manners of the society are taken from the English, who are here more numerous and considerable, in proportion to the other rich inhabitants, than at Lisbon,' wrote the German.

An Englishman who visited Oporto at that time speaks of being hospitably entertained in a Portuguese household, where 'English comforts were found in every department of the establishment.'

The effects of the Methuen Treaty extended far beyond the limits of Oporto. Lord Carnarvon, who travelled in

Portugal during 1827-28, describing a visit to the house of a gentleman of large fortune, in the interior of the Minho Province, tells us his host had adopted many English customs, 'much of his furniture was English, and the china was all English and mostly costly.' And on visiting another gentleman near Tamego, the traveller was shown into a room with a comfortable fireplace, and that ' greatest of earthly blessings in a fireless land, a fire!' and on entering the drawing-room after dinner he was surprised to find a handsome Newfoundland dog and a pug somnolescent upon the hearth, before a blazing fire. 'This complication of delights transported me to England,' he wrote. But still another surprise was in store, for, on retiring, he found a roaring fire awaiting him in his bedroom.

He further remarks on the alteration of the dinner-hour, in the houses of the better classes, to four o'clock, a result, he says, of 'the connection which has so long existed between the British and the Portuguese inhabitants of the wine district.'

The results of the Methuen Treaty are, even now, observable in north Portugal, for it is affirmed by people acquainted with the country that porcelain from the famous works at Worcester, Derby, Chelsea, and Bow may still be met with in Portuguese cottages.

The extent to which British influences have affected native manners and customs is not, of course, perceptible to the casual visitor, and has escaped the notice of most recent writers. Whether these influences are as potent to-day as they were in the past, is perhaps doubtful. It has even been averred that notwithstanding the presence of a considerable British colony at Oporto, British influence has waned of late. Many causes contribute to this, the chief being one that is operating all the world over—the facility with which expatriated Britons can run backwards and forwards between the land where duty calls them and their own dearly-loved island.

For the reasons I have stated, Oporto must always possess a deep interest for Britons, who, on beholding the fine city on the Douro, cannot help feeling a pride in the share their race has had in the making of it.

Political troubles and civil wars during the past eighty years—to say nothing of bad government—have done much to obliterate the effects of British intercourse, while the inhabitants have become so habituated to the existence of foreigners in their midst, as to have grown indifferent to the origin of customs which, by dint of long usage, have become a part of their daily life;—they would probably resent even the imputation of their dear old town having been indebted to England for anything.

And yet, the besom of progress notwithstanding, there is much in Oporto to charm the eye, while in the older parts many a quaint 'bit' has escaped the ravages of municipal vandals who are intent on reducing everything to a dead and monotonous level of uniformity.

The river-side is the quarter where the most characteristic views must be sought, for modern enterprise has stopped short there, disdaining to meddle with the breakneck alleys and rickety houses which cling to the hillsides, imparting an air of venerable antiquity to the entire city.

At this point the town of to-day differs but little, if at all, from the Oporto that Wellington gazed on the evening before that amazing feat of arms which cleared the city of its tyrants. The very houses are, I believe, *in situ* from whose windows the inhabitants waved their handkerchiefs in transports of joy, while the church-bells above crashed out their noisy welcome to the British deliverers.

It is pleasant to turn from 'improved' Oporto, with its spick-and-span houses and monotonous street-alignment, to the old quarters with their narrow lanes, capricious windings and turnings, dark passages and overhanging houses, where every turn discovers a succession of pleasant surprises: here some quaint dwelling, with projecting balcony that almost shakes hands with its *vis-à-vis* across the way; here a venerable church, tacked on, as it were, to a vast, gloomy, tenantless, and half-ruinous pile of monastic buildings, with their barred windows, not as a protection against intruders so much as to prevent the monkish occupants from straying,—a very necessary precaution, if half of the rumours that are floating about concerning the manners and customs of those gentry are to be trusted; while ever and anon a lovely vista of river and distant mountain is framed, as it were, at the extremity of some dark and dingy alley leading out on to the Douro side.

When tired with poking about the *circumbendibus* 'wynds,' as they would be called in Auld Reekie, it is pleasant to linger awhile on one of the projecting spurs that commands the windings of the river as it rolls along on its way to the Atlantic; or to rest the eye, by way of contrast, on the pine-woods and terraced gardens, with their walks and vine-clothed arbours, their moss-covered walls, and bright flowers clothing the heights over Villa Nova de Gaia, the port-wine town across the Douro.

A traveller of last century, describing the city, says there is scarcely a house in it with four right angles, 'whence,' says he, 'a stranger would be led to suppose that the 47th proposition of Euclid had not yet found its way there.' And he explains this by pointing out that the corner-houses of the streets being obliquely disposed, render the adjoining houses of the same figure, 'as every one follows the crooked plan of his neighbour,' and thus 'all become rhomboids and trapeziums.'

Were this to meet the eye of the 'Progressive' Councillor, he would exclaim with pride, 'But we have changed all that!'—and changed, alas! the old town has been within the last decade. What it will be when that demon of destruction, the municipality, has worked its wicked way for another ten years, I hardly care to forecast.

Considering its immense antiquity—Oporto was under Roman as well as Moorish domination—the town is singularly deficient in marks of its former masters. But this is not surprising when we remember how many links-with-the-past have been swept away in the attempt to bring the town up to the modern municipal standard of tasteless architecture, by people who profess to labour in the interests of straight streets and wide thoroughfares.

The 'standard of perfection' aimed at may be studied to advantage in the modern quarter, where everything that can be done to make a place hideous and characterless has been conscientiously carried out. The only mark of genius about the new houses that I could discover was the cunning way in which the water-spouts are arranged to discharge their contents exactly on to the heads of pedestrians. I quite longed for a downpour to watch the effect.

The roofs of the houses here, as in Lisbon, afford curious evidence of the Oriental influences which have been at work in Portugal: a result doubtless of the old intercourse with India and the far East, when the countries of the

Orient poured their treasures into the peninsular kingdom, and received in return——? an army of Jesuits and the Inquisition!

The roofs of Portuguese houses invariably follow what may be called the 'pagoda-ish' style. That is to say, the slope of the roof, at a point about two-thirds down, turns gradually outwards till it approximates the horizontal—the corners being turned up and finished off with a fantastic design in pottery or metal-work—the pagoda-ish appearance being still further emphasised by the practice of colouring the under side of the projecting eaves a bright red colour. This custom, combined with that of colour-washing the outside walls of the houses a bright tint, compensates in some measure for the hideous monotony of the street architecture.

Oporto still possesses one remnant of the dark ages which might well be dispensed with. I refer to the street paving, which, judging by the size of the cobble-stones and the wide interstices between them, must date back to a period when these fulfilled the purpose of stepping-stones. They are worse laid than was ever the case in old Edinburgh, which is saying a great deal; and under existing conditions carriage exercise within the city limits is a penance, while to walk on the cobbles with a steady gait one must needs be an expert.

One could wish the municipality no worse fate than to be driven for ever and ever on their own abominable cobble-stones, as a mild description of everlasting punishment.

There are sights, too, that greet the eye in public thoroughfares—ay, and in the resorts of fashion—which savour too strongly of mediæval times to commend themselves to strangers habituated to the conventionalities of modern life. The unaffected simplicity of both sexes in some matters is positively astounding, though the old saying that 'where ignorance is bliss 'tis folly to be wise,' can hardly be held to apply to all customs. A fondness for 'olo custom' is by no means confined to China!

One agreeable trait of national character has remained unaffected by the British alliance—the love of bright colour. For although the 'classes' have most unwisely adopted what is known the world over as 'Paris fashions,' the 'masses' show their sense and good taste by adhering to a simple, and therefore becoming, form of dress. Eschewing the awful 'creations' with which the 'maids of merry England' sometimes elect to deck themselves out, the women here content themselves with a bright handkerchief for a head-covering—cotton for everyday use, and silk for high days and holidays—tied in a knot under the chin, and forming a pretty frame for the bright and often handsome faces that distinguish the poorer classes.

In the south a blue tone prevails—the natives of the southern provinces seem, in fact, to be afflicted with 'the blues,' the result, perchance, of bad government and overtaxation. Here, in the north, red predominates, indicative, doubtless, of the difference in temperament and republican principles of the northern Portuguese; and this warm colour, diversified with brilliant yellows and vivid greens, imparts brightness to the streets.

If the visitor to Oporto is sceptical about the native love of colour, let him stroll up the Rua dos Clerigos, one of the principal streets, on a bright sunny morning. The *coup d'œil* is positively startling. For in this short space is gathered, it would seem, all the drapers' and milliners' shops of the town; not the resorts of fashion—those emporiums, after the Parisian style, are in quite another direction—but the shops where the 'masses' do their purchasing, and whose contents reflect the tastes of their customers with absolute fidelity. Here, in bright sunshine —and bright sunshine is the rule under the 'ever-blue skies of Portugal'—the scene will be a positive revelation to the stranger. For the greater part of the stock-in-trade of these enterprising shopmen is stacked up, or, rather, spread out, on the adjacent pavement, the better to attract the eyes and excite the desires of intending purchasers. The entire street is thus converted into a waving, scintillating mass of glowing colour—the products of native and foreign looms, composed of cottons and muslins, silks and satins, and all the infinite variety of material which goes to the building up of feminine attire, the cheapest fabrics and the brightest of colours predominating, just such as the dusky inhabitants of our West Indian Islands love to adorn themselves with.

'What barbaric taste!' I can fancy some dull Briton exclaiming. 'Long may it last!' say I.

What a contrast, in this respect, does Oporto, and most southern towns, offer to our own dingy and colourless streets! And if the visitor is fond of colour—personally, I must confess to a childish delight in bright tints—a succession of pleasant surprises awaits him as he wanders through the streets of old Oporto.

The markets are, of course, delightful everywhere in southern Europe, for there you see the natives *au naturelle*; and at Oporto you can always while away a pleasant hour therein, observing the quaint and pretty costumes of the country-folk, admiring their handsome faces, peering into the contents of their stalls, and sampling the luscious fruits, amongst which white strawberries of immense size seem to be the *spécialité*; but though tempting to the eye, they are fleshy and tasteless—poor substitutes for the 'British Queen' or 'Doctor Hogg.' Very attractive, too, are the flower-stalls, whose presiding geniuses have a pretty knack of making up 'button-holes.'

Taste, here, seems to run strongly in the direction of crimson carnations whose brilliancy absolutely dazzles one. Everywhere, even in the slums, you meet their bright and smiling faces—peering out of window-boxes, beaming down on you from the tops of high walls, or revelling amidst their green surroundings in trim surburban gardens. One feels sure the Moors loved carnations; for these bright and cheery companions almost monopolise the wall-top borders which the bronzed warriors are said to have introduced into Portugal, and which were certainly the invention of a race that disliked bending the back.

In the markets you may chance on certain quaint specimens of native manufacture which have long been spurned from better-class shops, and now only find a home in the houses of the poor. Amongst these are a sort of quilt or counterpane, cunningly contrived from scraps of old cotton dresses, into which are woven strips of bright worsted-work, and making an excellent portière.

Another cheap and pretty native product is the pocket, or purse, worn by the peasantry about Vianna, near the frontier. I never saw it in use about Oporto, and I only know of two places in the town where it can be bought—pokey little shops in the poor quarter. The purse consists of a piece of coloured flannel—usually scarlet—on which an ornamental pattern is embroidered in coloured worsted and beads, bearing the word 'Amor,' or some other device, in the centre.

We were so captivated with these purses—for native art-products are scarce in Portugal—that we bought up the entire stock-in-trade at one shop, to the astonishment and infinite amusement of the laughing damsel who presided therein, and to whose deft fingers we were indebted for our trophies. We even asked her when she would have a further supply, to which she laughingly replied it would take her some time to renew it.

In a street branching out of the Rua dos Clerigos, of bright memory, are the jewellers' shops wherein may be seen the gold trinkets which are so conspicuous amongst the country-folks' adornments on feast-days. Jewellery is the favourite form of investment amongst the poor, who place little reliance on banks as depositories for their savings, which they prefer to carry on their persons, in the form of gold ornaments, as these can be easily reconverted into the current coin of the realm.

There is a sort of barbaric simplicity about these ornaments, reminding one of the specimens of the jeweller's art to be seen at Tangier, and other Moorish towns. In fact, Moorish influence has been traced here, as in so much else in Portugal: 'the curious intermixture of Moorish emblems with symbols of the Christian faith' being specially noticeable, says Mr. Crawfurd.

Passing into a pleasant suburb, at the west of the town, we come to the charming houses belonging to the members of the British colony, who, in addition to golf-links, possess an excellent cricket-ground. Theatrical performances take place from time to time in the Crystal Palace, and many pleasant social functions help to minimise the bitterness of expatriation in this sunny land, wherein it seems almost an impertinence to ask if life is worth living.

The hospitality of the colony is proverbial, and, on certain occasions, is dispensed on a truly princely scale.

Such, at least, was my experience, on a certain memorable occasion which, after the lapse of thirty years, still lingers pleasantly in the memory.

The occasion to which I refer was the visit of a party of officers from the Channel Fleet at Lisbon, by invitation, to play a cricket-match, and take part in sundry other diversions not specified in the 'official' programme. As I happened to be something of a cricketer myself, in those far-off times, I was so fortunate as to form one of the noble company selected to defend the honour of the fleet.

Time being important, we travelled to Oporto by night, and were met on arrival next morning by a deputation from the colony, who detailed us off to the several houses in which we were to be entertained during our stay. It was a right royal welcome; and, I may say that, from the moment of arrival till the time of our departure, three days later, there was hardly a moment we could call our own. Excursions, visits to wine-lodges, drag-hunts, and last, but not least in importance, cricket, occupied the days; while dinner-parties, banquets, and a truly splendid ball at the Crystal Palace kept us merry, and on the go, till a very late hour every night. We were all of one mind as to the superlative merits of genuine port—that, in fact, the best wines we had ever tasted were ditch-water compared to the delicious nectar that lay prone in the cellars of the Villa Nova, and there alone. Port wine 'as she is drunk' in Oporto is a beverage to be remembered—a revelation to the British palate.

The cricket-match was rather a one-sided affair, the compiler of this chronicle enjoying the unique distinction of beating Oporto off his own bat, trebling the total score of the colony. It was rather a shabby return for so much hospitality. But what would you have?

I have always understood that this match was the first of a long series of pleasant social functions which have continued, almost without a break, to the present time. The annual match with the Navy came off about a month before the visit which supplied 'copy' for this book.

Results arose from the match above-described which do not come within the province of the chronicler to reveal; and doubtless very similar consequences have arisen since, and will continue to arise in the future. For it is in the nature of things that when young people are thrown together, if but for a few short days, friendships spring up which lead in due course to closer relationships.

Twenty-eight years, with all their changes, were destined to roll by before I set foot again in Oporto. The tradition of the cricket-match still lingered in the place. But where were the players? Only one solitary member of the British colony of that far-away time was *en evidence*. I annex an account of the match from *The Field*,[1] in case

[1] MARCH 23, 1868.

OPORTO.		CHANNEL SQUADRON.	
W. Tate, b. Mercer	1	Sub-Lt. Martin, b. Wroughton	46
R. Reed, jun., c. Miller, b. Mercer	5	Sub-Lt. Carpenter, c. Tate, b. Reed, jun.	19
L. Renny, c. Montgomery, b. Olive	2	Lieut. Mercer, b. Renny	15
W. Teage, not out	4	Sub-Lt. Shore, c. and b. Renny	50
F. J. Cobb, b. Olive	0	Lt. Olive, R.M.L.I., c. Wroughton, b. Reed, jun.	4
R. Reed, sen., b. Olive	0	Sub-Lt. Tabor, b. Wroughton	0
W. Cassell, c. Montgomery, b. Olive	1	Lieut. Miller, b. Reed, jun.	5
O. Crawfurd, b. Olive	0	Lieut. Gambier, not out	11
W. Wroughton, b. Shore	0	Lieut. Montgomery, R.M.L.I., b. Wroughton	7
J. Jones, b. Shore	0	Lieut. Musters, b. Reed, jun.	10
C. Wright, run out	4	Sub-Lieut. Giffard, run out	1
		B. 13, l.b. 2, w.b. 17	32
Total	17	Total	200

In Second Innings of Oporto: Tate (not out) 9, Reed, jun. 3, Renny 21, Teage (not out) 1, Cobb 0, Reed, sen. 3, Cassell 5, b. 6, w.b. 1: Total, 49.

any one of my readers who happened to have assisted at it may like to be reminded of his achievements on that particular occasion.

One thing, at any rate, has survived all changes—the hospitality of the British colony.

'The first thing that strikes the mind of a stranger, on his arrival here,' wrote Murphy in 1789, 'is the devout appearance of the inhabitants. Religion seems to be their only pursuit. The clattering of bells, the bustling of processions, and the ejaculations of friars, engage the attention by day, whilst every part resounds by night with the chanting of hymns.'

Many changes have passed over the city since those happy, innocent days. And if Murphy was to revisit the scene he would be impelled to exclaim, in the words of the poet—

> 'It is not now as it hath been of yore:
> Turn wheresoe'er I may,
> By night or day,
> The things which I have seen I now can see no more!'

Assuredly the modern Portuense would never recognise their dear old city in the fascinating picture touched in by the English traveller a hundred years ago.

> 'Whither is fled the visionary gleam?
> Where is it now, the glory and the dream?'

The 'devout aspect' of the inhabitants, which so delighted Murphy has, alas! disappeared with much else.

In most continental cities of the size and antiquity of Oporto, the visitor turns to the churches with the assurance of finding architectural merit without, and artistic beauty within. Here, at Oporto, however, there is little to attract or commend in either respect, such attractions as the churches possess internally being almost entirely due to a lavish—not to say wasteful—profusion of gilding. And gold, as an old author justly observes, 'is certainly a very effectual thing to conceal the want of art, or science, or'—devotion he would have said.

Here in Oporto, as at Lisbon, the churches and ecclesiastical establishments have ever been chiefly remarkable for their number, vast extent, great wealth, and, lastly, for the hordes of strong, healthy, full-blooded bipeds, endowed in a pre-eminent degree with the appetites and passions of average humanity, which they maintained, in a state of insufferable boredom, within.

The friars of Oporto would seem to have been a singularly frolicsome lot—even for Portugal. In fact, after studying the old writers, and putting two and two together, one is forced to the not altogether regrettable conclusion, that the monks of Oporto enjoyed a 'real good time.' To be sure, as we know, 'stone walls do not a prison make, nor iron bars a cage'; and the truth of this aphorism was strikingly exemplified in the history of monasticism hereabouts.

The Father Guardian of the great Franciscan convent told an English traveller, in 1779, that he had constantly to be on the watch to prevent the young friars from rambling, and to send the old ones abroad to preach, exhort, absolve, and bring back charities to the community: 'that between the gadding disposition of the young Fryars and the laziness of the old, his choir was never more than half full,' and that therefore 'the daily services were neglected.'

In the year 1827 the monastic garrison amounted to over 5000. The monks mixed freely in society; many lived out of barracks, with their friends; and these gallant and accomplished, if not over cleanly, gentlemen were doubtless in great request at the social functions with which the Portuense of those far-off and 'devout' days were wont to beguile the tedium of existence. An Englishman who visited one of these palaces of 'plain living and high thinking' was surprised to find his monastic friend's 'chamber of penance and ascetic virtue' as 'beautifully furnished as a lady's boudoir.' At the same time, the churches were 'so filthy and unwholesome, and the behaviour of the lower orders so indecent, that the better classes were wholly prevented the services.' At one of the principal churches the altar was made, 'through the corruption of the attendants, a regular channel of communication between persons who had not yet arrived at personal interviews, and thus connections took place which would otherwise never have been formed.' The bishop of the diocese, a most learned man, had not held a single confirmation during the ten years he had occupied the post. He had a library of thirty thousand volumes 'which engrossed all his attention,' with the lamentable result that 'the conduct of the clergy in his diocese was profligate in the extreme.'

'Protestant prejudice!' I fancy I hear some 'serious-minded' reader ejaculating. Well, all I can say is, let any one go to Portugal and study the matter on the spot. The results will appal him. I dare not even hint at the 'goings-on' that were tolerated by the Church authorities in the good old days of ecclesiastical domination. Some idea of the manners and customs ecclesiastical may be gathered from old authors, who discuss matters with a freedom and wealth of detail which almost takes one's breath away, and assuredly would not be tolerated at the present day.

Oh, depend upon it, the friars and churchmen of olden

time quite understood the art of good living, and were by no means insensible to the joys this poor world affords! 'If you cannot be chaste, be discreet,' was the rule of life inculcated on the young monks by the older hands.

The monasteries of Portugal contained a great many jolly boon-companions, as well as some really good men. And judging from facts made public, we may safely infer that there were other religious brotherhoods besides the particular one that built itself a little nest at St. Edmondsbury, that needed the cleansing broom of an 'Abbot Sampson.'

'Of what use to the State,' wrote a Portuguese Secretary of State, a hundred and fifty years ago, 'are so many fat Benedictines, and so many proud Augustines, who live in their convents eating and drinking, except when they disturb the peace with their peculiarities, and send large sums of money to Rome?' It was enough to make a recruiting-sergeant weep to think of the splendid fighting regiments that might have been made of those 'sturdy beggars.'

The standard of intelligence prevailing amongst the church-folk of Oporto, in old times, may be gathered from the following incident. The tower of the Clerigos had been struck by lightning. An assembly of clergy and congregation was at once convened to concert measures for preventing a repetition of the disaster; and, after much debate, the question was narrowed down to the choice between a lightning-conductor or a lamp, to be lighted every night in honour of the lady patroness. The matter being put to the vote, the lady carried the day, a unanimous vote being cast in favour of Santa Barbara and the lamp.

With such frivolities did the inhabitants of those days beguile the tedium of existence.

Or take the following: Towards the close of last century, the post of Consul for Great Britain was held by a gentleman of wide culture and high scientific attainments, who employed his leisure moments in dabbling in astronomy and other abstruse sciences. He even had electrical machines of his own devising, amongst which was a singular contrivance for the purpose of protecting his house from lightning, in the form of a horizontal bar of iron stretching right across the roof, from one end of which a chain depended, the end being buried in a flower-bed. On several occasions, during thunderstorms, the electric fluid had descended with such force as to make a large hole in the ground, and scatter the flowers all over the garden. In due time this was noised abroad the priests and common people, both equally ignorant, declaring that the Consul was a magician, who, by his art and the help of the devil, drew the thunderbolts from the clouds into his own garden. The clamour grew so loud that the shepherds of the Infallible Church could no longer ignore the scandal; for the Oporto priests, moved to alarm at the prospect of a competitor in the particular department of miracles of which they enjoyed a 'monopoly,' and exploited in fine style, invoked the aid of the Holy Inquisition of Coimbra—a city then, as now, the great seat of 'light' and learning. In due course, commissaries from this important State department paid a visit to the Consulate; but though they came to curse, they were moved to bless. For it so happened that Pombal, the great enemy of ecclesiasticism, was in power; and the commissaries, being men of the world, as well as Holy Inquisitors, and not willing to run foul of the great

Marquis, or lay themselves open to ridicule, investigated the matter with open minds. The Consul, on his part, received them courteously, explained the process of his experiments—not omitting the particular instrument which had caused all the fuss—and sent his visitors away perfectly satisfied, and 'enraged at the ridiculous accusations of their ignorant countrymen.'

The state of education prevailing in the monasteries of Oporto may be inferred from the following anecdote. In old days there stood, on the south side of the Douro, at a point about half-way between the Villa Nova and the bar, the convent of S. Antonio, in the midst of the most beautiful gardens to be met with anywhere around the city, and furnished with everything that could make life enjoyable. Now, the pride and boast of the monks of S. Antonio were the statues with which the terraces and balustrades were most liberally besprinkled. In addition to all the saints of the Christian calendar, there were representatives of most of the heathen gods and goddesses, all mixed up, higgledy-piggledy, in most incongruous style, with the inevitable result that there often occurred instances of mistaken identity of a most ludicrous character. For example, to take a few typical cases: Venus was often paraded as the Virgin Mary; Jupiter as St. Peter; while Apollo, with his harp, was introduced as the King of Israel; and a certain gentleman with wings to his heels, and an implement of some sort in his hands, was invariably believed to be the angel Gabriel. 'But it mattered little,' says an old writer; 'the pious crossed themselves with equal devotion as they passed, and never failed to return home highly edified by the spectacle.' After all, when you take to bowing down to statues, one bit of stone is as good as another.

When the 'Castles of Idleness' were suppressed throughout the kingdom in 1834, the convent of S. Antonio was put up to auction, and bought for use as a wine-lodge.

Near this spot is another which possesses a melancholy interest for Englishmen, for it was here, 'in former days of bigotry,' that English and other Protestants were taken for burial. To judge from the accounts of old writers, the obsequies were not always conducted with the decorum that befitted the solemnity of the occasion. No English clergyman ever officiated at the last rites, which, owing to strong local prejudices against 'heretics,' were usually performed by the English Consul. But this high official, conceiving the office to be derogatory to the dignity of his post, deputed it to the Vice-Consul, a foreigner, who in turn delegated the duty to some one else; until at last funerals were conducted by a drunken watchmaker. This obliging mechanic being observed, on the occasion of an evening burial, to be afflicted with nervous hesitation while reciting his part, was discovered by a bystander, who had the curiosity to peep over his shoulder, to be studying a 'history of the late war'!

In delightful contrast to the laxness and indifference of those far-away days stands the existing English cemetery, on the outskirts of the city, with its pretty church, tasteful surroundings, shady bowers, and bright flowers, wherein you are tempted to exclaim, in the words of a German traveller of last century: 'We seem almost to have quitted Portugal, and to be suddenly transported to England.'

The churches and conventual establishments suffered much diminution of wealth, and parted with many of their treasures, during the troublous times at the beginning of the century; especially during Soult's occupancy, when those light-fingered liberators of oppressed peoples, the French, 'nipped up' all the superfluous ornaments of a portable nature—for their better preservation in France, it is to be presumed! They showed a nice taste, too, it is said, in their selection of specimens of local ecclesiastical art. But the 'cream' of these had been skimmed before. And it was in connection with this particular 'skimming' that a curious incident took place at Oporto a year previously, which wellnigh proved fatal to the church thieves. A detachment of French troops were embarking, under the terms of the Convention of Cintra, and in the course of shipping their 'private baggage' a military chest fell to the ground, and, bursting open, displayed a fine collection of 'church plate.' This so enraged the populace, that, forcing their way on board the transports, they seized all the baggage, re-landed it, and carefully rummaged the contents of the boxes. 'When it became apparent that, under the head of private property, the pillage of the most sacred edifices in the kingdom was about to be carried away, the lives of the soldiers were placed in imminent danger,' wrote Lord Londonderry.

After all, these 'disciplined brigands,' as Sir Walter Scott called them, were only acting up to the maxims of their emperor, who laid it down as a guiding principle in warfare that the country must support the war. And, of course, no well-ordered religious services could be conducted without plate; and a French army, as we all know, was *très exigeant* in this matter, when campaigning.

Not content with annexing several small and unimportant mementoes of their all-too-brief sojourn in the capital of the north, the French soldiery shamefully ill-treated the brotherhoods, besides perpetrating many wanton acts of cruelty on the inhabitants, by way of enforcing their mission in the cause of 'Liberty, Equality, and Fraternity,' which, being interpreted, meant 'Might is Right!'

During the Miguelite wars the friars displayed *trop de zèle* in the cause of absolutism and clerical domination, and in the manifestation of their sympathies drove several very long nails into the coffin of their orders. They even took arms and fought with carnal weapons, proving in many an encounter as tough customers as the wild beasts at Ephesus; though, to be sure, for want of proper training, their methods of conducting warfare were neither correct nor chivalric—as witness the attempt of certain misguided brethren to set fire to the Franciscan convent, wherein lay a regiment of the Constitutional army, in the hopes of burning the soldiers as they lay asleep.

This was part of a diabolical plot to fire the whole of the convents of Oporto, which had been converted temporarily into barracks for the Constitutional troops. But in their anxiety to make sure of their prey, the infernal miscreants who had been intrusted with the task of firing the Franciscan convent set it alight an hour too soon, and although the flames burst out in three different parts of the building, the alarm was given in time to enable all the troops to be got out. In the midst of the confusion, three friars were observed cautiously gliding from the convent, and trying to mix with the crowd. They were seized by the soldiers; one was instantly shot, and the other two were arrested; but in spite of the strongest evidence of their guilt, they were never even brought to trial.

During the confusion which it was supposed would prevail throughout Oporto consequent on the general conflagration, it was further proposed to assassinate the Constitutional king, Dom Pedro: 'and this pious office,' says an English officer who was present, 'was undertaken by a Capuchin friar, a man as well known for his profligate habits as for his utter disregard of personal danger.'[1]

But why continue the tale of their misdeeds? Suffice it to say, the orders were suppressed in 1834, in none too merciful style, and the members dispersed—'never more, I trust, to reunite,' piously ejaculated an English writer at the time, 'unless they find some snug corner in enlightened England, whence they may issue forth to preach a fresh crusade against freedom and education.' Prophetic words!

Oporto is making praiseworthy efforts to live up to the reputation it has long enjoyed of being a go-ahead city. The chief hotels and other important establishments are lit with the *luz electrica*, or the incandescent gas-burner, which is in high favour all over Portugal—as would be the case with other modern conveniences did not a besotted, and, alas! corrupt administration use its best endeavours to keep the land in the darkness and discomfort of the Middle Ages.

Tramways intersect the city wherever the gradients are not prohibitive—for the remark of an old traveller still holds good: 'Many of the streets are so steep that a man may be said rather to climb than to walk them'—and they run along the Douro to its mouth, and beyond to Matosinhos. A journey by tramcar in Oporto is a curious experience, seeing that by dint of twelve-mule power the cars are dragged up the most break-neck ascents, even when crowded with passengers, who, I verily believe, would rather stay the night in the city than walk up twenty yards of hill to ease the load.

A steam tramway takes one along at a fine pace to Foz and Matosinhos, the Ramsgate and Margate respectively of

---

[1] The confessional was shamefully abused, and assassination openly preached from the altars, during these troublous times.

the Oporto folk; and arrangements are in progress for the construction of a railway station in the heart of the city.

When I last visited Oporto, the station and terminus was on the south side of the river. Now the railway crosses the Douro on a bridge which seems to have been constructed of spiders' webs, so fragile is its appearance. Assuredly, its designers never had heavy traffic or express speeds in view!

It has always been a legitimate subject of chaff against the Portuguese that their ambitions have been wont to outrun their resources. They have been called a nation of big ideas and small means; and there are two erections in Oporto which may be cited as cases in point—or, to quote an old writer, as 'lasting monuments of the folly of not proportioning the design to the public purse.'

The first is the Seminary, or Jesuits' College, a building rendered famous for all time by Wellington's brilliant exploit. For it was the seizure of this post that enabled him to effect the crossing in the face of the French army. Begun in the last century, on a magnificent design, and partly constructed in a truly cyclopean style, the edifice remains almost exactly as it was on the ever-memorable morning of May 12, 1809. The 'Jesuits' Folly,' it might well be called.

The other is the hospital, a building of imposing appearance, in the centre of the town, and which I confess to have gazed on with considerable interest, having routed out several curious particulars relating to it from old writers. The front is decidedly imposing, and might lead the uninitiated to suppose the building was complete; but look at the back! Its history is a curious one, and much too characteristic to be ignored. Commenced in 1767, from the designs of an English architect, the building was intended to consist of a square, measuring about 560 feet on each face, a design, as a writer of the period justly remarked, 'much too immense for the place, and better calculated for the purpose of a general infirmary for London.' This, however, was a consideration not likely to trouble the projectors, who, like their sovereigns, were intent on 'going one better' than their neighbours, the Spaniards. So the structure was taken in hand; but as the available funds only amounted to £1000 a year, very little progress was made during the first twelve years; 'and there is no great danger of its ever being finished,' wrote an English traveller, who saw it at this stage, with singular prescience, for, he adds, 'the whole estimate has been laid at £300,000 sterling.' We learn from another visitor, who saw it later, that 'twenty years had only just sufficed to complete one of the wings of one of the pavilions': the rest was raised but a few feet above the ground, and 'is likely to remain in this state.' However, the front is now finished, and the city has thus 'saved its face'—*à la Chinois!*

I was presumptuous enough just now to speak disrespectfully of the administration. Perhaps I was unjust. Let the reader judge for himself. I will take the liberty of citing a few recent examples of administrative wisdom and forethought, culled at haphazard from the experiences of certain influential members of the commercial community of Oporto.

For reasons best known to the authorities, but which may be surmised, the Post Office from time to time issues a new series of stamps, and the fact is sometimes brought home to business men in a curious way. For example, a gentleman, in a large way, told me the first intimation he received of the fact was a letter from his German agency telling him that all his letters had lately been charged for deficient stamping. On inquiry at the Oporto Post Office, he was calmly informed by the officials that those particular stamps had been recently cancelled. A very short time after, a notice was issued by the Post Office that in consequence of a fresh issue of stamps all the old pattern ones would be cancelled on such and such a day. A day or two *before* the new issue took place, my friend applied at the office for the new stamps. 'Oh, they are not out yet!' A day or two *after* the issue had commenced, he carried all his old supply to the Post Office and asked to have them exchanged for the new stamps. This was refused. 'The stamps had been cancelled, and were useless!'

Now these are the 'dirty tricks' by which the Government of Portugal debases itself in the eyes of all self-respecting citizens. But even the case above mentioned was not nearly so bad as one that came under my cognisance a short time ago at Lisbon, and was, I believe, made the subject of official complaint. And well it might, for the transaction was nothing more nor less than a piece of downright rascality.

A seaman, a British subject, desired his friends in England to remit to him the balance of his wages, about £30, by Post Office order on Lisbon. Little did the poor fellow know the trap he had laid for himself; for on presenting the order at the Lisbon Post Office, he received payment in paper money, the currency of the country, but at par value. The infamy of it all will be apparent when I say that this 'filthy lucre' was depreciated to the extent of about twenty per cent., so that the poor fellow was robbed of some five pounds by the transaction. Remonstrance was useless, for this honourable Government refused to recognise the depreciation of its miserable currency.

The question is, What became of the balance? for we may be sure the Portuguese Government claimed and received the full amount from the British Post Office in gold. This is one of the unexplained mysteries of Portuguese finance. I understand that the British Post Office afterwards declined to issue money-orders on Lisbon.

Just one more specimen of administrative 'cuteness; this time from official sources. The Mint of Portugal has the privilege of issuing notes of the value of 5d. and 2½d. respectively. One of these series was called in some time back, with a notice to the effect that all notes not presented by a named time were to be cancelled and declared valueless. Now as eighty per cent. of the inhabitants of this enlightened kingdom can neither read nor write, such a notification was of little use; and of that issue £4400 worth were never presented, 'involving a profit to the State which does not figure in the accounts.' What became of it? 'It is alleged by some,' says the official document from which I quote, 'that the equivalent received in exchange for the notes has been applied to the expenses of the State.... It is this and other ambiguities in the national book-keeping which give rise to the prevalent idea that things are worse than they really are, and that from one moment to another a crisis may arise consequent upon the discovery of some large deficit now lost sight of and forgotten' (Foreign Office Report, 1895).

And now for lighter things.

There is one department of State here which provides a never-failing fund of entertainment, or annoyance, according to the standpoint of the spectator—namely, the Customs. I must explain that there exists in Portugal a deeply-rooted belief—an article of national faith, one might call it, to doubt which is anathema—that if it had not been for the perfidious English in times past, with their infamous Methuen Treaty, Portugal would have been a great manufacturing country—the industrial workshop of the world. Consequently, it has been a guiding principle of the fiscal policies of successive governments to enable the marvellous industrial genius of the Portuguese people to have a fair chance of developing its natural bent. To that intent there has been raised up around the country a sort of Chinese wall of protective duties, to bolster up such wretched little 'jobbing shops' as already exist, and *pour encourager les autres!* The results have astonished the Portuguese, though not exactly in the manner anticipated.

The following example shows how this fiscal policy affects the importations of certain conveniences of civilisation which the industrial genius of the native Portuguese is incapable of supplying.

A foreign merchant ordered a Chubb's safe from England. On its arrival he found that the duties payable on it would almost equal the value of the article, because it was 'painted.' Had the safe been plain and unadorned, the duty would have been comparatively small; it was the paint that made it so valuable in Portuguese eyes. The merchant refused either to pay the duty, or to remove the safe from the Custom House; so, after the usual interval, the safe was put up for auction and bought for a mere song, because it was locked, and no key was forthcoming. The Customs officers had previously asked for the key, but of course the owner declined to part with this interesting accessory, and these innocent officials, thinking to outmanœuvre him, wrote to the manufacturer for another key. Messrs. Chubb replied that they were not in the habit of making duplicate keys, so the Customs authorities were nonplussed. Meanwhile the merchant 'sat tight,' and in due time got possession of his safe for a merely nominal sum from the purchaser, who could find no use for it in default of a key. Truly the biter is sometimes bit!

In the course of a speech at the Bradford Chamber of Commerce, it was recently stated that, 'on some of the goods produced at Bradford, Portugal had excelled herself in fiscal extravagance by levying a duty of 235 per cent. on the first cost.' And yet, with all this incubating, the Portuguese cannot even make a decent match! A resident assured me that the only amusing things he had ever found in Portugal were the matches; for you never knew what they would do!

Oporto, like Lisbon, is subjected to the intolerable nuisance of an octroi—'an unjust and infamous tax,' as it has been called by a high authority. To facilitate the levying of this, an immense line of fortification has been constructing during the past ten years, enclosing the whole of Oporto, as well as the suburbs. This noble monument of an 'up-to-date' system has already cost untold sums, and was still in progress when I had the privilege of gazing on it. A military guard will furnish a line of sentries along its entire length, as at Lisbon, and Oporto will then be in the 'state of siege' in which the governments delight in placing their longsuffering subjects. It will take many years of octroi to pay the costs of this fortification; but that is a mere detail to a wealthy corporation like that of Oporto.

Of 'protected' industries and 'monopolies' there is no end. Monopolies indeed have ever been a popular policy with Portuguese governments—the last refuge of virtually bankrupt States. There is one thing, however, which no system of monopolies or protection has ever brought into being—an honest administration, the one thing needful.

Amongst the titles the Portuense love to bestow on their dear old town is that of the 'leal e invicta cidade,' which, being interpreted, means 'loyal and unconquered city.'

It is a pleasant conceit, if not historically true. And the inhabitants lay claim to the distinction on the strength of the brave defence their city made when besieged by the troops of Dom Miguel, the usurper, in 1833.

As a matter of fact, Oporto has been twice conquered during the present century; and but for British help, on a recent occasion, the town would again most assuredly have had to succumb to the tyrant. Three several times within the past hundred years has this 'loyal and unconquered city' been rescued from the oppressor's grip by friendly Britons; and on as many occasions has the Portuguese nation shown its appreciation of favours received by insulting and abusing its deliverers, and in several instances by breaking faith, in a shameless manner, with the men who had risked life and limb on its behalf.

Few towns in Europe have been the scene of more stirring events, or of more fighting and bloodshed, than Oporto. Twice under the heel of a foreigner, the town has subsequently passed through all the horrors of civil war and a siege. Of late years this 'classic home of liberty and industry' has become the stronghold of republicanism, and was recently the scene of a revolution, which was not suppressed without bloodshed.

Of the troublous times through which Oporto has passed, the shattered remains of the once splendid Serra convent, with its domed church pitted with shot-marks, now stands as a ghastly memorial. It survived the Napoleonic wars only to be desecrated, and almost destroyed in the civil troubles of later years.

Taking one's stand on this commanding position, and gazing down on the waters of the swift-flowing Douro, two memorable scenes in the grim drama of the wars rise before one. Both were connected with the French usurpation; both were enacted within the short space of three months, and at points but a few hundred yards apart. One took the form of an awful tragedy; the other was a feat of arms which, for audacity in conception and brilliancy of results, stands unsurpassed in military annals.

The reader, if he be conversant with the history of the Peninsular War, will hardly need to be reminded of the incidents to which I refer. But as that long struggle is now chiefly regarded as a chapter of long-forgotten history, all interest in which has been superseded by later occurrences, a few observations may not be out of place.

The first scene was on the occasion of Soult's capture of Oporto in 1809. At that time a bridge of boats, nearly three hundred yards long, connected Oporto with the south side, and it was at this point the tragedy which Napier has so graphically described took place. The bridge offered the only means of escape from the victorious French who were pouring into the city; and towards this point the terrified inhabitants and retreating soldiery converged in a compact, surging mass. 'And there,' says Napier, in one of the most thrilling passages of his book, 'all the horrid circumstances of war seemed to be accumulated, and the calamities of an age compressed into one doleful hour.' More than four thousand persons, old and young, and of both sexes, were seen pressing forward with wild tumult; some already on the bridge, others striving to gain it, and all in a state of frenzy. At that moment a troop of Portuguese cavalry, flying from the enemy, rode furiously down one of the streets, and remorseless in their fears, bore at full gallop into the midst of the miserable, helpless crowd, trampling a bloody pathway to the river. Suddenly, the nearest boats, unable to sustain the increasing weight, sank, and the foremost wretches tumbled into the river as they were pressed from behind, until the heaped bodies, rising above the surface of the waters, filled all the space left by the sinking of the vessels.

Meanwhile, in the city itself, the most horrible scenes of rape, pillage, and murder were being enacted; and 'what with those who fell in battle,' says Napier, 'those who were drowned, those sacrificed to revenge, it is said ten thousand Portuguese died on that unhappy day!'

The man who beyond all others was responsible for having brought these calamities on the city was the Bishop of Oporto. For Soult, before commencing the attack, had urged him to spare so great a city the horrors of a storm, but this hot-headed prelate was obdurate. The rest we know.

The Bishop's subsequent behaviour was characteristic, affording a curious instance of a mistaken vocation. 'Having brought affairs to this awful crisis,' says Napier, 'the Bishop's courage gave way.' Leaving the Generals Lima and Pereiras to command, he repaired in the evening to the Serra convent, on the left bank of the river, from whence he beheld in safety the horrors of the next day.

In after years the cunning ecclesiastics of Oporto turned this horrid tragedy to account for their own base purposes. Immediately facing the bridge, on the Oporto side, there was to be seen attached to a wall a large picture representing the catastrophe—the river almost filled with fugitives and the bodies of the slain, while Soult, mounted on a white charger, is giving orders for a cessation of the carnage.

Close beside this wretched daub was hung a representation of souls enduring the flames of purgatory—from which merry company the Bishop was missing! And underneath was a box bearing the legend, 'Give alms for masses for the souls of those who died.'

The French were allowed but a brief space of time for the enjoyment of their triumph. Wellington was on their track; and within three months of their capture of Oporto the French were flying, a disorganised mob, destitute of guns, ammunition, military chest, or baggage, before the conquering British, back into Spain.

This sudden reversal of fortune was brought about by one of the most daring and masterly strokes of military genius that history records—the passage of the Douro, on the morning of 12th May 1809—a date ever memorable in the annals of the British army.

The scene of this dramatic incident lies a few hundred yards above the spot where the tragedy above described took place, at a point where the river takes a sharp bend to the southward. Here a deep gorge, which contracts to a width of a couple of hundred yards, obscured all movements from the observation of Soult's lookouts, and was besides a most unlikely spot for a crossing to be attempted.

Wellington, who had arrived the evening before, quietly massed his troops in the early morning behind the high grounds and wooded knolls of the Serra convent, and awaited the development of events.

Soult, in leaving this gap open, had mistaken his man; for Wellington, as Napier justly says, 'habituated to the command of armies, was endowed by nature with a lofty genius, and capacious for war.' The Douro still rolled between him and the French; for the bridge of boats had been destroyed, and the problem that faced him was, in Napier's words, 'How pass a river, deep, swift, more than three hundred yards wide, when ten thousand veterans lined the opposite bank? The Macedonian hero might have turned from it without shame!'

Wellington took post on the ground where, a few weeks before, a leader of a very different mould had stood—the Bishop of Oporto. Suddenly a large building called the Seminary caught the English general's eye, the direct line across the river being hidden from the city by the rock on which he stood. 'Here, then, with a marvellous hardihood, Sir Arthur resolved, if he could find but one boat, to force a passage in face of a veteran army and a renowned general.'

The story of finding a boat by Colonel Waters, the crossing in the little skiff with a poor barber and the gallant Prior of Amarante, their return with three barges, and Wellington's laconic order, 'Let the men cross,' with all the consequences that arose therefrom; is it not all written in the book of the war? If the reader does not know the story, he should lose no time in rectifying the deficiency; for it was a most dashing feat of arms, and one of which Englishmen may justly be proud.

Such are the scenes which rise before the spectator as he gazes down from the Serra rock. The landscape has undergone many changes since those memorable days; but the convent of the Serra, wherein Wellington is said to have passed the night before the crossing, as well as the imposing pile of the Seminary, still remain, fitting memorials of a brilliant exploit.

War has left its indelible marks around Oporto. The

splendour and beauty of the once-admired Serra convent, with its immense gardens, orchards, and chestnut woods, exist only in tradition. The finishing stroke was given to it all during the Miguelite siege, when the copses were cut down, the gardens destroyed, and the convent turned into a defensive post. It was in recognition of the gallant defence of Oporto at this time that Dom Pedro bequeathed to the city his heart—the only piece of real estate he had power to will away,—and this interesting relic reposes in one of the city churches.

Such portions of the Serra convent as exist are now used for military purposes, one large apartment being utilised for carrier pigeons. The tiny clay saucers, in which — according to military regulations — the birds deposit their eggs, were handed out for our inspection.

The grounds at the back of the Seminary,—the scene of a gallant exploit by British soldiers during the siege, are now occupied by a cemetery.

There are some curious mementoes of the last revolutionary outbreak to be seen in one of the principal streets of Oporto, in the shape of bullet-holes, with the inevitable starring of glass, in the shop-windows. These interesting perforations remind one of a phase in the national character, already alluded to—a proneness to grandeur of ideas, with a total inadequateness of means for carrying them out.

The story of the bullet-holes is a tale of folly. A regiment of the local garrison, headed by a few ambitious officers, having revolted, rushed to the principal square, and proclaimed a revolution. This act was the measure of their capabilities, as also of their military knowledge, for the square is in a hollow commanded on all sides; and while these foolish revolutionists shouted for a republic, they were being gradually hemmed in. The Guarda Civil—a sort of military police, which is always to be depended on in such crises—having ensconced themselves snugly behind a balustrade commanding the principal street up which the 'revolutionary army' was about to advance, waited their opportunity; and from this safe post potted at their foes directly they appeared, until these misguided men cried, 'Hold, enough!' The bullet-holes through the shop-windows prove how wild was the firing. A little preliminary target-practice would have been the means of saving both ammunition and plate-glass.

An excursion to S. Joao da Foz, or to Lecca and Matosinhos, is an agreeable way of varying one's peregrinations about Oporto; for by this means a whiff of sea air is obtained as well as a sight of the blue Atlantic—almost as blue here as the Mediterranean itself.

During August and September these little bathing resorts are thronged, and then is the time for lovers of quiet to flee elsewhere. For a Portuguese bathing resort, with its entire lack of shade or verdure—with nothing, in fact, to relieve the hideous monotony of long conventional lines of staring white one-storied cottages—is depressing enough at any time. What it becomes in the season, when crowds, dust, brass bands, and perpetual glare 'impart life and animation to the scene,' must be experienced to be appreciated.

One of the sights of Foz in old days, when the friar was a common object of the country, was the 'bathing parade' of the monks from an adjacent monastery. And an amusing story is told of a fat friar whose aquatic exploits were not only the talk of the town, but the source of endless amusement to laymen. This corpulent ecclesiastic had been ordered a matutinal dip, and having the proverbial dislike of his order to cold water, a little gentle persuasion was necessary to get him to undergo his penance. The needful stimulus was applied by ten people—six men, who stood on the beach holding a rope tied round his corpulency, and four women, who led him into the water, and forced him to take the prescribed number of dips, ducking him most unmercifully, and forcibly pressing his head under, until at length his holiness emerged from the briny sputtering, crying, praying, and actually swearing!—Yes, alas that I should have to say it! but it is recorded on the testimony of an eyewitness that this holy man was in the habit of swearing over his matutinal ablutions like a common layman.

I can never pass through S. Joao da Foz without being reminded of the fat friar and his bath.

The town—which is at the Douro mouth—has an interest to Britons from the fact that it was here Captain Charles Napier, afterwards the famous Sir Charles of Acre and Baltic renown, landed on his arrival in Portugal during the Miguelite war, to take command of the naval force intrusted to him by the Emperor Dom Pedro. The story of his exploits and adventures, the departure of the fleet, and the brilliant victory he won in the battle with the Miguelite force off Cape St. Vincent—a feat of arms which made the world ring at the time, and certainly contributed more to the shattering of the Miguelite cause than anything accomplished by the Constitutional generals on shore—is it not all recorded in the book of *The War in Portugal*?

A grateful people would have marked the landing-place of their deliverer by a suitable memorial. To suggest, however, to a modern and up-to-date Portuguese that his most ancient nation had demeaned itself so far as to accept—much less solicit—help from such a perfidious power as Britain would be to invite an incredulous smile—if not some strong language. 'Portugal for the Portuguese,' varied with the refrain, 'Down with the English,' is the cry at the present time.

The fact is, the *fin-de-siècle* Portuguese *fidalgo* is so entirely satisfied with his country's achievements in mediæval times, that he thinks himself entitled to 'rest on his oars' till the end of time. Hence the inertia which characterises his nation at the present day.

A pleasant way of reaching Foz is by the tram-line, along the Douro side; for by this route you soon escape the streets, and following the windings of the river, obtain an uninterrupted view of the pine-clad hills on the opposite bank, with many exquisite vistas up-stream. Ever and anon, too, you get visions of paradise, in the form of some beautiful garden, with its terraces and half-ruined walls, its arbours and bright flowering shrubs, and the vine-trellised walks so dear to the natives of this sunny clime. And to crown all, the 'lovely Douro glides placidly before you, blue as the blue heaven its bright waters reflect.'

Once we accompanied some friends to Matosinhos, while the great religious festival was in full swing. This merry-making takes place at Whitsuntide, and lasts an entire week. The motive of it resides in the Church of O Senhor de Matosinhos, in the shape of an image, concerning which some astonishing legends are treasured up for the delectation of the faithful.

We arrived on the scene about sunset, and plunging into the midst of the merry, good-tempered, orderly, and picturesque crowd that thronged the streets of the small modern town that is encroaching on the village, followed the stream until we found ourselves converging on the centre of attraction—the Church of our Lord of Matosinhos.

The streets were patrolled by mounted police, but more with a view to imparting the right direction to the moving stream of humanity than anything else; though, to be sure, there was a little excitement as we alighted from the car, owing to the attempted arrest of one man by six policemen—for what reason we failed to discover. It ended in an unseemly scuffle; for instead of marching their would-be prisoner to the police-station, these valiant 'bobbies' sought diversion by shoving their victim about and pommelling him with their fists.

Drifting with the crowd for half a mile or so, we arrived at the fair which was being held in a wide, open thoroughfare, terminating at the church. One side was occupied by booths for the sale of sweetmeats and eatables—a most unappetising display; while the other, consisting of a grass bank, perhaps thirty feet wide, presented one of the most strangely picturesque sights eye ever lighted on. For here was displayed, in one continuous line, the most remarkable collection of pottery that was ever got together. Amidst jugs and water jars of graceful design, bowls and cooking-pots, and sundry other triumphs of the potter's art of a purely utilitarian description, was a vast assortment—there must have been thousands of pieces—of the very quaintest objects in glazed pottery I ever beheld. These consisted of the most rude, not to say barbaric, representations of birds and beasts—four-legged and two-legged, bullock-carts, instruments of agriculture and husbandry, insects and crawling things, and what not, all 'conventionally treated' in red clay and roughly glazed, which imparted a mottled red and yellow or chestnut tone. Some of these were laughable caricatures, intended evidently to appeal to the native sense of humour. But the most singular feature of the collection was the fact of every single article containing a whistle. It seemed incredible; but you had only to poke about, and turn the thing round and round, and sure enough a little mouthpiece would presently discover itself. The air literally resounded with whistles in every conceivable key; for, of course, it was *de rigueur* to buy some memento of this most holy pilgrimage, and then to give utterance to the spirit of devotion in a prolonged whistle. To be sure, the connection between O Senhor de Matosinhos and a whistle was not exactly apparent to the stranger; but what of that? Every one whistled, and every one was jolly!

Now, as all the company perambulated the scene with a clay trophy, and seemed mightily well pleased with themselves, we began to think there must be some occult virtue in these bits of baked earth, and determined to fall in with the prevalent humour. Indeed, I am bound to confess we had been seized with an irresistible longing, at first sight of these delightful toys, to buy up the whole show, and transport it bodily to England. They were absolutely fascinating in their quaint, uncouth, barbaric simplicity and colouring; and in spite of their weight and most uncompromising shapes, and the absence of any convenient means of transport, we fell to there and then, and only came to a standstill at last from sheer inability to carry more—arms and handkerchiefs being already loaded to their full capacity. To be sure, there were willing hands in abundance standing around; for, knowing the ways of the eccentric Ingleses, several stalwart young fellows had tacked themselves on to our party.

ART POTTERY
(Height, 6 to 10 inches)

But as we were not returning to Oporto till late at night, it was useless enlisting their services.

What fun it was choosing the specimens and making the bargains! For, of course, the laughing senhoras who presided asked quite three times as much as they ever hoped to get. And after we had loaded up, there was the inevitable 'one thing more' that had to find a place, and just one more, until in very desperation we tore ourselves away. It was then we stood absolutely aghast at our wanton extravagance. For, I am convinced, in spite of all assertions to the contrary, that we squandered at least two shillings over these 'childish gewgaws'; but while the fever of squandering was on us it was impossible to stop. Had we been provided with a cart and a ship I don't know what might have happened; for really one could not gaze on these piquant toys without falling under their spell; and I shall always look back with regret on certain triumphs of art which for want of space, we had to forgo the delight of possessing. I can only compare them to the things you see in museums—unearthed in Mexico or Central Africa—links with a forgotten past, sorts of Jumbos, black men's devils, the Lares and Penates of some long extinct race of 'clay-worshippers.'

To what influence are these native manufactures to be attributed? None of the writers on Portugal—and they are many and learned—have ever alluded to this particular phase of native art. It surely cannot be a relic of the Moorish domination, for the disciples of the Prophet were forbidden to make representations of animals, in case these should enter into competition with the Prophet; for Mahomet was a man of the world, and knew a thing or two. The whole matter is a mystery, for none of our

Oporto friends could tell us where these things were made. All I could discover was, that they never appeared at any other time or function—were, in fact, especially reserved for the *romario* of O Senhor de Matosinhos. The mystery awaits solution.

As we trudged through the crowd, bowed down with the weight of our iniquities—for we remembered, when too late, that it was Sunday!—the thought occurred to us, on beholding the looks of commiseration that our bent forms called forth, as well as from whispered remarks, that the pious pilgrims mistook us for evil-doers of some unclassified type, who were 'working out' their penance—a most comforting reflection which cheered us up amazingly.

Meanwhile, our friends had gone to work in a much more business-like way. Having been intrusted with a commission to buy largely for a bazaar at home, they had engaged a porter, and were dispensing their patronage in royal fashion.

But I have forgotten all about the shrine. We must certainly take a look into the church, if only for curiosity's sake; for though it is neither grand without nor beautiful within, it contains a fine display of gilding, which, like charity, covers a multitude of faults. Everything is sadly in need of soap and water—the imagination kindles at the future that awaits some of those images, under the influence of Monkey soap and elbow-grease, judiciously applied by a healthy, vigorous charwoman, not a priest— and there is a deal of 'matter in the wrong place'; for the Church of Rome in Portugal has long ceased to recognise the old connection between cleanliness and godliness. Even the priests wore an unwashed, late-to-bed-on-Saturday-night appearance, though they turned out smart enough as far as clothes could make them.

The priceless treasure enshrined within this humble edifice has an interesting story attached to it, and such is its fame as to attract every year enormous crowds to the festival. From thirty to thirty-five thousand is said to be the average attendance.

The 'true story' of this relic affords a measure, not only of the audacity of the priests, but of the credulity of the illiterate multitude, and is more in keeping with nursery story-books or Grimm's *Fairy Tales* than with Christian tradition.

Once upon a time—in ages so remote that history is silent on the matter—an old woman who was walking along the sea-shore chanced on an image, and on the discovery becoming known to the priests the waif was promptly installed in the church of Boucas, near where it was found. True, the figure was minus an arm, but things were so pleasantly arranged that some fifty years later the missing limb miraculously turned up, the discovery being made in this wise. Amongst some drift-wood picked up on the beach was a piece endowed with miraculous properties which there was no way of accounting for, seeing that it eluded all attempts, either at cutting it up or burning it, by promptly jumping aside. The priests were called in, and, with the prescience of their order, instantly recognising the nimble faggot as the missing arm of the image, it was at once re-united with the parent stem.

Another curious fact concerning the image is that, it dates can be trusted, it found its way into the church before the introduction of Christianity! which seems to confirm a statement of Mathews, that 'some traces of the old heathen superstitions are constantly cropping out from under their Catholic disguises.' And he goes on to ask,

'What is the modern worshipping of saints and images but a revival of the old adoration paid to heroes and demi-gods?'

The image was eventually removed to the church of Matosinhos, where it has proved as effectual a 'raiser of the wind' as any in the church's possession.

It was quite in keeping with the antecedents of this bit of paganism that it should be credited with some occult power over the destinies of people who go down to the sea in ships and fishing-boats. It was therefore installed as patron saint of the seafaring classes, who hold it in high favour. The mere enumeration of all the feats of life-salvage performed by it would stock a fair-sized volume, and prove vastly more entertaining than the 'new humour.'

Of course every one who has benefited by this inexpensive yet efficient system of life-salvage has felt it incumbent on him, or her, to present an offering to the image as a mark of gratitude, and the church is heavily stocked in this particular line—so much so, indeed, that a 'stock-taking sale' might be held with advantage. Even art has been called in to assist in giving expression to the feelings of pious pilgrims; and the art of Portugal—especially the devotional-marine art—is something quite original and unique in its way; with the result that the church possesses a picture gallery of some magnitude, if not of high merit.

The pictures that adorn the walls of O Senhor de Matosinhos are no mere 'pot-boilers,' but the products of native painters who have worked from the highest motives that can inspire man to labour. They would assuredly cause the heart of the most obdurate and inartistic British churchwarden to sing for joy. The very sight of the shipwrecks and other nautical horrors depicted here, in all the crudeness of native colour, in marvellous perspective, and with an imaginative power that quite compensates for any deficiency in nautical knowledge, and absolutely defies criticism, should make every one of the thirty thousand pilgrims who come to worship at the shrine vow on the spot to renounce the sea and all its works. It would have been impossible for the church to have devised a more effectual means of driving sailors from the vocations of their fathers into the prosaic paths of agriculture, and other shore-going pursuits.

May not the existence of this pious cult be held to account for the steadily decreasing number of Portuguese who take to a seafaring life every year?

'These pictorial offerings and their doggerel inscriptions, though miserable and absurd productions,' remarks an old author, 'yet do not excite so much mirth as inspire pity for the slaves of a deplorable superstition.' Southey, on the other hand, says it is folly to grieve for systems we cannot amend, 'and the wisest way is to laugh at them'!

It was with deep interest we watched the happy, perspiring, and odoriferous crowd marching round the church, past the goal of their pilgrimage, where they 'paid up,' and received in exchange the priest's blessing. For even blessings have a market value, and are not dispensed free-gratis-and-for-nothing by the shepherds of the Infallible Church.

The very last thought to enter the brain of the spectator of this strange scene would be its connection with religion, or that the laughing, gossiping crowd was on devotion bent. As a matter of fact, the *raison d'être* of this popular *romario* is—as it always was—the raising of money. 'Mak money; mak it honestly if you can, but mak money!' is the ruling principle of the Church in Portugal. And with such childish, not to say fraudulent, follies does the Roman Church in Portugal debase the cause of true religion, and multiply scoffers. But 'twas ever thus.

Dear me, how one scene recalls another! As I stood watching the festa of O Senhor de Matosinhos, I seemed to be carried back to old China, and to be gazing once more on the annual festival held near Tientsin in honour of the God of Medicine. Like the one I have been describing, this festival is the great merry-making of the year; and certainly, with the exception perhaps of the Portuguese, no people have a greater aptitude for combining religion with pleasure than the natives of the Flowery Land. The neighbourhood of the temple was, as at Matosinhos, converted for the nonce into a fair, where pious pilgrims bought some little mementoes of the occasion. The inhabitants of the surrounding country flocked here in their thousands, and so close was the resemblance between the two scenes that, barring the costumes, a spectator who happened to be transported suddenly from one to the other might have supposed the festivals to be one and the same, and with identical objects—the raising of money. At each there was the same merry, chattering crowd, passing in at one door and out at the other; the same conclave of dirty, money-grasping priests raking in the oblations of the devout, and the same total absence of reverence, or even of respect, for the shrine containing the object of so much pretended veneration.

Alluding to the absorption of heathen rites and practices by the Roman Church, Mathews points out that even the processions are closely copied from ancient patterns, 'and the lustral water and the incense of the heathen temple remain, without any alteration, in the holy water and the censer of the Catholic Church.'[1]

As if to complete the resemblance, there were Chinese devotees performing the very identical description of penance that was once in favour at Matosinhos. One, a woman, had accomplished the whole ten miles from Tientsin on her knees, rolling a brick in front of her, which she touched with her forehead after making a certain number of revolutions. Another, a man, progressed by measuring his full length along the ground, while carrying a lighted taper in one hand. And these penances were performed with precisely the same object as those of the Matosinhos devotees—with a view to propitiating an enraged Deity.

Now there is no irreverence in scoffing at all this, for it is not religion, but pantomime, which wicked men have invented for their own sordid ends.

It is a remarkable fact that self-inflicted torture—or, as the Roman Catholics prefer to call it, penance—as a means of propitiating the Deity, and securing happiness hereafter, is a prominent feature of Buddhism, and leads to the same abuses and degrading practices as exist under the sanction of Rome. In outward resemblance and ceremonial there is a striking similarity between the ritual of Roman Catholicism and Buddhism. For example, at Tientsin is a temple dedicated to the Queen of Heaven, who, like O Senhor de Matosinhos, is the patroness and protector of the seafaring classes; and this, like the shrine at the latter, contains a marine museum, well stocked with models of all sorts and sizes, though better made and more skilfully rigged than the offerings of the Portuguese

[1] *Diary of an Invalid.*

devotees, while around are suspended a bewildering collection of model legs and arms, deposited in grateful recognition of favours received, in the shape of perfect cures effected, it is supposed, through her agency.

And what almost clinches the extraordinary analogy is the presence in this Chinese temple of a figure with child in arms, known as the 'Conferrer of Sons,' and one of the principal deities of the Buddhist Pantheon. The existence of this figure, and its striking resemblance to the Virgin and Child of the Romish Church, filled the early Jesuit missionaries with delight, until they discovered it was a two-edged sword which might be turned against them with fatal effect. Thereupon they attributed the likeness to satanic agency.

And here, again, everything was designed with a view to 'raising the wind,' money being 'the sole nexus,' as Carlyle would say, the *raison d'être* of the entire establishment and its ritual.

Comparisons of this nature may seem odious to people whose religion, if it can be called religion, is founded on a system of fraud, which they are too weak to investigate; but they are unavoidable if we would live in an atmosphere of reason and truth. 'To see variety in human nature,' says an old writer, 'one must go further than Europe.' And the after-digestion of all one sees and hears in strange countries leads inevitably to comparisons, which, however odious they may seem, are certainly profitable.

That the abuses by which the Romish priesthood have degraded the character of their faith in Portugal have disgusted all liberal and enlightened Catholics is well known, and it is worthy of note, that amongst the various sources of profit to the papal government, in time past, were (1) the sale of permission for domestic oratories in private houses; (2) the sale of licences for people to contract marriages otherwise illegal by their degrees of affinity, the fees being regulated according to the wealth of the applicants. But it was estimated that not more than the third part of these fees reached the papal treasury. Such was the dishonesty of the agents.

The remark of a devout Catholic apropos to this is worth quoting: 'When such an abundance of graces are bought for money, may we not hope that a time will come, and the sooner the better, when Heaven itself will be purchased by other and better means? I hope so,' he added, 'for if it does not come to be so, I am sure I do not know what will become of me for not believing in the efficacy of these bounteous graces of the See of Rome.'

When Dom Pedro attended the first high mass in the royal chapel at Lisbon, after his victorious entry into the city in 1834, he made several observations to Admiral Napier on the ceremonies that were observed on this occasion, and ended by asking him 'if he did not think a man might be a good Catholic and a good Christian without so much mummery?'

A Portuguese Secretary of State, himself a Catholic, thus expressed himself with reference to the religious orders in 1740: 'These men lay the people under contribution in the name of alms; and they absolve those who defraud the revenue without enjoining restitution. . . . I should be reconciled to them if they did not mingle their practice with so much superstitious devotion.' And speaking of the saints' days and other holidays, he says: 'Such is their number that our peasantry and people are allowed to labour only a third part of the year. Indeed, in their mode of worship the Protestant countries have considerably the advantage. Their service, which lasts nearly two hours, is heard with reverent attention, whereas we think one half-hour's mass very tedious. On their holy festivals they examine their own hearts and take the sacrament devoutly, after their heretical manner, which we submit to only to satisfy the forms of the Church, and for fear of excommunication.'

There is one more point of similarity between Portugal and China which is too significant to be passed over, namely, the repudiation by the 'educated classes' in both countries of religious belief. Religion, say they, is very necessary for the poor and ignorant, but we know better. The causes of this dreadful state of things are the same in both countries. As regards Portugal, listen to what an observant traveller said in 1827, a few years before the so-called 'religious orders' were suppressed: 'When the Constitution of 1820 took place, a great deal of light was let in upon the public mind in a variety of matters; religion gained little by the change. Too many began to question the necessity of religion at all, and to point their sarcastic remarks against the discrepancy discoverable between its precepts and the lives of its professors, which were admitted to be universally bad. The effect of these scandals has been to chill the feelings of respect amongst a large portion of the rising generation for the principles of the Christian faith; and there can be no doubt that the most serious results will follow, unless a very speedy reform takes place among the clergy, and unless the useless convents are abolished.'

Since then, the progress of Portugal along the down-grade has been rapid indeed, and 'the most serious results' have ensued. I can give ample authority for this desponding view of the country. Meanwhile, let me remark that, after spending some time in both China and Portugal, and making a particular study of their respective conditions, I have been so much struck with the resemblance between the two, as to be more than half inclined to call Portugal the China of Europe, and the remark of a foreign resident in Portugal has gone far to confirm this view: 'You must not look on Portugal as a European nation: it is a bit of the East tacked on to Europe.'

It is significant that the Romish faith is not only losing hold, but is being slowly spurned from the very countries which have been regarded heretofore as its strongholds. Indeed, the only lands where this sensitive plant appears to flourish at the present time are precisely those which have been saturated through and through with Protestant sentiment. The Protestant atmosphere would seem in fact to be essential to its existence as a form of religion. Portugal, and even Italy, have long given the Pope the cold-shoulder, and even Spain—poor, benighted, besotted, superstitious, bull-fighting Spain—the last refuge of the Papal cult, is in course of dissolution.

And yet this is the Church which is not only held up to our admiration, but with which a certain school of hot-headed, high-minded Englishmen desire to effect re-union. But how can any union be effected between health and decay? New wine cannot be put into old bottles, or new cloth into an old garment, without disaster. Let the worthy folk who yearn for union with Rome go and study Romanism on the spot, and observe its effects in those lands where it has exercised undisputed sway for hundreds of years; and where, if it was ever intended to bear sound and wholesome fruit, the results would be palpable to the eye and ear. If the investigations are undertaken with an open mind, the results will appal them, and they will come back wiser if sadder men.

Turned out of its own preserves, the Papacy is casting about for a new habitat—the old lands having been overcropped—these years past. It is even rumoured that the kindly old gentleman who occupies the throne of St. Peter is sighing for real estate, in spite of the shocking incapacity displayed by his infallible predecessors in their management of landed property. Can we wonder at the Papal leech turning under these circumstances with envious eyes to England? Why, the very thought of plucking such a rich and juicy orange is enough to set the Papal mouth a-watering! The tentacles of the Roman octopus are already stretched forth. There has been the usual preliminary sowing of ground-bait—the establishment of a special fraternity for the 'conversion of England'—as it is piously put. But in vain is the net spread in sight of the bird. The day for these follies has gone by. The world has already had some experience of the 'Union of Christendom'—the 'Boss' system in Church matters, with its pleasant accessories of furnaces and branding-irons, racks and thumbscrews, and other gentle methods of propagandism, and the experience was not such as to encourage a yearning for re-union. Napoleon did much towards upsetting the imposture of Papal government, and it is well known what an Augean stable of indolence, corruption, and incompetency he found. Papal supremacy is played out in this hemisphere.[1]

Let us take a last peep at Matosinhos fair.

The sun has sunk into its Atlantic couch in a halo of orange light, and the afterglow, with its exquisite blending of tints, is suffusing the sky, already a glowing sheet of

---

[1] See 'The "Black" Pope and the "White" Pope,' *Spectator*, Dec. 31, 1898; also a remarkable article in the *Contemporary Review*, Feb. 1899, 'The Policy of the Holy See,' by Professor Fiamingo.

colour, ranging from saffron to delicate lavender. The scene which now greets the eye, with such a setting, and in the clear atmosphere of this pleasant land, is one of enchanting loveliness. Under the mellow evening light, local colouring asserts itself strongly, and wherever the eye turns a perfect wealth of colour awaits it. There, for example, spread out on the greensward, in bewildering variety, is that wonderful collection of pottery, its deep reds, bright yellows, and chestnut browns all glowing by contrast with their verdant surroundings. But the most attractive sight is the crowd—a shimmering, scintillating mass of glowing colour. For every one, of course, is decked out in holiday attire. The women—who greatly predominate—arrayed, either in old-time costume, and resplendent with jewellery, or wearing a simple cotton dress, with bright shawl, and a dainty handkerchief as a framing for the face.

It is in the selection of the head-covering that the 'colour-craving' finds expression; and on great occasions this will always be of silk, and of the brightest colouring. The *coup d'œil* is startling in its brilliancy, almost beyond power of words to express. Never, indeed, was such a feast of colour spread out before mortal eye. I know nothing in our own rather sombre-tinted island to compare with it: unless it be the kaleidoscopic effects of a well-arranged ballet at the Alhambra; or, to turn to nature's palette, the effect of a long perspective of tulip-beds, in the London parks, under brilliant sunshine.

As the mass moved, the most exquisite harmonies were evolved, presenting just such a scene as the great Turner would have revelled in and turned to account—just such an effect as his biographer tells us he once obtained by dabbling his fingers in the colour-box and repeating the operation on a bit of paper. Had the great man visited the fair he would doubtless have carried home a vivid impression of it—as he once did of oranges bobbing about in a rough sea, and afterwards evolved, from his 'inner consciousness,' one of those magnificent colour-schemes he was wont to dazzle his contemporaries with.

Not one jarring note disturbed the perfect harmony of it all. There was hardly a hat or bonnet to be seen in the whole vast assemblage, while those wonderful creations of the '*modiste,*' the Paris fashions, were happily conspicuous by their absence. In fact, the most striking and agreeable feature of the 'show' was the unaffected simplicity of attire. There was none of the pretentious, tawdry trappings with which the women of the wage-earning classes at home love to deck themselves out, under the belief they are 'in the fashion'—a vulgar, snobbish affectation of a higher position in the scale of life than they really occupy. And yet the people were clean, well-dressed, and good-humoured, and courtesy prevailed everywhere. And, if the mother-tongue of Portugal is not musical, 'as she is spoke' amongst the 'masses,' the strident voices of 'Arry and 'Arriet out for a holiday, and intent on publishing the fact abroad, did not jar on the ear. There was a pleasing absence, too, of that detestable form of savagery which seeks to derive enjoyment from the annoyance of others.

It was with difficulty we could tear ourselves away from the enchanting scene; but that arch-tyrant hunger would not be denied, and with many regrets we obeyed. But the recollection of that vision of bright colours will never entirely fade away while life lasts; and when oppressed with the grime and gloom of our cold northern towns, or when November fogs darken the land, memory's eye will always turn fondly to that delicious evening at Matosinhos.

After spending an hour or two with friends at Foz, we drove back to Oporto, in the soft, balsamic air which steeps this favoured land after sundown, reaching our hotel at midnight.

A hot spell had now set in, and we determined to set off in search of green fields and shady coppices, and see something of the lovely inland scenery in the cradle of the race which built up Portugal's greatness in times past. It was the sturdy peasantry of the Entre-Minho-e-Douro and the Tras-os-Montes (Anglice, *Between the Minho and Douro* and *Beyond the Mountains*) that furnished the Portuguese fleets and armies with their best and bravest men, and who preserve even now something of the independent spirit of their ancestors.

These northerners still cling to their ancient customs and their picturesque costumes, and are noted for their love of song and frolic, and much else which the besom of progress would sweep away, if it could. They are still essentially Portuguese—a pleasant, kindly, light-hearted race, endowed with many sterling qualities which have withstood the disintegrating effects of time and external influences.

Everywhere in Portugal the peasantry are courteous and kindly to the stranger; and our own experiences exactly accorded with the observations of a traveller in the last century, who, on entering the country from Spain, wrote: 'We found the peasants surprisingly courteous, and ready to give us any information required: and this struck us the more, as the Spanish peasants are in general remarkable for the very opposite disposition, being haughty, rude, and brutal to strangers.' And after a longer acquaintance, he referred to them as 'affable and courteous to a degree hardly to be found in any other country.' In fact, we can fully indorse the dictum of a later writer, that 'the civility of the labouring classes, if it has not already done so, ought to pass into a proverb.'

How long will these agreeable traits survive 'modern tendencies'? Only the other day I heard of a clergyman of the Church of England discouraging the respectful salutation of school-children, on the ground that 'we are all equal, you know'! Here, in Portugal, the custom of giving and returning the salute, as a mark of respect due from one human being to another, still survives.

The inhabitants of these favoured regions are by no means insensible to their natural attractions; for they claim that neither the rest of Portugal nor any known portion of the globe can compete in beauty with their valleys—that, in fact, heaven alone possesses such scenes of true enchantment.

This beautiful district has inspired many a native poet; and, even after experiencing the devastating effects of war, Lord Carnarvon could still say of it: 'All in the Minho seems redolent of joy, the country pleasing, the climate fine, and a perpetual sunshine in the face of man shows that oppression has no entrance here.'

Unfortunately Portugal is a country wherein art has done little to render the pilgrim's path either smooth or agreeable; and much remains to be done before worshippers in the temple of Nature can move about, or perform their devotions in comfort.

Hotels, wherein the traveller who cherishes some regard for the conventionalities of civilised life can rest and be thankful, are few and far between. And before setting

From specially prepared Photographs

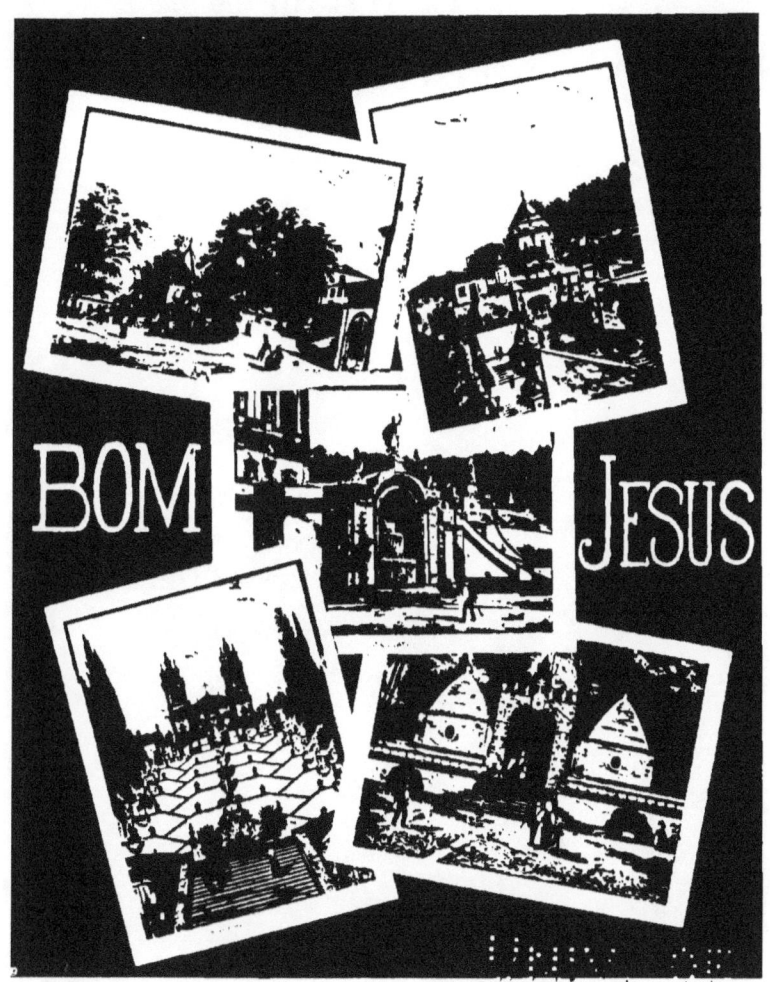

In front of the Hotel   *The Hotel*
Cascade in front of Church
The Grand Approach   *Entrance to the Grounds*

UNIV. OF
CALIFORNIA

forth on a journey—especially if ladies are of the party, —it is essential that careful inquiries be made as to accommodation *en route*. Native certificates of character must be accepted with caution. For the Portuguese, even of the well-to-do classes, are simple in their tastes, and easily satisfied, and their ways, it must be remembered, are not our ways.

Of course, in every land there are hotels and hotels; and it would be unreasonable to look for the home comforts one finds, as a matter of course, at the 'Red Lion,' or the 'White Lion,' or the 'Golden Lion' of an English country-town in the rural *estalagems* of Portugal. But even the conveniences and comforts of a common village 'pub' are lacking here. And it is hopeless to look for reform until public opinion has been educated up to the requisite pitch. At present, the traveller's complaints are regarded as displaying a want of respect for old Portugal.

Our friends had assured us we should find excellent accommodation at a place called Bom Jesus, one of the most lovely spots in the north, near the ancient town of Braga. So for Bom Jesus we packed, and in due course departed.

Since Lord Carnarvon wrote, the railway spider has spun its web over the land, and a line now connects Oporto with Braga, about thirty miles off, as the crow flies; and although in a journey by rail one misses the curious experiences described in old books of travel, it is not a bad way of seeing the country, so leisurely is the progress, and so long and frequent are the pauses for contemplating the landscape, or botanising.

Leaving Oporto at eleven, we ran through a pleasant country, wherein, half-hidden by roses, myrtles, and vine-clad bowers, stood quintas and cottages, with vines and creeping plants swarming over and almost smothering their roofs.

At Nime Junction we changed on to the branch line for Braga, and while waiting, chanced on an antiquarian discovery of considerable interest—a locomotive, bearing the legend, 'Beyer, Peacock, and Co., Manchester, 1854.' This curious relic of the dark ages was actually in the possession of its faculties, and puffing off steam! No traveller should omit seeing this interesting specimen of the antique.

The remainder of the journey was performed in even more leisurely fashion than the first part; but there was nothing to regret in this, for the air was fresh, and redolent of fruit blossom, the heavens were an expanse of deepest blue, and the country lay steeped in the brightest of sunshine, while each little roadside stopping-place was a picture in itself as it stood enveloped in verdure, with its trellised vines and fruit-trees, and so richly decked out with geraniums and other bright flowers, as to more nearly resemble a graceful arbour than a railway station.

The jagged peaks of the Serra de Gerez now towered up in front, and, ever and anon, we discerned through breaks in the low hills, a detached mountain, from whence there stood forth, in bold contrast to the dense wood surrounding it, a glittering white edifice, which we at once recognised as the goal of our pilgrimage—the church of O Senhor do Monte, more commonly called Bom Jesus.

Outside Braga station—a mere shed—stood the steam tramcar that was to carry us to the foot of the mountain; and into this we transferred our belongings, and awaited the pleasure of the conductor. The car was American built, comfortably seated, with open sides, the occupants being neither numerous nor exigent.

At last we got off, puffed noisily up the incline into the great square, and pulled up at the tram-office, where we managed to while away twenty minutes. Why we waited, Heaven only knows, unless it was to give the engine a chance of pulling itself together for the tough bit of collar-work in front.

The sun was searching out the streets with four-furnace power; not a breath of air stirred, and, what with the glare from the white houses, and the hot and dusty road around, we felt no inclination to quit the shelter of the car. In fact, the little we saw of the ancient city, added to what our friends had told us, excited no longing to increase our knowledge of the place. For, with the exception of the church, which is historically interesting, and contains some relics, there is absolutely nothing here to detain the traveller.

The tram-officials—to judge from the oppressive sense of boredom that stamped their faces—were evidently of the same mind. But it was their duty to remain in this broiling spot for twenty minutes, without any valid reason, for not a passenger got in or out, and I must admit they performed it conscientiously.

Off we went again, our route lying through a fashionable suburb where spruce villas, 'pleasantly situated within their own grounds,' abounded on all sides. Very lovely, too, were the gardens surrounding them, and these, interspersed with orange-groves, orchards, and vineyards, make pleasant retreats for the shop-ocracy of Braga to retire to after working-hours.

'The Portuguese,' wrote Beckford, apropos to the Prior of S. Vincent's behaviour on one occasion, 'have a strong relish for coarse, practical jokes.' A striking illustration of this trait was afforded during our passage through the suburbs; for, as we passed a showy little villa, our fellow-passengers—male and female, well-dressed folk—were suddenly overcome with hardly suppressed merriment. Following the direction of their gaze, I just caught a fleeting glimpse of the cause—a fountain, in full view of the road, whereon the marble figure of a child, life-size, was utilised in a manner that would scarcely commend itself to people of refined taste in other lands.

Nearly three miles separates Braga from 'Our Lord of the Mount.' And as we wound up the circuitous road which constitutes the 'pilgrim track,' the sanctuary loomed up conspicuously in front, as was doubtless intended by the monkish builders who perched it thus loftily. At length we ran under a bank of grand old trees, and drew up at an imposing gateway, the entrance to the Sanctuary grounds, at which point, in the devout and athletic days of old, the pilgrims were wont to commence on foot the ascent of the steep and crooked path that led to salvation.

An excellent carriage road is now carried zig-zag fashion up the face of the mountain, under shady trees, emerging, about 150 feet short of the summit, on a terrace or platform, from whence the ascent may be completed, by those who are so disposed, by a flight of marble steps, forming a noble approach to the church of O Senhor.

This approach is quite the feature of the place, and is certainly unique; but, in the absence of elaborate drawings, it is almost impossible to convey a correct idea of the structure, seeing that it is really a very complicated and cleverly contrived piece of architecture, a strange monkish 'conceit,' devised, one would suppose, for the purpose of taxing the physical powers and self-control, in the matter of language, of the pilgrims.

As viewed from below, it has the appearance of a continuous flight of steps. In reality, however, it is a series of platforms or terraces, communicating by short flights of steps carried zig-zag fashion, and adorned on each side with chapels, or oratories, containing groups of clay figures representing scenes in the last hours of our Lord, at each of which it was incumbent on the pilgrims to pause and uncover.

As climbing up stairs is apt to induce thirst, the monkish designers provided for this by conducting limpid streams of the purest water into cunningly wrought fountains on each stage. Nowadays, if the pilgrims can only hold out till the top is reached, there are other sorts of waters, and stronger things.

I believe in old days it was *de rigueur* for the truly devout to perform all this part of the ascent on their knees; it is not recorded if knee-caps were allowed, but in any case, the results would tax the powers of any humanly devised trousers-stretcher to remedy. But this part of the performance is rather slurred over nowadays, for the modern pilgrim is, alas! a sadly matter-of-fact fellow. He makes the ascent by—a lift! Pilgrims and lifts. How dreadfully incongruous the words sound! It is a fact, though. And what is worse, the lift has been led up the mountain-face, alongside the old 'track,' those trying steps which, doubtless, in many cases, proved the proverbial 'last straw' to the 'pumped' pilgrims.

The lift conveyed us to the door of the Grand Hotel, which is on the same level, and but a hundred yards from, the Sanctuary, in a magnificent situation, with views commanding the entire Braga valley, right away to the far

Atlantic. Here we selected our little cell, and having settled in, set forth to investigate our surroundings.

This finely situated domain, now the property of Government, is very extensive, and of surpassing loveliness. Shady walks interlace every part, so that one may wander for hours under the most varied foliage, radiating from trees of great age, whose gnarled and crooked branches, arching overhead, form impervious canopies of green. The grounds are excellently well kept, and altogether make a delicious hot-weather retreat.

After wandering about until we had fairly lost ourselves in the maze of paths, we came suddenly on an expanse of artificial water, with bridges, islands, rustic arbours, and other abominations of the 'cockney' type—a modern exotic, intended, doubtless, to 'enhance the attractions of the place,' as the Guide-book would say. We fled in disgust; there were even boats on it, and it is called a 'lake'!

Our explorations showed that this particular mountain was but a spur from a much loftier range at the back—bleak, bare, and wind-swept, which makes the Monte seem all the more lovely by contrast. But our wanderings were cut short by the dinner-bell, which rang out at the early hour of 4.30. Hitherto, when on our travels, we had usually arranged to eat at civilised hours. But as there seemed to be some little difficulty about it here, and as our stay was to be brief, we did not press the point, seeing that it was a question of disorganising the establishment and disturbing the cook's siesta.

And now, for the benefit of intending pilgrims to this most famous shrine, let me place briefly on record our hotel experiences. And first let me observe that there are three hotels here, all within handshake of each other.

But the Grand is by far the best, and its position unrivalled, for the cool Atlantic breezes search out every cranny of the house after arriving at these altitudes uncontaminated by man or beast. The proprietors, two brothers, are courtesy personified; and as one of them speaks French, we found it easy to explain our requirements. Moreover, as they are also owners of the best hotel in Braga, visitors staying at either are permitted to take their meals at whichever hotel may happen to be the most convenient, an arrangement which facilitates sightseeing.

The hotel contained a fair sprinkling of visitors, considering the time of year; but we by no means relished the intelligence that by Saturday night it would be full, owing to the great Whitsuntide festival which was to commence on Sunday. Truth to tell, no Portuguese hotel is a congenial resting-place for Britons in the season; for, although scrupulous cleanliness reigned everywhere throughout this particular establishment, so agreeable a state of things could hardly survive the influx expected later on, when entire families would take up their residence with nurses and children, and time-honoured customs would certainly begin to reassert themselves.

There was a large and airy *salon de leitura*, and, oh! luxury of luxuries, plenty of comfortable easy-chairs, sofas, and couches, by no means common objects of native *estalagems*; and, to our intense surprise, the establishment was lighted with the *lux electrica*. As luck would have it, the engineer elected to fall sick the day after our arrival, leaving us all very much in the dark; but as no sane person, unless a confirmed bookworm, would have dreamed of spending his evenings indoors amid such surroundings, and in such a climate, the deprivation was not a severe one.

The *quartos de dormir* were delightfully fresh and clean, as indeed I am bound to say they are in all the best hotels. But who, I should like to know, is responsible for the invention of the orthodox mattress of Portugal? He must have been a true Spartan; for anything less sympathetic or responsive to pressure I have never met with than the pillows and mattresses of this ancient realm. They almost compel the weary traveller to follow the sailor's injunction, and 'prick for a soft plank' on the floor! Our couches here exactly tallied with the description of beds given by a traveller of seventy years ago, showing how attached the people are to 'olo custom.'

The cooking was good, and the table liberal, but the meal-hours were a relic of early civilisation. Briefly, there were but two meals a day, according to the ancient custom of Portugal: the first at 9.30, the second at 4.30, an arrangement to which no self-respecting stomach can readily accommodate itself.

Breakfast began with thick, unappetising, schoolboy slices of cold veal and bacon, eaten without accompaniment of any sort. And when this course made its appearance the first morning, we concluded it must be the *pièce de résistance* of the meal, and set-to accordingly. My *vis-à-vis*, a refined, delicate-looking lady, who I should have expected to see toying with an egg and a bit of toast, quite alarmed me by putting away two immense slices of this cold delicacy, while I, an Englishman, was brought to a standstill before I had got half through my ration!

After a decent interval there appeared, steaming hot, the favourite national dish, stewed salt cod with potatoes—

'Bacalhao,' as it is called—which takes the place of porridge in Scotland. This light refection was attacked by every one with as hearty good-will as if they had fasted for a week. Even my fair *vis-à-vis*, who had already made what I considered a 'hunter's meal,' pegged away as cheerily as any one at the table: the veal and bacon had been a mere appetiser. And now, thought I, the breakfast *menu* must be exhausted. Not a bit of it! Beefsteaks with omelet next appeared, the dish being attacked in the same fierce way as its predecessor was. Overcome with wonder, I stole a glance across the table, but the fair one was still well in the running, and showed no signs of distress.

At last the company, having taken the edge off their appetites, began to toy with rolls and butter and jam. Coffee appeared with hot milk, and tea for those who preferred it, the excellent red wine of the country having been the beverage so far.

'Stand at ease' was the order of the day, and a very perceptible air of weariness now stole over the company, all of whom, let us hope, were beginning to experience what is called 'a comfortable sense of repletion' after the ample justice that had been done to the good things provided. The stateliness and dignity which had prevailed hitherto disappeared, and the company resolved itself into a 'free-and-easy.' Every one's knife dived promiscuously into the nearest butter-tin—for the butter is not removed from its original packing-case in fair Lusitania,—and from thence travelled backwards and forwards to the roll. Elbows were planted on the table, toothpicks set forth on voyages of discovery, and every one did what seemed good in his or her eyes, regardless of conventionalities.

And, to be sure, after nearly two hours of hard exertion,

a little relaxation was excusable, and it was refreshing to see the 'naturalism' that distinguished the company. A sense of calm pervaded the assembly—a kind of *dolce far niente*, which no one seemed anxious to disturb. The temperature of the room all the time, owing to the tightly closed windows, which are *de rigueur* during meal-hours, had been gradually rising to tropical heat, and had resulted in flushed faces, not pleasant to gaze on, but inevitable after so much hard work.

The physical exercises which follow eating in Portugal having been completed, the company betook themselves to—pedestrianism? Not a bit of it, they just lolled about in the *salon*, or outside, till dinner-time.

Now dinner at 4.30 is a very serious and substantial repast, as well it may be after so long an interval of fasting, and was excellently well served and done justice to. But what tries the patience of restless Britons is the dreadful amount of time wasted over these gorges; for the dinner lasts even longer than breakfast; and before one-half of the courses had appeared we nearly expired of *ennui*.

Early dinner has, however, this advantage: it enables one to enjoy the cool of the evening out of doors. And this is the period of the day when the natives do really indulge their legs in a little gentle locomotion. There is no rushing up mountain-tops, and other mad freaks, but just a leisurely, dignified crawl, which so well becomes the descendants of Albuquerque.

At half-past nine, or ten, the table is again set out with a light refection. I am not quite sure what it is called, though a resident assured me the proper name for it was 'tea-water'; and 'tea-water' it certainly was, for the faintly-tinted decoction that made its appearance, and was taken plain or with hot milk, certainly merited no other appellation. This light beverage, a poor substitute for the 'cup that cheers,' was sipped to the accompaniment of sweet biscuits or bread-and-butter. I must confess that after an evening on the mountain-top, where the breezes were cool and invigorating, we thoroughly entered into the spirit of this particular entertainment, light as it was.

Altogether the native hours proved a veritable thorn in the flesh, which somewhat marred our visit; though, to be sure, it was the only penance we performed here.

The monks certainly knew what they were about when they selected this particular spot for the building of a shrine, seeing that the abundance of shade—the woods reach to the very door of the hotel—make it a most delectable retreat. And I have often wondered what Portugal would have been like without her monks; for it may be said of them, as of those of Buddha in far Cathay, that 'they had an eye for the picturesque and a taste for natural beauty of no mean order, to judge by the position of their temples and monasteries, which occupy all the most beautiful spots in the country.' And in Portugal, as it was in China during the Tang dynasty, 'every beautiful spot amongst lakes, waterfalls, and mountains was selected for a hermitage or a monastery.'

Of the church of O Senhor do Monte, or, to give it its full title, 'Real Sanctuario de Bom Jesus do Monte,' little need be said. The shrine, which looks so mighty imposing from afar, has no architectural merit, though built of a beautiful white limestone resembling marble. The towers are provided with a suitable equipment of bells, which, when rattled with proper energy, emit the unmusical jingle which is, alas! the characteristic of church bells everywhere. The interior has been described as 'striking in its plainness,' and plain it is; in fact, with the exception of a certain carved ivory crucifix of some value, the church possesses few treasures.

A side-chapel contains a fine collection of anatomical specimens in wax, the gifts of pious admirers; and there is a remarkable 'art gallery,' containing some pictures selected from the well-known realistic school of Portuguese painters of fifty years ago, whose praiseworthy efforts have done so much for devotional art. The *motif* of one of these fine works is sufficiently remarkable to call for a more detailed notice than can be given here. Let me just sketch in the outline. A man is in bed, vomiting blood into a basin, which is held by a friend, while a Franciscan monk grasps his hand—probably containing money. Some of the family are kneeling before an apparition of 'O Senhor do Monte,' while the wife stands by, holding up some of the intestines which have come away from the invalid during a violent fit of coughing. The particulars of this astonishing malady, and the miraculous recovery therefrom, are set forth in a legend below. From this brief account of a really fine work, some idea may be formed of the character of these compositions. It struck me the collection had been got together with discrimination and taste.

There are also some noble seascapes in oil and water-colour, forming a fairly representative collection of works by this particular school, while the museum contains some specimens of ship-modelling, nicely carved and neatly rigged.

If the executive skill of the artists whose works were displayed here could only keep pace with their imagination, Europe would ring with their fame.

An inscription informs pilgrims that the first stone of

the present edifice was laid in 1784, and that it was designed by a captain of engineers. In an appeal to the generosity of visitors, we read, 'The Sanctuary is not rich, and much remains to complete it,' to which is appended the information, that it is 'a spot endowed by nature beyond any other in Portugal and Europe.'

Making every allowance for monkish bombast, it must be admitted that the view from the terrace is surprisingly fine. It has even been compared to that from the Superga over the fertile valley of the Po and the city of Turin. Every evening we wandered out here to enjoy the magnificent panorama, and every evening the prospect seemed more lovely. It was so ordained, too, that the sunsets were arranged with extraordinary splendour.

Mr. Oswald Crawfurd, in his pleasant *Round the Calendar in Portugal*, dwells especially on the remarkable beauty of the sunsets in this particular latitude: 'The cloudscapes at sunset-time are magnificent beyond the words of the writer, beyond the brush of the artist, and almost beyond the fancy of the poet'—a circumstance which he reminds us is in accordance with Humboldt's statement that the finest sunsets are to be seen in about latitude 40°, in mountainous regions in the neighbourhood of the sea. Oporto lies in about 41° N.

Here we would often linger till the valley beneath was steeped in a purple haze, through which flashed the diamond lights of Braga. But under such a sky and in such a balmy atmosphere we might have loitered till midnight, without risk of damp or chill, the stones being so thoroughly saturated with sunshine that they not only retained their store of heat for hours afterwards, but warmed the air all round.

Every evening, after sundown, the 'fairy lights' of the

fireflies would flash out bright against the dark forest background as they commenced their revels, which lasted long after the 'lords of creation' had gone to roost.

Sometimes we would vary our rambles by a climb to a loftier peak at the back, where, on a commanding height, about 600 feet above the Real Sanctuario, a 'rival establishment' was in course of erection. It seems that the ecclesiastical powers are of opinion that a little healthy competition in the matter of shrines ought to be encouraged in the interests of true religion. And so, in hopes of catching a few stray pilgrims whose zeal has not been 'worked off' at the lower level, a rival shrine is being 'run up' at this most breezy altitude.

There is already a church in embryo, as well as a few buildings for the shelter and refreshment of pilgrims. But really, until the locomotive powers of the Portuguese show a vast improvement, I should fancy there would be little eagerness to take the 'refreshment contract' up here.

In front of the church-to-be, on a detached knoll, overlooking the Braga valley, is a raised platform supporting a pedestal, whereon is perched a colossal statue of——I really forget who the lady is! For, truth to tell, the prospect from this particular platform is so grand, that all counter-attractions sink into utter insignificance. Nature claims precedence here over everything, and will, I feel confident, be accorded undisputed sway by all who visit these scenes of grandeur. I cannot even remember the name of the shrine. But what matter? It is only one folly the more, in the land of follies.

One particular evening effect has imprinted itself indelibly on the mental retina. We had reached the summit at sunset, and on turning to the west, such a glory of colour met our gaze as would baffle the efforts of the greatest colourist in oils or water-colour to give expression to. It almost seemed impious essaying to transmit a faint echo of its splendour to the pages of a pocket sketch-book. Just in front rose up the figure of the saint, a great purple mass, silhouetted against an orange sky. The Braga valley lay far beneath, spread out like an exquisitely tinted map, wherein a distant curve of the lovely Cavado caught a momentary gleam from the sky above. Towns and hamlets were faintly suggested by veils of light blue smoke, while mists were creeping up the slopes of the distant serra. The whole valley seemed steeped in sleep. Not a sound rose up to these serene heights; and, but for a few lights which had begun to speckle Braga, and scintillated like stars in a summer sky, and an occasional rocket with its fiery trail and star-shower, the city might have been under a spell of enchantment.

And now, what means this sudden effulgence like the flashing of diamonds on a purple cushion? Only 'switching on' the current. For, marvellous to relate, Braga is lit by electricity — a proof of her Municipality being wide awake in more senses than one.

But, after all, what are sunsets? I hear some reader exclaim. There is no novelty about them! They come round as regularly as the days of the week, and, for the life of me, I can see nothing in them to gush about. I'm all for novelty.

Well, the power of appreciating the beauties of nature are, I know, a mere matter of temperament. But if Nature doesn't paint pictures in the sky for our particular delectation, why does she waste all this fine colour? Surely these displays are intended to excite admiration and afford pleasure. 'What that pleasure is would be perhaps more difficult to describe than the landscape itself,' says a justly esteemed author; 'for how much more will one person see in a landscape than another, and even the same person than himself, at different times?' It has been asserted that beauty does not reside in things themselves, but in the eye that sees it, and every eye sees a different beauty.

The curious thing is that people who rarely, if ever, notice beauty in nature, and would never look at a sunset sky, will go into raptures at a crude imitation of nature on a bit of canvas. A well-known author tells us that he once heard a man argue that there was nothing in nature to equal the *scenery* of Covent Garden. Perhaps it is the fact of having to sit and stare at a thing that first opens the eyes of the blind; and the 'Oh, my!' and 'Lor, ain't that fine!' that rise up in chorus from the pit of a theatre, are the outward and audible signs of an inward and spiritual sense of the beautiful which lies latent in many an unsuspected bosom. 'He is little to be envied,' says the above-quoted writer, 'who is dead to the enthusiasm of Nature; whose heart and feelings are out of the reach of her influence, and who is insensible to the tranquil enjoyment which is derived from the contemplation of her charms.'

The spot whereon we stand is historic. For it was on this very mountain that Soult, when entering Portugal at the head of his army of devastating locusts in 1809, halted his troops, and, pointing to the rich valley below, extending far away to the shores of the Atlantic, addressed them in the following words: 'Venez, soldats! Venez, voir le paradis qui vous attend!'

Now, when a French army is invited into a 'paradise,'

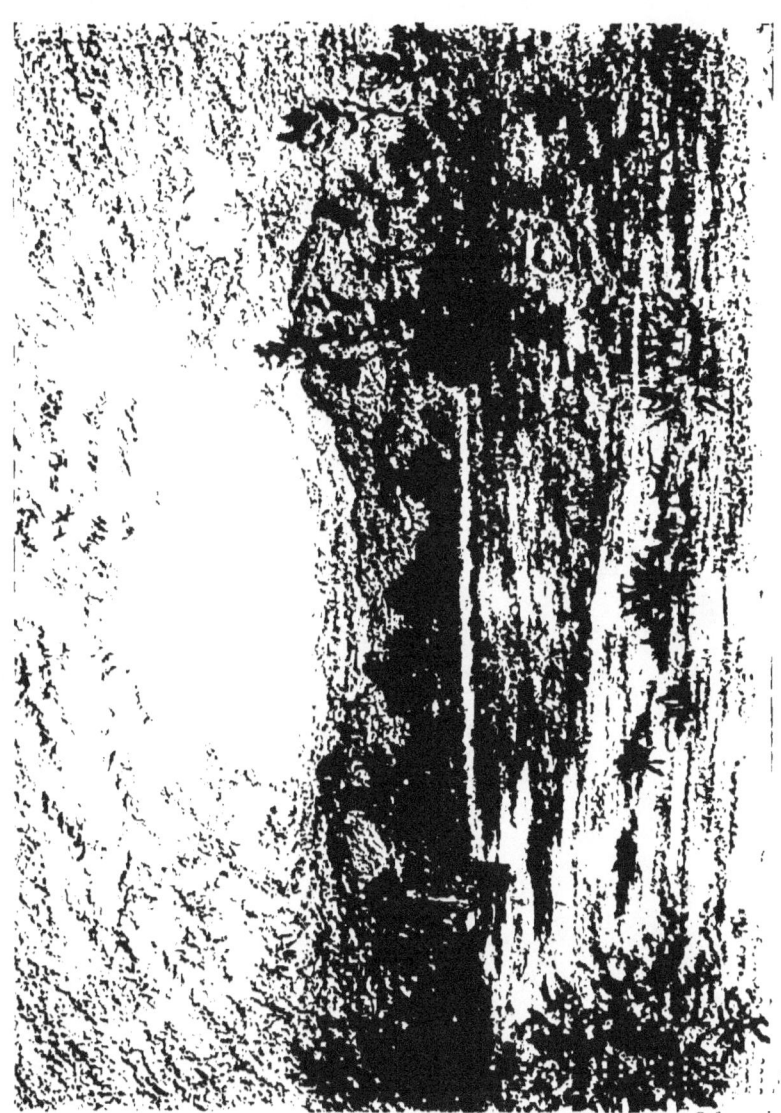

'THE RIVER OF OBLIVION,' FROM PONTE DE LIMA

UNIV. OF
CALIFORNIA

it very speedily converts it into a hell; and the particular occasion to which I allude formed no exception. Smoking ruins, with all the horrors comprised in the word rapine, marked the track of these 'liberators of the oppressed' wherever they marched in Portugal.

Perchance this is the reason why the modern Portuguese have discovered an 'affinity of soul' with the French nation. For, assuredly, no people ever kissed the rod so assiduously as the inhabitants of fair Lusitania.

And now, a wonder appeared in the woods.

On the evening of the day after our arrival, while seated on our favourite terrace, the stillness was broken in upon by faint musical sounds. 'Listen!' we exclaimed simultaneously, 'listen! Why, surely it must be sheep-bells far up on the mountain: how very pretty!' The silvery tones of those far-away bells came rippling down the mountain-sides in one continuous peal. It seemed like magic. For no sheep or goat bell we had ever heard emitted silvery tones like these. And yet, what else could it be? The air was full of the sound, as if the mountain was bewitched, and the fairies had peopled it with silver bells and ringers. Had we fallen under a spell of enchantment?

While lost in wonder, a tiny bell began ringing out its fairy chimes at our feet. It was quite uncanny! And yet it could not be a real bell, for the stones were much too solid to contain bells in their interstices. Besides, as we listened, we detected a distinct hoarseness; and then, of a sudden, the voice broke into a most palpable croak, and the spell was broken. It flashed on us, in a moment, that it was a 'bell-frog,' and that the fairy chimes which filled the air were the silvery voices of hundreds of these singular little creatures. It was wonderful!

A friend at Oporto had assured us there were such animals in Portugal—but we had our doubts! Newcomers are apt to have their 'legs pulled'; and we were decidedly of opinion that this was a case in point. But hearing was believing; and never again, after listening night after night to those fairy chimes rippling through the still air, shall we doubt the existence in Nature's strange menagerie of the bell-frog—we actually saw one.

Truly, a fitting accompaniment to so enchanting a spot were the silver chimes of the bell-frog. The last sounds that rang in our ears as we closed our eyes in sleep, night after night, were these fairy bells.

Is it not singular that in no book of travels in Portugal is a single allusion made to these interesting creatures?

We were so completely in harmony with our surroundings that there was little attraction in the idea of quitting the shady glades and going a-gadding. Still, there was one particular spot, within easy driving distance, which we had been earnestly enjoined not to miss seeing—Ponte de Lima.

This town stands on the beautiful Lima—the 'river of oblivion,' as it was called on account of the exquisite scenery that marks its course; indeed, according to native writers, this part of Portugal was the Elysium of the ancients. It was here that the stern victors of the ancient world—the Roman legions,—little prone to the soft emotions of our nature, were vanquished by the bewitching beauty of the valleys of the Lima and the Cavado, and, 'in a fit of passionate enthusiasm, threw down the national eagles and refused to leave that happy land': they mutinied, and, according to the best authorities, even 'forgot the ties that bound them to their distant homes, and renounced the glories of Imperial Rome for the pastoral and peaceful seclusion of the Minho.' And really, after becoming acquainted with this fairy land, one could almost forgive this act of mutiny. One would fain hope, however, that the stern legionaries of Rome showed more consideration for the inhabitants of this Elysium than did the latest intruders—the French.

We felt irresistibly drawn to these regions, and, shaking off the lethargy which had crept over us, determined to brave the heat and dust of the lower regions, and do our duty.

The arrangements for the excursion were soon completed. A carriage was to meet us at the bottom of the lift at 6.30 A.M.; while, to ensure punctuality on the part of the lift-man, this individual was enjoined to be at his post at six, soon after which hour we were foolish enough to appear. But as the Illustrimo Senhor did not put in an appearance until long after the appointed time, and had, first of all, to walk half-way down to grease the wheels and look to the points, it was late before we started.

However, the morning was delicious, the air crisp and cool, and as we sat under the spreading limbs of a grand old cork tree, enjoying the view, we felt that ill-humour would be out of place. Besides, it was our own fault for being unreasonable enough to expect punctuality. Our 'copy-book maxims,' if rendered into Portuguese, would read—'Procrastination is a virtue,' 'Punctuality is the thief of time,' etc. etc. We had forgotten this.

Our road lay through Braga. 'Its situation,' justly remarks an old traveller, 'renders it a perfect oven.' It was already shimmering in the heat, and we were glad to escape from its ugly, glaring streets, and still more so to get clear of the dirty, smoky suburb, and breathe country air again.

Braga calls itself a manufacturing town, hats and hardware—an elastic term—being its chief products, the particular suburb through which we passed being the 'seat of industry.' But we were in no humour for investigating the noisy 'hives of industry,' those filthy hovels, wherein work was going on.

After labouring heavily for a couple of miles, over an abominable road—a succession of pits filled with boulders, —we escaped from the busy haunts of men with their lumbering bullock-carts, and breathed freely once more, and our spirits rose. For how true it is that 'our very physique changes with our surroundings. We expand mentally and morally and physically in one atmosphere, and we close and shrink and fade in another.'

We had now entered a truly delightful country, which extended all the way to Ponte de Lima. High hedges, which, like our English ones in early spring, are gay with wildflowers, skirted the road, while the trees were interlaced with vines climbing to their topmost branches.

Nothing is more characteristic of north Portugal than the manner in which the vine is allowed to follow its own sweet will amongst the branches of the oak, the chestnut, or the cork tree, disporting itself in luxuriant festoons, as it struggles with its ally for distinction. The picturesque appearance of the vineyards is also greatly enhanced by the intermixture of orange, lemon, almond, peach, cherry, fig, plum, and mulberry trees.

In south Portugal the vine is pruned as it is in France and Germany. Here it is permitted to run wild over trees or trellis-work, as in some parts of Italy, where bunches of laburnum flowers peeping through the young vine-leaves surprise as well as delight one. In this method of viniculture the farmers of the north still follow the practice of their former masters, the Romans. 'To this day,' says Mr. Crawfurd, 'the Minhote farmer grows the vine as the ancient Italians did, still "marrying it" to pollarded trees; while the grapes are crushed, and their liquor fermented, just as Pliny and Cato directed.' Even the flavour of the wines is said to be identical with that which the old Romans smacked their lips over, which shows what a conservative fellow the Lusitanian farmer is.

A curious feature of the naturally-grown vine is that it enjoys immunity from the ills to which the pruned and dwarfed species have fallen heir—the only way the poor vine has of showing its particular aversion to being civilised,—stunted and reduced to one dead level of monotonous uniformity, by having all 'character' and 'individuality' crushed out of it, like much else in modern life.

To push the resemblance, it is worthy of remark that just as the 'noble savage,' in his wild natural state, displays few of the higher attributes of man, the fruits of long ages of 'culture' and 'mental training,' so it is found impossible to get the finer wines—the 'great wines,' as they are called, the ports and sherries and burgundies—without stunting the growth of the vine by pruning, dwarfing, and other artificial devices. The brain-fag, nervous exhaustion, and other ills of latter-day life, come out in the vine in the shape of phyloxera, and other diseases unknown in their natural state.

Such are the penalties we have to pay for our exacting tastes in grape-juice.

The inevitable result of over-culture is that the old stocks get worn out; and of late years nearly the whole of the vineyards of Portugal have been re-planted, as in France and elsewhere, with the imported American vine. But this has entailed enormous expense, especially in the port-wine districts, seeing that in many vineyards, in order to allow room for growth, the underlying rock has had to be quarried out—often blasted—to the depth of several feet. The old native stock, on the other hand, had a kindly way of insinuating its roots into the interstices of the rocks, an accommodating habit which the American vine repudiates entirely, in accordance with the spirit of independence which characterises the land of its origin.

We crossed the Cavado, one of the most admired of the northern rivers, and presently drew up at a wine-shop—a sort of half-way house,—where we ordered wine, for the good of the house and the refreshment of 'coachy,' who, poor man, to judge from the beads on his honest brow, was feeling the heat as severely as his cattle.

Whether the great poets of the Augustan age would have smacked their lips over the particular vintage we sampled, I cannot pretend to say, but we found it extremely agreeable to the palate; and, judging from a sly twinkle in the driver's eye, as he tossed off his allowance, we thought he detected that very particular sharpness so highly esteemed by connoisseurs, and called the 'soul' of the wine. It has long been suspected that the native wines contain 'spirit'; and it is comforting to know that they also have 'soul.'

While the horses were resting, and having their faces and legs dashed with water, we strolled off to watch some ploughing operations in an adjacent field, where a yoke of oxen were dragging a 'crooked bough' through the rich yielding loam. For, in this pleasant land, 'where all things always are the same,' as one who knows it well truly says, 'a man may look about him and almost forget that the world has grown older and sadder. Here he will see the ploughman and the carter guiding an ox in size and shape such as the ancient Romans bred, yoked to such primitive ploughs and carts as we see on Greek and Roman coins.'

The particular point that struck our inexperienced eye was the prodigious expenditure of physical effort and lung-power that was required to coax the pretty soft-eyed oxen along. The farmer and all his progeny—from baby upwards,—with several dependants, found occupation in urging on the cattle; for each animal, it seemed, had to be dragged forcibly along, while the illustrious senhor, the proprietor of it all, guided the plough, throwing in 'swear-words' now and again amidst the volume of unmusical sounds escaping from the throats of the attendant angels. It was magnificent, but it was not—well, business, from a Briton's point of view. In fact, the conclusion we arrived at, after watching the process intently for several moments, was that it would have saved time and trouble, and possibly much strong language, if the senhors and senhoras who were making so much noise and fuss over it, and waxing excessively hot, had harnessed themselves to the plough, and turned the beautiful, patient oxen out to grass. Compared with what these poor folk go through, the British agriculturist has 'real good times.'

But if we dawdle on like this, we shall never get to Ponte de Lima. So, leaving the farmer to finish his ploughing, we set off at a rattling speed, and the kilometre-stones flew past us. 'I rode on, through the same lovely country and execrable roads,' wrote a traveller eighty years ago. Since those days an excellent road has been engineered the whole way, over which we bowled in smoothness and comfort, thoroughly enjoying the scenery.

Scarcely sixty years have elapsed since macadamised roads were introduced into north Portugal. The first one is said to have been that from Oporto to Matosinhos, and was the result of private enterprise, combined with the diligent use of little baskets. For, at first, the senhors whose services were enlisted in this beneficent work objected to carrying the materials in any way but on their heads; because, said they, with irresistible logic, the illustrious senhors, our ancestors, for untold generations before us, carried dirt on their heads, and who are we that we should do differently? Then English wheel-barrows were tried, and the senhors, pocketing their pride with their earnings, pushed and pulled, and behold, the road was made. Other roads followed suit, and now the country is fairly well provided with these channels of communication.

Amongst the common objects of the country, hereabouts, are curious sorts of sheds raised off the ground on stone pillars. They look like toy houses, are very long and high and narrow, with tiled roof, and wide, projecting eaves, reminding one of the Noah's Ark of childhood. Another peculiarity is that the upright planking forming the sides is so constructed as to allow a free passage of air through the houses, making them true 'castles of the wind.' They were empty at this time, but later on, when the maize harvest is garnered, every house would be filled with the ears of Indian corn, which are left here to dry, so as to harden the grain and cause it to start from the husk in the process of threshing. These sheds are, in fact, drying-barns, without which no farm is complete.

At last, we found ourselves entering Ponte de Lima; and, with a suitable flourish, our *cochiero* dashed up to the door of the principal 'hotel.' I forget its name, but it is on the south side of the Lima, which it faces, not far from

PONTE DE LIMA

UNIV. OF
CALIFORNIA

the bridge, and is, I have been assured, a very fair specimen of a country *estalagem*. I should advise every one to avoid it.

Before starting off on a voyage of exploration, some food was essential; so, clambering up a dirty, rickety stair, we found ourselves in the *sala de jantar*, wherein two sets were absorbing such provender as the establishment afforded. A lady and gentleman near the window were evidently newly married—honeymooning, or its equivalent in Portugal. The bride, a comely young woman, was decked out in her gayest apparel; both were young, and behaved with great decorum, clasping each other's hands under the table, and gazing fondly into each other's eyes. The particular dish they had been discussing, as we entered, appeared to be a cow's hoof—*au naturelle*, and it seemed to suit them to a nicety.

At the other end sat a country priest and a couple of well-to-do farmers—perhaps it was a tithe dinner. Anyhow, they were doing excellent justice to the viands, the padre appearing to have set his particular affections on the wine-bottle; and as the wine went down—which, to be sure, it did at a great pace—so the spirits of the party went up, and when at length the senhors rose to depart, they formed a very merry trio, their faces glowing almost as crimson as the wine they had been consuming.

We made the customary obeisance to the company, which was as courteously returned, and taking our seats near the window, looked on while food was being prepared.

The newly married couple having finished their repast, the bride proceeded to wash her hands at a basin in a corner of the room, and then both departed.

From the dissolving views we had obtained of dishes that had occupied our predecessors, we did not expect an *embarras de richesse* here; and when a plate of fried fish appeared, we hailed the apparition with joy. But a whiff of the rankest oil quite put us off it. The fact will scarcely be credited, but these descendants of De Castro cannot be prevailed on to refine their olive oil; the consequence is that the whole of the oil used for their sardine tinning has to be imported at great cost from France.

Every well-ordered hotel has one particular triumph of the culinary art on which it prides itself; and the *spécialité* here consisted of cows' hoofs, just as they had been cut off—boiled, to be sure, but without garnishing or accompaniments, and in all their pristine repulsiveness. I greatly regretted that my command of the language was not sufficiently comprehensive to hint that the most suitable resting-place for such odds and ends was the knacker's yard, or the glue-maker's. And the waiter's feelings were evidently hurt when we waved the dish aside. After a decent interval, another dish arrived, and we gave a sigh of relief as the removal of the cover disclosed beef-steak and onions, evidently the *pièce de résistance* of the repast; and a veritable *pièce de résistance* did it prove, for that slice of ox resisted all our efforts at mastication. We had to give it up in despair and fall back on fried eggs—the *dernier ressort* of the weak-jawed, in Portugal and elsewhere. The wine of the country and the oranges were excellent.

On emerging from the *sala* an object revealed itself that fairly drove us into the street; and a passing vista of the kitchen confirmed us in a determination to avoid the 'best hotel,' when next we found ourselves at Ponte de Lima. Think of this being the Elysium of the ancients!

I am convinced that this inn must be the identical *estalagem* wherein, some seventy years ago, the Rev. Kinsey and his *compagnon de voyage* passed a most unpleasant night with the inhabitants, two-legged and four-legged, not to mention other little friends. Like him, we felt inclined to echo Dr. Clarke's apostrophe to his own country: 'O England! decent abode of cleanliness and decorum, it is only in viewing the state of other countries that thy advantages can be duly estimated. May thy sons but know and guard what they possess in thee!'

As one gets older, one inclines more and more to the opinion of a pious American that 'no landscape is worth looking at without a comfortable hotel in the foreground.'

And now, before dilating on the charms of the place, I must confess that, owing to the intense heat, we were unable to do justice to all the sights, contenting ourselves, in fact, with a stroll across the narrow, picturesque, old bridge of twenty-four arches which spans the river, and a saunter along the banks.

The Lima, whose bed is perhaps a couple of hundred yards across here, and which in winter rolls down with great force, had shrunk to the dimensions of a brook; so that the boats which carry down produce found it difficult navigation, while the *lavadeiros* were rather 'put to' to find pools deep enough for their rinsings.

The town is of great antiquity and of historical interest, seeing that it was the Forum Limcorum of the Romans. Remains of an ancient castle and walls still exist. But its great charm lies in the beauty of its surroundings. 'I thought I had never gazed upon a lovelier scene,' wrote Lord Carnarvon, as he watched the 'sun set gloriously behind a range of bold mountains, then robed in the deepest purple, and illuminate with its last beams many peaceful and picturesque hamlets, built of cork and thatched with broom.'

As we sat in the portico of an old church, watching the 'river of oblivion' gliding peacefully over its sandy bed, with the quaint old bridge above and the background of mountains beyond, the dark green of the pines, with bits of bright colour dotted here and there along the golden strand, and, over all, the 'ever-blue skies of Portugal,' we more than sympathised with those stern legionaries who mutinied on the banks of this delightful stream, and who, like the Lotos-eaters, doubtless exclaimed, in their best Latin—

'We have had enough of action, . . .
. . . .
Let us swear an oath, and keep it with an equal mind,
In the hollow Lotos-land to live and lie reclined
On the hills like gods together, careless of mankind.'

Like many other places in the north, Ponte de Lima witnessed the horrors of Soult's invasion; while later, it was the scene of those fratricidal struggles which devastated Portugal in the years succeeding the Peninsular War.

But of all the strange sights the inhabitants of this fair spot ever gazed on, the strangest must have been the passage of Admiral Napier's 'ever-victorious army,' in 1834. His march through the province was a continuous triumph, the mere terror of his name being enough to cause towns to throw open their gates, and garrisons to lay down their arms without fighting; with the singular result that the entire province was won for the Queen, without bloodshed, by a British sailor, fighting under a *nom de guerre* at the head of a force chiefly composed of adventurous Britons—'broken-down shoemakers, tailors, drapers, men-milliners, poachers, disappointed lovers, resurrection-men, and it was even said there was a Burker or two in the party.' Such is the 'Admiral-General's' description of his 'army.' Nevertheless, he tells us they were 'generally very well behaved.'

The Admiral—'fighting Charlie,' as he was nicknamed in after years—must have cut a sorry figure on his pony, which had been captured from the Governor of Caminha: 'a most beautiful little animal, but as wicked a brute as ever I saw, and he attacks every one he sees. The staff was mounted on mules and donkeys, or whatever could be found.'

And when the business was finished, the Admiral wrote to a friend: 'This is one of the finest countries I ever beheld. I have much enjoyed my campaign, and we have done wonders with a handful of sailors and marines'; and he added significantly: 'If there is any gratitude in Portugal, they will not forget our services,' which shows how superficial was his acquaintance with the official character at that time.

Our driver had reckoned on resting his horses till the cool of the evening; but by four o'clock we had thoroughly tired of the place, so we ordered the carriage and set off forthwith.

The heat was fearful, and in spite of careful driving the horses were so completely done up by the time we entered Braga, that the driver begged us to take the steam-tram for the remaining three miles, pointing pathetically to the limp and thoroughly done-up horses. We were only too glad to meet his wishes; and I may mention a little incident as illustrative of the character of the rural folk. On tendering the tram fare—only a few pence—to the conductor, he indignantly rejected it, explaining that the driver of our carriage had arranged all that.

We had purposed spending an hour or two in Braga, but the clouds of black smoke drifting through the streets of the industrial suburb, and well-nigh choking us, combined with the stifling atmosphere, effectually choked off all enthusiasm in the cause of antiquarian research.

In justice to Braga, let it be observed that it is a place of historical interest, and of high antiquity, though its attractions to sightseers are almost *nil*. It was a place of importance in Roman times, and was called Bracara Augusta, the remains of an amphitheatre and a fine aqueduct once bearing witness to the splendour which distinguished the place. But not a vestige of these can now be traced, the ruins having shared the fate of our own Glastonbury—carted away by local Vandals for building purposes, a century or more ago. Tradition even assigns the town a higher antiquity, declaring it to have been founded by the Greeks, after the fall of Troy; but when tradition busies itself with these remote times, verification becomes difficult. The subsequent history of Braga has been eventful enough—Suevi, Romans, Moors, and other conquering hosts, having all in turn rested for a while in its enchanting valley.

The chief interest centres around the cathedral—an unpretentious affair, built, it is alleged, before the Moorish domination. But the *pièce de résistance* consists of the relics, which pious souls really believe to be genuine. The most precious of these are, or were—first, a thorn from our Saviour's side; second, a phial of milk from His mother's breast. But to educated travellers the chief attraction of this establishment is a certain chalice which tradition affirms to have been used at the christening of the first great Portuguese king, at Guimaraens, in 1109. This precious relic is believed to be of very great antiquity, and is most carefully preserved in an elaborately carved case of ivory, with an inscription in the Kufic character, believed to be even older than the chalice itself. Mr. Crawfurd, who has gone into the question of its origin, believes the ivory casket to be Arabian work, or possibly Christian work under Arabian influence, and not less than eight hundred years old, perhaps older, seeing that the Kufic character ceased to be used about the year 1000.

But the most remarkable feature of the casket is the fact of its being carved with designs exactly similar to those seen on Portuguese ox-yokes at the present day: 'the same intricate combinations of circles, squares, and crescents, and, what is stranger still, the same twisted Runic ornament between leaf, spray, and Rune knot.' Mr. Crawfurd suggests that this ornamentation may possibly represent the coming together of the art influences of the North and the East—of Christian Gothic with Moslem art.

A British gazetteer, which is justly esteemed for its bulk and good printing, gravely informs us that Braga is 'defended by a citadel, and is surrounded by walls flanked with towers.' We saw no signs of these important appendages; perhaps they have been spirited away.

On the whole, our impressions of the place differed but little from that of a traveller of the last century, who wrote: 'Except in a few by-streets, where some hatters and nailmakers were at work, everything wore the appearance of that melancholy stillness and quiet whieh but ill agrees with the character of a thriving city.'

As an object of pilgrimage, the Real Sanctuario de Bom Jesus de Monte rivals Matosinhos. The annual *festa* takes place at Whitsuntide, when thousands of devotees flock up from far and near, and keep up high-jinks for three days.

Strange to relate, in spite of the wave of scepticism

which has swept away many a landmark of the faith in fair Lusitania, the devotional instinct still lingers amongst the peasantry of the north; of whom it may still be affirmed, that 'devotional expeditions to their chapels, placed like landmarks on the highest hills, are generally combined with feasts and merry-making, and many vows, besides those addressed to their saints, are there offered up; and many a maiden looks forward to the day when she shall accompany her family to some favourite shrine with a throbbing heart, and thoughts with full as much of earth in them as heaven.'

These Romarios are, in fact, excellent matrimonial agencies.

It seems surprising that the priests have managed to retain influence over the people. But the explanation is a simple one. As Beckford's French *chef* remarked, on being twitted with an unwonted display of pious fervour: 'Ah, monsieur, Monseigneur rend la religion si aimable!'

In the devout days of old—and, for aught I know, the practice still survives—a convenient arrangement existed by which the image of O Senhor do Monte was let out, on the hire-system, to other churches; though whether the 'consideration' took the form of 'gate-money,' or a percentage on the takings inside, is not recorded. Anyhow, a traveller, who visited Braga sixty years ago, found the image ensconced in a church, whither it had been brought during a long drought to hear the prayers and receive the alms of pious agriculturists.

As a means of propitiating O Senhor, or 'getting round it,' as we should say, the image was encircled with roses, balsams, hydrangeas, rhododendrons, cockscombs, and sweet marjorams. And as, by a chance coincidence, rain fell a few days later, every one cried, 'A miracle!'

At the time of our visit there had been a long drought, and farmers were in despair; but the image was still on its perch in the Real Sanctuario. Perchance its owners had been trying to drive too hard a bargain, and had overshot the mark.

The great festival was to commence on Sunday. It was now Friday, and preparations were in full swing, under the direction of 'Mother Church,' in the shape of the clerical staff, every mother's son of which was busily employed from early morn till late at night superintending the erection of bandstands, poles and banners, festoons of Chinese lanterns, and all the sundry and various emblems of religious devotion displayed on these solemn occasions.

Some nimble young fellows had even climbed to the topmost pinnacle of the temple and hung out flags, while within a regular spring-cleaning was going forward, all the gorgeous panoply of religious processions being dragged forth into the light of day, brushed up, and laid out, in readiness for the great event.

The fireworks display was to 'cut' all previous 'records,' —there was even to be a 'set piece,' I believe, but of this I cannot be sure; for in this pleasant land rockets are what chiefly bring joy to the hearts of the devout. A rocket affects the Portuguese in a way our cold northern temperament can hardly understand; with the curious result that the heavens are seldom quite free from rockets, and whenever an explosion strikes the ear, you say at once 'some pious soul is easing his feelings!' After all, this is better than smashing street-lamps or knocker-wrenching, after the mode of impious young Britons.

But there were more important matters to be attended to—the feeding of the people in this mountain wilderness.

Their spiritual requirements were easily met; their bodily wants required far more extensive provision, and it was evident from the preparations going forward, that those who were answerable for the catering for the vast crowds expected during the next few days were quite alive to their responsibilities. The entire forest resounded with the crash of the hammers, the creaking of bullock-wagons, and the 'still, sad music of humanity,' if the discordant voices of industrious Portuguese merit so poetical an appellation. A large expanse of open ground—a sort of terrace—was being converted into a vast open-air restaurant; a row of strongly-built cooking-stoves and ovens, which appeared to be what we should call 'permanent fixtures,' occupying all one side of the terrace, showed a wise prevision on the part of the Church authorities, who, doubtless, regarded the 'letting them out' to enterprising restaurateurs as a valuable source of income.

Nothing that could contribute to the solemnity of the occasion or the jollification of the pilgrims seemed to have been omitted, and on all sides a most successful *romario* was anticipated. From early dawn till far into night a ceaseless stream of people kept pouring into the woods, the winding road—a mile or more from top to bottom, presenting a continuous line of bullock-carts, laden with the paraphernalia of trade—tables, stools, tents, cooking-stoves, and crockery; and every available bit of camping-ground was soon annexed and arranged for the entertainment of man or beast. The whole mountain seemed in labour, to judge from the discordant creakings of the carts as they dragged slowly and painfully up the incline; and, to be sure, if the mountain did not bring forth a mouse, it was speedily peopled by a busy and right merry multitude.

The forest seemed to be converted, for the nonce, into a vast gypsy encampment, every foot of vacant space under shade of the trees being turned to account. Tables were erected, tents pitched, rude fire-places built up of stones and clay, the proprietors camping under their carts, or in a sort of Robinson-Crusoe hut made of bent sticks and rags, or boughs of trees.

What happened at night I really can't say, for the preparations went on to so late an hour that sleep entirely overcame my curiosity; it was past midnight when I closed my eyes, the merry hum of voices still ringing in my ears.

The silvery chimes of the bell-frogs were, alas! drowned out, or perchance the wise creatures reserved their music for quieter times. For my own part, much as I grieved at leaving this enchanting spot, I sorrowed most of all that I should hear the silver voices of the bell-frogs no more.

The primitive arrangements above described being complete, other cargoes began to arrive, conspicuous amidst which were enormous casks of the famous Minho wine; and these on reaching their destination were carefully adjusted in the carts that bore them, decorated with green boughs, and then tapped and tasted; while, as an encouragement to thirsty souls to try the contents, each cask bore the legend, in large letters, 'From the celebrated Quinta of Camoens,' or 'the noted vineyard of De Castro,' and so on.

And what a sight were the 'wine-cups'! huge mugs, holding a quart, at least, and often bearing an inscription, the single word 'Amor' (love) occurring most frequently. And assuredly, after toiling up to these altitudes, the nimblest of pilgrims would need refreshment, and, let us hope, performed his devotional exercises all the more blithely for a draught of the rich Minho wine!

It was delightful to see a people entering heart and soul into the business of converting a religious function into a source of so much pleasure; for every one anticipated a 'real good time.' There was no anxiety about the weather. The very heavens smiled on the scene, and all the world was gay.

Early on Saturday, the first of the pilgrims began to arrive, and soon entire families might be seen wending their way up the steep ascent, pausing at each chapel or shrine, and reverently examining the contents, with bared heads. The chapels wherein the scenes from our Lord's Passion are represented, though of no artistic merit, are, no doubt, well adapted for the purpose they are intended for—exciting the devotional feelings of the unlettered peasants, by means of appeals to the only sense that can be reached by external influences. To the credit of these simple folk, let it be recorded that they used their legs instead of the lift, and accomplished the entire round of chapels before refreshing themselves.

As the country folk grouped themselves about tables and wine-casks, or reclined under the trees, the effect was delightful, many of the women being decked out in picturesque costumes, and wearing the beautiful jewellery which is so highly esteemed by connoisseurs. The sound of the guitar, too, was heard in the land, and here and there joyous spirits burst forth into song.

Taking up our post at a corner of the great terrace, now entirely occupied by tables ready spread for the feasting to come, the view was enchanting; and as we sat watching some policemen doing justice to the good things set out for their delectation, an enormous wagon, drawn by a pair of powerful oxen, drew up beside us, and a load of splendid oranges was shot out on to the turf in a golden heap.

We spent the morning in wandering about the busy scene, now watching a party of fresh arrivals, all agog with wonder at sight of the gorgeous preparations for their entertainment, their faces beaming with delight and happiness; now listening to a party of itinerant musicians, twanging their guitars assiduously, and gathering in contributions from onlookers, and anon investigating the contents of an *al fresco* kitchen, peering into bubbling pots, or exchanging greetings with the amused *chef*. What a fascinating scene it was! The diversity of costume, the bright colouring of the dresses, the rows of little arbours; the endless vista of bullock-carts with the patient, handsome cattle, unyoked, and munching their piles of green fodder; the vast assemblage of people with their pleasant, good-humoured, and often really handsome faces and fine figures—all contributed to the making of a scene that imprinted itself indelibly on the mind.

As the time of our departure drew near, we began to regret the step that was to sever us from a scene we might never again have the opportunity of gazing on. But our decision was irrevocable.

Seeing that this festival is one of the sights of the country, our friends thought it the height of folly running away on the eve of the event. But we had really come here for coolness and quiet, and were in no mood for the racket and bustle of the next few days. We had already seen a very similar gathering at Matosinhos, and moreover, were loath to have our pleasant impressions of the place spoilt by fireworks, and brass-bands, and other cockney abominations.

But there was another aspect of the *romario* which had

to be considered; for collections of human beings, no matter how merry or gaily clad, give rise to odours, which, if allied to sanctity, are not of the hay-field, and are none the less strongly developed under a hot sun. The space, moreover, was far too confined for the enormous gathering that was anticipated, and the prospect of spending the next few days in the midst of—to put it mildly, extremely insanitary conditions, effectually clinched our determination to be off.

The hotel, unfortunately for the perfect enjoyment of so picturesque a scene, was in the thick of it all. You could not stir out without finding yourself at once in a dense throng of hot and perspiring country folk, of all ages; and already there were thousands of people camped-out in the surrounding woods. The heat was intense, the paths had already been tramped into a mass of fine dust, which every movement of the crowd raised aloft, and the natives of the Minho, albeit picturesque and interesting, are —well, aromatic! The hotel, too, was filling up fast; the overflow house at Boa Vista, half a mile off, was ready to receive guests, and we learned that every hole and cranny would be packed. The weary hours we had wasted already, sitting in a hot room while the two daily gorges were being patiently plodded through, had been trying enough in a half-empty house. What would happen when the hotel was full we hardly dared contemplate. We fled.

Saturday night found us back in our comfortable quarters in the Grand Hotel d'Oporto.

Well, it had been a delightful experience, and looking back on it, we could heartily endorse the remark of a traveller of eighty years before: 'His heart must be insensible to external influences who can behold without delight, or quit without regret, such a favoured country.'

TO BUSSACO

And now in default of discovering other places in the north where the comforts of civilisation could be obtained, we turned our faces south, with the intention ultimately of reaching Lisbon.

In journeying south, there is a convenient half-way house at Coimbra, which, as it possesses a decent hotel, is often chosen as a halting-place.

But there is another place within easy reach of Coimbra, where friends assured us we should find a comfortable hotel, and they spoke in ecstatic terms of the scenery, declaring it to be one of the loveliest spots in Portugal.

It so happened that Bussaco, for that was the name of the place, was a spot I had always felt a very particular desire for seeing. For besides having read tantalising accounts of it in old books of travel, the name is encircled with a halo of glorious associations; seeing that here was enacted one of the most dramatic, romantic, and glorious episodes in the annals of the British army—the ever-memorable battle of September 27, 1810.

On this account we determined to make Bussaco our next resting-place, and on mentioning our plan to the manager of the 'Grande,' he replied, 'You cannot do better; a great friend of mine, who keeps the hotel, was *chef* at the Braganza in Lisbon for many years, and was the best cook I ever knew; oh! his cooking was famed, I assure you. I will write to him if you wish, and let him know you are coming, so that your rooms may be prepared; for the hotel is only just opened for the season, and you will have it almost to yourselves.'

This was excellent news, especially the last part; so, having ordered rooms in advance, we left Oporto by the mid-day train, and crossing the cranky-looking iron bridge, entered a pleasant if not a particularly striking country; though, as a matter of fact, wherever the spirit leads you in fair Lusitania there is something pleasant to gaze on, which the regulation jog-trot enables you to enjoy without straining the eyes.

A few miles south of Oporto, there was once a quinta, and for aught I know it is still *in situ*, on the old Ovar road, which was occupied by Wellington, when on his way to accomplish the passage of the Douro. The room wherein he slept used to be shown with pride by the owner, together with the very log whereon the great man was found asleep, in the court-yard, wrapped in his military cloak, while preparations were going forward for his reception.

It would be interesting to know what has become of these relics, as well as many other warlike mementoes, which formerly abounded in Portugal.

The bright colouring of the gardens and the rich greens of the fields are agreeably contrasted by pine-woods, which extend for miles along the sea-coast; and albeit monotonous, Mr. Crawfurd tells us that these forests have a particular virtue, which is recognised by the faculty, who send consumptive patients to places where they can breathe the *ar dos pinheiros* in all its fragrance and purity.

The most extensive one in Portugal lies north of Leiria. It was planted in the thirteenth century by good King Diniz, who has been called 'the wise lawgiver,' and was the enemy of the old feudal system, the promoter of agriculture, and the protector of the peasantry. There are people who think Portugal would be the better for another King Diniz.

This excellent monarch also founded the university of Coimbra, from which useful institution, and from the forest of Marinha Grande, 'Portugal has derived more advantages,' says an old author, 'than from all the victories of King Emmanuel.' The peaceful triumphs of good King Diniz, and the useful results that flowed therefrom, are they not set forth in the book of Camoens?

The forest was Crown property, and proved an excellent investment before America was discovered, as all the timber used for shipbuilding was drawn from it. It also served to arrest the encroachments of the sand upon the fertile districts inland. What this devouring element can do, on a small scale, is shown by the fate of Peranzabuloe church, in north Cornwall.

But the chief interest to Britons of 'this superb forest of venerable pines' is its connection with an enterprise initiated here in 1760, by William Stephens.

The story of William Stephens and the glass factory has so entirely faded out of recollection, that some notice of it may be acceptable, especially as the old authors amongst whose works one has to quarry for the facts are not accessible to the general public. The story is creditable to our countryman, and moreover affords another instance of Portugal's indebtedness to English enterprise in times past.

When the Marquis of Pombal turned his attention to the reconstruction of Lisbon, after the great earthquake of 1755, he derived great assistance from the English residents, both in the matter of advice and in the execution of his schemes. And his attention having been drawn to the indifferent nature of the lime then used for building purposes, he complained of this one day to his English friends, one of whom replied that, 'with the assistance of his Excellency, he would undertake to remedy the difficulty.' 'Very well,' said Pombal, 'try what you can do,' and he directed the Englishman to be supplied with the requisite funds. The result was successful, and Lisbon, built with an entirely new sort of lime, sprang up like a phœnix from its ashes, and ever since, the Portuguese have boasted, and with justice, of the excellent qualities of their lime. It would be as well, however, if they were to remember, that before an Englishman taught their countrymen how to make lime, the preparation of it for building purposes was but imperfectly understood.

The 'friend in need,' on this occasion was William Stephens. And although this, his first speculation, did not prove a remunerative one, his next, from which Portugal derived equally important advantages, was more profitable.

Pombal was so deeply impressed with the superior abilities of his adviser that he employed him on other business, consulting him, amongst other matters, on the subject of establishing a glass factory, with a view to competing with the imported article. For it was one of the great Marquis's fads that nature had intended Portugal for a great manufacturing country, in pursuit of which chimœra he started factories all over the country. Mr. Stephens again tendered his services, and being supplied by his patron with money and workmen, he designed and established the first glass factory in Portugal, which remained without a rival for nearly half a century. From this establishment Portugal and her colonies derived every article of glassware, bottles excepted; and though its situation was not without drawbacks, owing to its distance from the ports of shipment, the journey of eighty miles to Lisbon occupying the carriers three days, these were compensated by the abundance and cheapness of the raw materials on the spot—sand, kelp, and wood being all at hand, Mr. Stephens having the privilege of drawing his supplies of wood from the Crown forests.

William Stephens died in 1826, having amassed a large fortune by his successful enterprise, the result of which he bequeathed to Government, for the nation.

The memory of this benefactor of Portugal is still perpetuated in the name of a square which he built after a plan supplied by the illustrious Marquis, his friend and patron, the 'Largo do Stephens.' And here, in the year 1822, resided his only surviving relative, who, says a contemporary, 'must feel gratified upon being surrounded by such honourable monuments of the talents and respectability of his race.' The wealth of this gentleman was reputed to be immense, his hospitalities were proverbial; indeed, for any English resident not to have partaken of Mr. Stephens's hospitality was to argue himself unknown.

Such is the story of Marinha Grande; and yet, how few Briton's nowadays are familiar with the name of William Stephens, the benefactor of Portugal and the founder of the glass factory.

After the death of its founder, the factory was intrusted to a Mr. Lyne. 'It is much to be feared,' wrote Kinsey, who visited it at this time, 'that the Government will allow this important factory to fall to the ground for the want of proper encouragement, as is the case with everything submitted to its blighting influence.'

A German traveller, describing a visit to the factory, says: 'The glass is very good, though it does not possess the lustre of English glass.' There was a considerable import of Bohemian glass at that time, in spite of an almost prohibitive duty; in fact, according to an English traveller of that date, 'the glass most frequently seen is of German manufacture, but its only recommendation above the British article is its cheapness, the colour being exceedingly bad.'

There are depots at the present time for the sale of the produce of the 'Real Fabrica de Vitros de Marinha Grande,' both at Lisbon and Oporto, a proof that the factory is still working.

But memories of a widely different nature are awakened in the minds of Britons by a journey over this classic soil. For the entire country between Oporto and Lisbon was traversed and retraversed by opposing armies, during the earlier stages of the war—now swept bare by the devastating French, now occupied by the conquering British, and constantly the scene of fierce combats between the invaders and the raw native levies. The very railway stations bear names which have a familiar ring about them. And if the traveller is not insensible to feelings evoked by scenes hallowed by the shedding of British blood in freedom's cause, he will derive a genuine pleasure from a visit to this portion of the Peninsula.

Sunset tints were beginning to suffuse the sky, when our attention was drawn to a bleak mountain range to the eastward. The position and lay of the range immediately proclaimed it to be the Serra de Bussaco, of glorious memory, and I confess to have gazed on those rugged heights for the first time with interest.

The train presently drew up at Milheada, and then a short run brought us to Pampilhosa Junction, whence the mail route branches off to Madrid. A capital buffet is provided here, and there is a halt of twenty minutes to enable passengers to take in provender.

Philosophers tell us that nature abhors a vacuum, and I certainly never saw more expert or expeditious stevedores than those who were busily employed at the moment of our arrival in humouring nature's prejudice.

We had been warned to look out here for 'mine host' of the Bussaco hotel, and soon spied him, ensconsed behind the counter, with sleeves tucked up, hard at work ladling out soup for hungry *voyageurs*. Watching for a pause, we introduced ourselves to Monsieur Paul Bergamin, who, I may observe, besides being managing proprietor of the hotels at Luso and Bussaco, 'runs' the buffet at Pampilhosa, and is doubtless amassing the pile which so much enterprise deserves. He is a Swiss.

Mons. P. B. beamed on us: 'Were we on our way to Bussaco?' The question surprised us. 'Certainly, did you not get a letter to say so?' 'Oh, my friend at Oporto wrote me some days ago to say you were coming, but I have not heard from him since. However, I will telegraph to the hotel to prepare for you.'

The letter in question turned up some days later, having been on a cruise in Spain; for letters, unlike the natives of the country, have a way of taking circular tours in strange lands.

A run of a few miles through a hilly country clad in fragrant pine-woods, skirting the foot of the serra, brought us to the Luso station, where on alighting a very small carriage was in waiting. But as there happened to be another party of three bound for the same goal as ourselves, the driver had to rush up hill and get a larger conveyance, so that by the time we got off the shades of night had fallen, and we could but dimly discern the features of the landscape. And when, at length, we plunged into the forest depths, all was blackness. After a steep climb, lights gleamed in front, and we drew up at a huddle of buildings, out of which rose a vast pile, which had the appearance in the gloom of a cathedral or a palace. A French-speaking waiter led us through a labyrinth of dark vaults, fitting cellars for the bluebeard's castle above, and crossing an untidy sort of stable-yard, entered a detached building where he ushered us into a nice, airy bedroom, comfortably furnished, the window, as far as we could judge, looking on to a garden, with forest-clad mountains beyond. It was tantalising to arrive so late that we could make out nothing of our surroundings, and we longed for daylight.

Bright sunshine streaming in next morning revealed the beauty of the situation; while a rose peeping in at the window seemed a fitting introduction to the horticultural treasures awaiting us. For in this enchanting spot many of nature's choicest products are nurtured by skilful husbandmen.

Before chronicling our movements here, let me describe the Hotel da Matta—*Anglicé*, Hotel of the Forest. The establishment has been evolved from the original convent of Carmelites, to whom the whole of this domain once belonged, and which was surrendered to Government on suppression of the orders. It stands in a hollow, which has been compared to the crater of a volcano, whose western side has fallen away, disclosing a magnificent panorama of the country lying between the serra and the Atlantic. Every part of the mountain and crater is clothed in dense forest, which completely embosoms the convent.

It is approached by a steep, zigzag road from Luso, a village about a mile below, where there is a thermal establishment and hotel, and where, in former days visitors to Bussaco used to lodge. But since the opening up of the estate and the construction of roads over the serra, Luso has fallen out of fashion, and is now only patronised by people who are taking the waters.

The convent grounds extend down to Luso; and on entering the hallowed precincts all view of the surrounding country is shut out by forest. The property is a valuable one, and the woods, which are well cared for, contain many noble trees—oak, chestnut, walnut, cork, several varieties of pine, cedar, cypress, and other varieties which are strangers to northern lands.

Winding upwards, through the gloomy and silent forest—fitting abode for the disciples of La Trappe,—the monastery is at last espied through a magnificent avenue of giants, often mistaken for cedars. These marvellous trees rise majestically upwards, like the columns of an Egyptian temple, to a height of perhaps forty feet, before throwing out a branch. At this point massive limbs extend horizontally outwards, as if emulating the beams of a temple roof; so that, as has been justly remarked, 'you walk under a canopy of leaves, in a vast sacred grove,' where the branches of the trees, whose stems form the pillars of the arches of verdure, are intertwined and laced together overhead, forming a lofty verdant roof.

These noble trees are veritable curiosities of arboriculture, an examination of their foliage and fruit, especially in the youthful stage, disclosing a close resemblance to the *arbor vitæ*. In fact, it was only after reading Lord Carnarvon's book that the mystery of their genus and origin was cleared up. In his description of Coimbra he says: 'The cypress that grows in the Garden of Tears is the *Cupressus Lusitanica*, a tree of extreme beauty, and closely resembling in growth the cedar of Lebanon, though deeper in colour. It is so very unlike the common cypress, that I had at first no suspicion that it belonged to that class of trees. It was originally brought from Goa to Bussaco, but it is now only found in perfection in the midland parts of Portugal; for it has dwindled in the neighbourhood of Lisbon, and is no longer to be seen in the Algarve.' I understand that some specimens of this tree grow in sheltered spots in the West of England.

The convent was originally a straggling, one-storied building of no great extent, and is now engulfed by a palatial edifice which has sprung up of late years. Happily the vandals have spared the charming old entrance, with its quaint mosaic-encrusted portico, and diminutive side-chapel, whose floor is besprinkled with copper coins, the 'mites' of the poor pilgrims to this direlict shrine; while without, the seat-encircled quadrangle with its central cross remains intact.

Passing within, where the silence of the tomb, unbroken but by the rarely heard whisper of the Prior, was wont to reign, we enter the cork-lined cloisters, which present much the same appearance as of old, when the only feet that trod the stones were those of the barefooted Carmelites.

Paintings of sacred subjects, the work of monkish amateurs, whose ambitions far outran their executive skill, litter the walls, and bear silent witness, in the midst of a pushing, materialistic world, to the thoughts which sometimes flitted through the monkish minds, and served, let us hope, to buoy them up when struggling in the bitter waters of remorse, and encouraged them with hope when bowed down beneath the load of their self-imposed burden of dreary idleness.

A few more years of damp, indifference, and neglect, and these affecting memorials of the vanished life monastic

BUSSACO

SHOWING THE GROUND TRAVERSED BY THE RIGHT COLUMN OF ATTACK

← Crest held by the Light Division under General Crawfurd

occupied by the French army

where the French halted preparatory to the attack →

UNIV. OF
CALIFORNIA

will have resolved themselves into the elements from whence they sprang.

The deserted cloisters and ruinous empty cells seem haunted, even now, with a host of interesting memories, and might well incline the 'sentimental pietist' to sigh for a touch of the vanished hand, if only with broom and varnish brush. On each side, diminutive cork-lined doors give access to the cells—human silos, wherein the brothers moped away their useless lives like so many cabbages. What strange aberration of the mind could have led men to cut themselves off from all the beauty and occupations of the present world, to enter the gloomy precincts of a prison-house? 'I discovered from subsequent accounts, what, indeed, I then suspected,' wrote a traveller who visited the place when its 'activities' were in full swing, and enjoyed the unique distinction of being feasted on salt fish and sour wine, 'that the inmates of this convent had generally entered their cheerless abode from feelings of blighted affection, or mortified ambition, the most prolific sources of human discontent.'

The sequel, in too many instances, was just such as might be anticipated from the variety of temperaments that sought asylum here. Some sank into a state of mental lethargy. Others vainly desired to quit their living tomb. While with others who had entered from an exalted spirit of religion, the want of active occupation was supplied by the internal fire 'which supported while it consumed them.'

Even matches that 'strike only on the box' lose their vitality if laid by too long. The rough friction of human intercourse is essential to the development of fire in the human 'match.' The latent fire soon ebbs away under the disintegrating effects of monasticism.

Even the Prior was forced to fall in with the humour of the place, whatever his inward thoughts may have been. 'This spot is indeed delightful,' observed a traveller, on bidding him farewell. 'It is, my son,' replied the Prior, 'with the cold and melancholy smile of one who felt the truth of the remark, but had ceased to derive enjoyment from the objects of my admiration.'

The room which Lord Wellington occupied while making his dispositions for the battle, and which was always shown to visitors, has gone the way of much else.

The church, though small, is of great antiquity, and contains some interesting specimens of ecclesiastical art, amongst others a group of figures in clay, representing scenes in the life of our Lord, under a glass case. But the most valuable is a half-figure of a Magdalene carved in wood, the gift of a Pope, and of excellent workmanship.

There is no resident priest—or indeed any one here, who seems interested in the preservation of the monastic relics. The church is locked up during the week, and only opened for an hour or two on Sunday morning for the mass, which is celebrated by a priest who rides up from the wilds below, a few peasants dropping in to form a congregation. The 'congregation' was comfortably stretched out on the seats, snoring away most delectably, when I looked in one Sunday morning, but whether this little 'indulgence' was paid for in the paper money of the realm I cannot take on me to affirm. Anyhow, every one looked supremely happy, and I was careful not to disturb the slumbers of these devout souls, for to judge by the state of their shoes, they had performed a long journey on 'shanks' mare.'

A picturesque little bell-tower on top of the church has escaped the ravages of time and man, and carries, on its face, an ancient clock which chimes the half-hours and quarters on the bells above—the very bells, I doubt not, which tolled with due solemnity while the battle—on which much else besides the fate of the monastery depended—was raging on the serra above, and which also, when all was over, and victory declared, would ring out a joyous peal.

On this account I looked at those bells with profound respect, and could never listen to the chimes without being reminded of the battle.

As one paces the deserted cloisters—and in wet weather, which, by the bye, fell to our lot in more than due proportion, they make a pleasant 'quarter-deck'— the mind travels insensibly back to former times and long-forgotten scenes: and surely of all the strange sights Carmelite eye ever gazed on here, the apparition of a British general, with his staff, orderlies, cooks, and domestics, must have seemed the most incongruous.

Wellington's headquarters were fixed here for a week, and it is easy to picture the upsetting of the *dolce far niente* routine of the establishment that would ensue. Think of the dismay that would seize hold of these men of solitude when they learned the cause of the intrusion! —and of the unconventional style in which the lay brothers would have to bustle about. Though, to be sure, the opportunity for indulging the love of gossip, which is inherent in man, would help to restore the balance of their minds.

One can easily conceive, too, the dread that would take possession of their souls as the roar of artillery and the crashing of musketry came rolling down the mountainside, through the mist-laden air, on that fateful September morning. For who were these *Ingleses* that they should presume to block the path of Napoleon's legions? And, with defeat, which seemed inevitable, there would follow the desecration and pillage of the convent with all its precious contents. Perchance, though, the advent of the 'red-coats' had been the signal for burying the monastic strong-box; for even barefooted Carmelites must needs have a store of current coin, if not some odds and ends of church plate, which they would scarcely be so foolish as to leave lying about to tempt strangers.

And then, in the midst of their anxieties, there would be the arrival of the wounded from the battle-field, with ghastly faces and blood-stained clothes; for we know that, amongst others, Charles Napier and the French General, Simon, were brought to the convent for treatment: while, ever and anon, conflicting rumours, now of defeat, now of victory, would find their way to this secluded corner of the forest; and as the hours sped by the tension of feeling would be almost beyond endurance.

One wonders, too, if, when victory was finally declared, the monastic rule was so far relaxed as to permit of 'three cheers' and 'one cheer more.' History is silent on this point, but no doubt the monkish feelings, after being so long pent up, would find vent in some way, if only in a clashing of bells.

And so the rest of the day and the night following and the next day would pass, amidst such sights and sounds as were strange to these recluses, affording food for converse and meditation, too, let us hope, for years after. At last, late on the evening of the second day, there would be signs of packing-up, followed soon by an exodus. And all through the September night the forest solitudes would resound to the ceaseless tramp, tramp of infantry, and the rumbling of artillery, as men and guns and horses, in seemingly endless stream, and in the inevitable confusion of a night march in a strange country, swept majestically through the forest glades and vanished into the mists below. And still there were the wounded!

Fortunately for the monks, the French had taken another route. Though how the monastery fared at the hands of the marauding army of human vultures that hovers in the wake of an army, I know not. If any 'brother Jocelyn' has jotted down his reminiscences, after the manner of the quaint chronicler of St. Edmondsbury, I have never come across the work. There would be little demand, indeed, for such a piece of antiquarian lore, in a land where eighty per cent. are wholly illiterate.

The bit of convent that still remains is almost engulphed by modern buildings—partly hotel, partly dwelling-houses and workmen's cottages, forming the most extraordinary jumble conceivable. The most self-assertive feature of it all is the Tower of Babel, already mentioned—a kind of citadel, or castle-keep, which has been tacked on to one end without any *raison d'être* whatever, and will prove, when completed, the most costly and incongruous temple ever reared on mountain-top.

Mons. Bergamin assured us that it was to form, when completed, a part of the hotel. But this seems incredible. And as, at present, it is an empty shell without any provision for a 'lift,' some stretch of imagination is needed to picture the natives, whose aversion to leg-exercise is proverbial, toiling up to those breezy heights for fresh air which they abhor, or to gaze at views which have no interest for them. The tower is an enigma.

The whole vast pile is built of the beautiful cream-coloured limestone resembling marble that abounds in Portugal. And as every block of it has been brought here at immense labour, the cost must have been prodigious.

The tower is quadrangular, of a florid and peculiar style, in which Moresque ornamentation largely prevails. The structure is, in fact, eminently suggestive of the Torre de Belem on the Tagus. Even Batalha has, I believe, been drawn on for the decorative work, and it would be unjust to withhold credit from architect and workmen for the astonishing beauty of their handiwork.

Aloft, the tower gradually tapers into a kind of spire, crinkled and carved to the very apex; while, at a short distance above the base, a stone gallery is being carried round two of the sides; and on this portion of the structure both designer and sculptor would seem to have concentrated their skill and attention. From a strictly architectural point of view there may be faults, but the non-expert who admires beauty and grace in design, combined with marvellous executive skill, cannot help being impressed with the results. In fact, as one takes in the extreme intricacy of the design, and slowly realises the labour, thought, and skill which have been lavished on it, one stands aghast at the incongruity of the whole thing. I can only compare it to the Albert Memorial, erected in the middle of a highland deer-forest. It might be the work of some half-crazy millionaire,—a *fin-de-siècle* Fonthill in Portugal.

A native gentleman told me in confidence that the scheme had originated with a neighbouring landed proprietor, a member of a former government, who thus hoped to attract royalty to Bussaco, with a view to the place becoming the resort of fashion. I was assured, moreover, that the entire work was being carried out at Government expense.

Happy, happy country, which, with the heaviest load of debt in proportion to population of any European state, can, nevertheless, raise up a little cell like this on a mountain-top, without worrying over the expense. To the unsophisticated Briton the whole thing seems a wanton waste of a nation's resources.

The great charm of the Hotel da Matta lies in its pleasant surroundings. And with gardens, fine trees, and miles of walks through forest glades, to say nothing of the crest of the Serra—Wellington's battle-field—for those who like to go further afield, Bussaco is an ideal refuge for lovers of quiet and fine scenery.

On the suppression of the religious orders, this *terra incognita*, so jealously guarded that none but lay priest had ever set foot within, was thrown open to the public. And for the first few months, numbers of visitors, attracted to the spot no less by the love of novelty than the rumours that had reached the outside world of the wonders to be seen within, flocked there. But the first flush of curiosity having been satisfied, the remoteness of the spot—it lies about eighteen miles north of Coimbra—combined with the difficulties of access before railways and roads had brought it within touch of civilisation, caused it to be forgotten. Interest gave way to neglect; Government lacked the money for keeping up the grounds, and for many years the property was abandoned to nature and vandal tourists, who broke into the little chapels, destroyed the sacred figures within, and carried away everything worth pillaging, while the monastery was given over to the bats and the owls, and a monkish pensioner, who, between them, eked out a miserable livelihood by gardening and other things.

So matters dragged on, until, about twenty years ago, a piece of ground adjoining the convent was leased to a private company, who built a small hotel on it, constructed roads from Luso and Pampilhosa, and tried to bring the place into notice as a health resort—a sort of northern Cintra.

In a 'puff' issued at the time, Bussaco is described as 'exciting in the beholder mingled feelings of such rapturous admiration and profound religious awe, that no language has words of sufficient force and meaning to give expression to them.' But the reader of local guide-books is familiar with this sort of rhapsody.

Government has now taken the place under its fostering care. A school of forestry is established here; and, wherever man, or natural decay, has made a gap in the woods, young trees are planted to fill up the void, and everything betokens a desire to make amends for past neglect.

A high wall, the work of monkish enterprise, encloses the domain, which forms a rough quadrangle, perhaps a mile each way, access to which is afforded by a gate in each face. Of these, the most important is the Coimbra gate, facing south, from whence a paved road extends to the city. This once important causeway, however, is now a mere track, no attempt being made to keep it in repair, the large blocks of which it was once formed having been removed or destroyed.

The Coimbra gate is remarkable for its curious ornamentation, consisting of mosaic work formed of rough pieces of black and white marble, fixed in cement. The design has a good effect, and is an interesting relic of monkish times. The same scheme of decoration on a less pretentious scale has been carried out on the north gate. Outside the former, a raised platform or terrace, with stone benches along the balustrade, has been thrown out from the mountain-side, which is almost precipitous here, and with a few old olive-trees for shade it makes a delightful lounge of an evening. Many an hour did we spend here admiring the superb panorama spread out in front.

Standing in the gateway, a charming vista is obtained through the gnarled trunks and limbs of some venerable cork and olive trees, clinging to the Coimbra road, planted, doubtless, in times past for shade, and now looking reproachfully down on to the neglected and long-disused causeway of so many interesting memories. Underneath, the mountain tumbles away in a succession of pine-clad ridges of deepest green, to the valley, with its richly-cultivated fields bordering the distant Mondego, which shimmers through the misty distance as it pursues its devious course to the Atlantic.

Far away, in those mist-enshrouded regions, is the spot where a little army of Britons, commanded by a 'Sepoy general' called Wellesley, disembarked during those August days, in 1808, to undertake what was thought the hopeless task of expelling the war-trained veterans of France.

Little did the soldiers of that 'forlorn hope,' as it was called, dream, as they gazed on 'grim Bussaco's iron ridge,' that, three years later, those peaks were destined to witness one of the grandest feats of arms that adorn Britain's roll of glory.

To this lovely spot did we resort nearly every evening, to

> 'Watch while the sun laid down,
> At the gate of the west, his golden crown.'

And although, alas! the days were almost invariably wet and stormy, a break always occurred at the moment the sun sank to rest, and we were treated to some of nature's grandest transformation scenes. Here we would linger, sole spectators of those masterpieces of composition and colour which it pleased that arch 'impressionist' Nature to throw off for our particular edification night after night. Far away in the middle distance, the noble Mondego would flash back its 'good-night,' the towers and buildings of ancient Coimbra sparkling through the mist like the turrets of fairy palaces, while the peaks above shone rose-colour in the fading light.

Looking back over the dense masses of forest foliage, the effects were often singularly beautiful, affording a striking contrast to those we had been gazing on. For, after a heavy downpour, the mists would rise up through the trees from the warm soil like vapour from a bath, and frolic about in the fantastic wisps and curls that steam delights in, and then fly upwards in long streamers, which caught the tints of the sky above as they vanished over the mountain-tops.

At times, too, a gust of wind would stray into these forest solitudes; and then, behold! wisps and streamers would all be swept clean away, until, after an interval, the same effects would reappear, only in their turn to be swept off the scene.

On the outside of the Coimbra gate, engraven on stone, is a copy of the Papal Bull for the establishment of the convent, in which it is ordained that no females are to be admitted to this bachelors' club—not even for canvassing at election time!

An absolutely level bit of road leads from here to the convent, and is vaulted overhead with an impervious roof of foliage, in the composition of which the beautiful *Cupressus Lusitanica* largely partakes; the stems, like the pillars of a Gothic cathedral, forming a noble avenue, wherein it must be pleasant to lounge in hot weather, of which, alas! we had only samples.

Truth to tell, the 'clerk of the weather' muddled things, and instead of attending to our distinctly expressed wishes—we had forgotten to commit the orders to writing —he initiated us into the mysteries of tropical rain in a mountainous district, amidst high woods, and a dense undergrowth which has a wonderful knack of secreting raindrops for days afterwards.

To be sure, the kingdom of Portugal was crying aloud for rain. There had been none for months, and the crops threatened entire failure, with all the dire consequences attached; and the village priests were turning the occasion to useful account, for "'tis an ill wind that blows no one any good'! But what, after all, was the welfare and daily bread of millions of poor Portuguese when weighed in the balance with the lazy enjoyment of a couple of English travellers?

So the rains came down, and the crops came up; and by way of compensation we had the pleasure of watching the plains lose their parched appearance—more in keeping with September—and turn visibly greener every day, as the young corn shot up through the moist and softened soil.

High overhead, perched on almost overhanging crags, may be discerned from the convent little shrines, with hermit cells attached, wherein vegetated—it would be a libel on human nature to call it living—solitary Carmelites, who, bored by the rackety life of the mother convent, sought in these isolated, if breezy, perches the opportunities for remorseful contemplation denied to them at a lower level, and attained, let us hope, in every sense, the 'higher life.'

From these eyries the barefooted recluses would gaze down on that beautiful world from whence their disappointed ambitions and uncontrolled desires had driven them, deriving such solace as they might from the thought that its worries troubled them no more, and that they could earn at least their rations by a useless life of meditation.

To any one of these misanthropists might have been applied Wordsworth's verses on the 'Recluse of Esthwaite'—

> 'Stranger! these gloomy boughs
> Had charms for him; and here he loved to sit.
> . . . . . .
> Fixing his downcast eye, he many an hour
> A morbid pleasure nourished, tracing here
> An emblem of his own unfruitful life:
> And, lifting up his head, he then would gaze
> On the more distant scene,—how lovely 'tis
> Thou seest,—and he would gaze till it became
> Far lovelier. . . .
> 　　　　. . . And so, lost Man!
> On visionary views would fancy feed.
> . . . . . .
> He died,—this seat his only monument.'

The paths to these romantic perches are paved from bottom to top with round pebbles, carpeted in many places with the richest of mossy pile. And yet, even with these delightful aids to locomotion, the climb is a stiff one, and it is not always easy to find one's way through the mazes of the forest; though, to be sure, that incongruous tower makes a capital landmark for the return voyage.

On the loftiest peak of the monastic domain, a cross is reared on a massive stone pedestal—the Cruz Alta, it is called; and as from this spot you can examine a very considerable portion of the kingdom of Portugal, it is the favourite pilgrimage for visitors, the ascent being always accomplished with the aid of that useful if unfashionable animal, the ass. Hence it has come about that the Bussaco donkeys are so habituated to the climb, that I verily believe they could accomplish the ascent to the Cruz Alta in the dark.

The view from here on a clear day is magnificent. It is considered one of the finest in Portugal. A great expanse of country is spread out before you, including the entire course of the 'silvery Mondego' through the fruitful plain lying between Coimbra and the Atlantic; while to the southward, the towers and vast monastic buildings of the university city stand out conspicuously from their rugged surroundings.

No monkish community ever reared up its modest cot in a spot where there was not an abundant water-supply. For, notwithstanding the hereditary aversion of the cowled fraternity to tubbing—and Beckford's frequent allusions to the monkish 'odour of sanctity' show how unpleasant the consequences of this aversion must have been to laymen,—the use of water was imperative in gardening, as well as in the cleansing of pots and pans, to say nothing of cooking, which in some monasteries was not altogether neglected, if rumour may be trusted.

Here at Bussaco, embosomed in forest, with a dense undergrowth, springs gush from the mountain-side everywhere, and the precious rills have been turned to account in a variety of pleasant ways. It is strange, though, that while so much attention was bestowed on the cleansing of the mind—not always, it is to be feared, successfully,—there should have been such poor provision for sweetening the body: a monastic swimming-bath has never yet been discovered.

Fountains for use of man and beast abound on all sides. But the *chef d'œuvre* in the way of hydraulics is a curious sort of water-ladder, called the Fonte Fria (Cold Fountain) —somewhat after the manner of the approach to Bom Jesus, hidden away in a gully below the convent, and difficult to find by reason of the dense foliage.

To give importance to the rill, it is conducted down a series of steps, with platforms at intervals, extending perhaps fifty yards from base to summit. Fountains are fantastically arranged on each stage, the water finally plunging into a basin, around which seats are provided.

This quaint monkish conceit is overshadowed by the arching branches of trees, and though sadly neglected and out of repair, is still one of the features of the place. By no great stretch of imagination one can picture the shoeless brethren peopling this pleasant nook, all snoring away delectably, after the mid-day crust, 'the world forgetting by the world forgot.'

On our arrival at Bussaco there was but one family in residence, the younger members of which were just recovering from whooping-cough; and as the *meminos* whooped away at a furious rate, we protested against being set down to meals with such noisy companions, and were shown into another *sala*. This we shared during our sojourn with the couple who had arrived with us, of whom the lady was English.

The table was liberal, the food varied and excellent of

its kind, and the cooking a revelation, as was to be expected, seeing that Mons. P. B., when *chef* of the Braganza, enjoyed a European reputation. And although his time was too fully taken up now, with three large irons in the fire, to don the cap and apron, he took care that none but properly qualified deputies should preside in the kitchen.

Now, as it was our intention to make some little stay here, we determined on making ourselves snug. Accordingly, next morning we set off on a tour of the establishment, selecting a couple of rooms *en suite* on the first floor, with a pleasant southern aspect across the garden, from whence a delicious scent of flowers and aromatic plants stole in through the windows, the outside wall being garlanded with roses.

Having fixed our *locale*, we proceeded to make things homely. The courteous manager quite entered into the spirit of our enterprise; assured us we could have as many rooms as we liked until they were required, without any extra charge; and when we suggested a more liberal scale of furnishing, the reply was, 'Take anything you like.' So off we set on a predatory excursion, selecting here a table, there a sofa, from another room an arm-chair, and so on, till our equipment was complete.

We furnished number two as a sitting-room, which proved a most welcome addition to our *ménage*, as, owing to the perversity of the 'clerk of the weather' aforesaid, we had to spend a great many more hours indoors than was pleasant; and as the public salons were in another building, a hundred yards away, across an open space, to traverse which in a Bussaco downpour required some nerve, it was an advantage to have a retreat of our own.

I must say the rooms, and all pertaining to them,

were the pink of cleanliness, although the establishment was not in full working order, thus early in the season, preparations for which were going forward industriously in all directions. Underneath our rooms, for example, a 'mothers' meeting' was held daily, in the shape of an industrious army of women, with babies in arms, who were picking the straw mattrasses, and chatting merrily the while. Furniture was arriving daily from the depths of the valley for some newly-built rooms; and waiters were brushing and sweeping, and rubbing, and making things snug for expected guests; while worthy Mons. Bergamin's time was taken up with running from one hotel to the other—when not ladling out soup at the junction buffet, down the line.

Our cheery, good-tempered *femme-de-chambre* had evidently made up her mind to humour *os Ingleses* to the top of their bent, and was all eagerness to oblige. Her methods, though unorthodox from a British standpoint, were always excellently well adapted to the end in view.

I have already mentioned the national custom of carrying everything on the head, so as to leave the hands free. Now I wonder what a fine lady in England would think, if her housemaid was to enter the room of a morning with a 'forty-thieves' jar of bath-water beautifully poised on top of her head? And if this same fine dame recovered from her first surprise—without 'giving notice,' what would her feelings be, when surrounded with a cosy circle of friends, waiting for five-o'clock tea, to see the parlour-maid enter with the tray containing all the requisite equipment balanced aloft on her finely-modelled head? And yet, such were the 'demonstrations' in the art of head-porterage we were daily favoured with at Bussaco. Bath-water, breakfast, and five-o'clock tea were all carried across from the

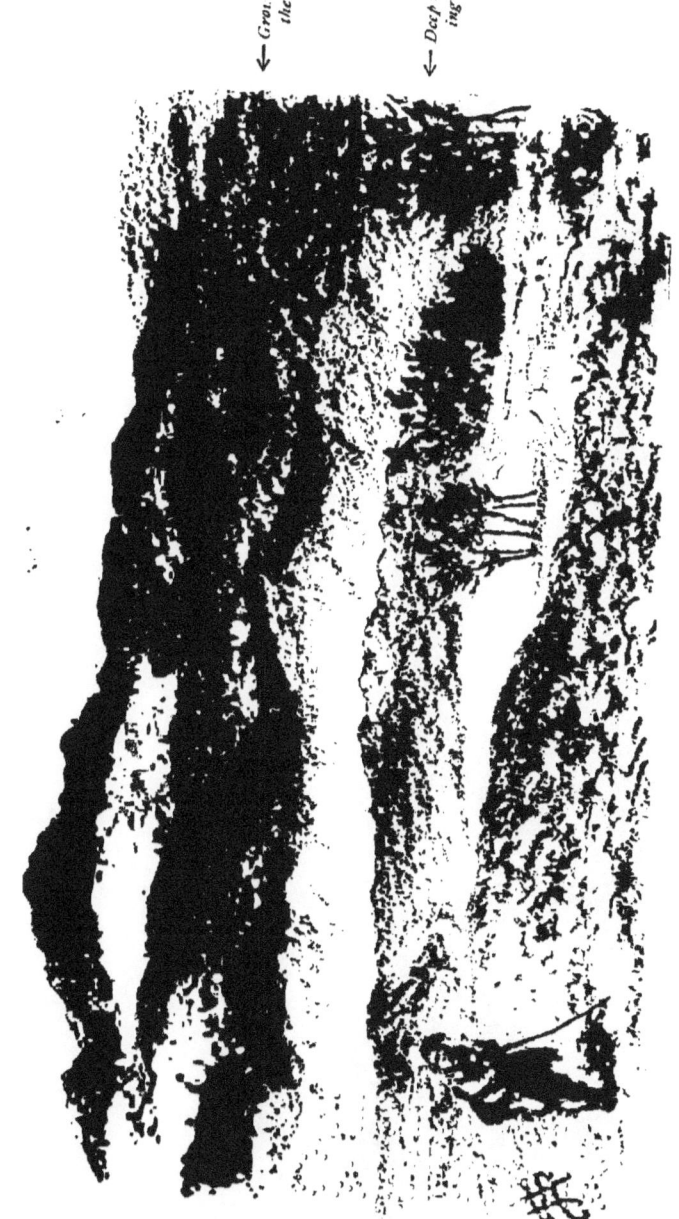

BUSSACO
SCENE OF THE NIGHT ATTACK

kitchen, a couple of hundred yards away, in this dainty fashion. And when it rained, the performance was still further improved upon, the dress being held up with one hand, while an umbrella was poised aloft with the other to shelter the tray—a feat of legerdemain which fairly astounded us. It was magnificent, it was sublime, and made us poor *Ingleses* feel our own national inferiority in the matter of porterage.

The grace of deportment and strength of limb the women thus acquire were shown in the easy *abandon* with which the maid aforesaid tossed aloft our portmanteaus, which were neither diminutive nor empty, on her head, as if they were bonnet-boxes, and trotted off with a cheery laugh.

This useful custom may be carried too far, as was exemplified during our sojourn in sundry ways. For example, we discovered that all the outside drudgery of the establishment, including garden-work, was performed by the fair sex—what had become of the 'lords of creation' we never could ascertain; and in the execution of these rather filthy tasks, the head was always made to bear the heat and burden of the day, for it was never covered, and the weights were considerable. In this stately manner, road material, garden soil, pot plants, manure, and even the superfluous matter from a pigsty, were all transported with consummate grace and indifference to their respective destinations; and right well did these 'strong women' perform their allotted duties, working from sunrise to sunset, with a suitable interval at mid-day, when, as I have already explained, the entire population of Portugal surrenders itself into the arms of Morpheus. Where the ladies who had been engaged in the healthful, if inelegant, occupation of 'scaling muck,' as it is called in

T

Cumberland, passed this welcome interval we were unable to discover, the pigsty being 'engaged'!

The only other member of the hotel staff who merits notice was the senhor who waited on us in the *sala de jantar*. This exemplary young man took a fatherly interest in our welfare and appetites, performing the duties of a foster-papa in most commendable style. Under his paternal care we made astonishing progress in Portuguese, 'as she is spoke' at Bussaco; and all went merrily as a marriage bell, until one evening we discovered a strangeness in his manner, an excess of parental devotion in the matter of pressing food on us, and tempting our palates with choice morsels. We wondered, but ate. When the pudding-stage arrived, our self-constituted guardian appeared with a triumphant smile on his face, and in his hands a most choice and really beautiful specimen of confectionery, which, on investigation, proved to be compounded of cream and caramel-sugar, cunningly arranged in the form of a castle, the destruction of which work of art seemed sheer vandalism. However, the matter was settled by the bearer of the trophy himself dashing in a spoon; we all ate, and rejoiced exceedingly, agreeing that it was one of the most toothsome and delicious dishes we had ever assisted in consuming. Our faithful servitor having satisfied himself of our entire satisfaction with the dish, proceeded to inform us, in strict confidence, of course, that we owed this pleasure to his ready wit in rescuing the dish, while still intact, from a party of early diners, in the other *sala*. After this we could do no less than return to the attack, our minds being filled with wonder at the motive of this act of unsolicited devotion. At length the secret leaked out, for, when the period had arrived at which all healthy diners are supposed to experience a sense of contentment, and their heart-strings are loosened and they feel at peace with all men, the attendant slave, who for some time had been labouring under a sense of embarrassment, and an evident desire to unburden his mind, informed us that he was about to leave; that, in fact, the hotel down at Luso was to be opened shortly, and that next morning he was to take up his abode there, and, like the elders of Ephesus, he was sorrowing most of all that he should see our faces no more. After so affecting an appeal, to say nothing of the diplomatic skill with which it had been led up to, we could do no less than dive into our pockets. Imagination can fill in the rest.

The chief—indeed the only—diversion at Bussaco in the season is donkey-riding, and every owner of an ass for miles around seemed to have scented our arrival, for the very next morning they turned up with their steeds and continued to impress on us daily—nay, every time we appeared—the necessity of performing the pilgrimage to the Cruz Alta. For three days their importunities ceased not, when at length asses and owners all vanished as mysteriously as they had appeared; some friends having probably dropped a hint that we were *Ingleses*, that all English were mad, seeing that they insisted on using their own legs instead of those so mercifully provided by Providence, in the shape of an ass, and that of all English we were the maddest, for we were always on the tramp.

After we had been here a week, a young and most bewitching senhora appeared on the scene with a couple of serviceable-looking mokes, and as the day chanced to be fine, and we rather wished to extend the range of our wanderings, we bargained with the fair one for a two-hours' ride. She took it for granted, of course, that the Cruz Alta was to be our goal, and remonstrated strongly when we turned out of the north gate on to the mountainside. It so happened that a sudden desire to investigate the crest of the Serra had seized us, and we struck into a rough track bestrewn with rocks, which unseemly proceeding so completely established in our fair cicerone's mind the fact of our insanity, that, after violent expostulations and much useless wringing of hands, she at last threw them up towards heaven in sheer despair, and plumping down on a stone, abandoned us to our own evil ways, vowing, no doubt, that she would see her donkeys somewhere before she trusted *os Ingleses* on their backs again. To be sure she wasn't shod for mountain climbing, but we were determined to have our money's worth, shoes or no shoes, and went merrily on, the fair Lusitanian resting on her rock the meanwhile.

Bussaco, as I have said, is essentially a hot-weather resort; and I may as well add, for the benefit of intending visitors, that there are neither promenades nor bands, beefsteaks nor 'bitter,' to be got here, and that the tourist who goes a-gadding in search of excitement will experience a sense of insufferable boredom before he has been here a couple of days.

For such attractions as Bussaco possesses visitors are chiefly indebted to those dull hypochondriacs, the Carmelite brothers, who, in their yearnings after the ideal, or from sheer satiety of the world's good things, fled from their allotted tasks, and amidst the solitudes of the Serra gave themselves up to a life of contemplation and landscape-gardening.

There is a craving discernible at the present day amongst dyspeptic folk for the return of the monastic system. Well, let it be granted that amongst the Bussaco brothers there were earnest and high-minded men; but what a useless life they led! It was a vegetable sort of existence at the best, and essentially selfish. If the world was so bad they could not live in it, why did they not try to reform it? If, on the other hand, they had sucked its pleasures dry, there was no self-sacrifice in quitting it. Whichever way we look at it, the act of leaving it was one of pure selfishness. It was an act of moral cowardice running away from the station in life they had been set to occupy. If a sentry quits his post in time of war, he is liable to be shot. Even suicides are held to be guilty of a crime; they are regarded as cowards, rather than as heroes. And what is the act of entering a monastery but an act of moral suicide, a desertion of the allotted post?

It seems to be forgotten that in entering a monastery the recruit does not leave human nature outside. Though he may change the colour of his skin, shave his pate, and wear sackcloth and ashes, his self remains. He may flee from other people's selves, but he can't part company with his own. The one dark spot in the monastic sunshine was ever the shadow of his own wilful self. And this self was ever wont to re-assert itself, with what dire results is writ so plainly that those who run may read.

There are folk who are for ever assuring you, that if they had not been 'misunderstood' when young, or if they had been put in some other profession than the one they happen to occupy, they would have 'set the Thames on fire.' And this is just the unwholesome state of mind which filled monasteries with idlers, and makes people nowadays think they ought to be barefooted friars—or the Lord knows what!

When any one feels a hankering after the monastic life, let him at once consult a stomach-doctor, or nerve-specialist, and make sure he is not suffering from a 'gin-drinker's liver'—or, perchance, a 'housemaid's-knee,' or even 'phossy-jaw'! Further, let him read up the monastic chronicles, take a run abroad, and drink a little mineral water for the good of his stomach and his often infirmities. But don't let him be so mad as to suppose he will benefit the world by shutting himself up in a cellar—unless, indeed, he is a *mauvais sujet*,—or by erecting palatial abodes, and calling them monasteries, and stocking them with healthy, full-blooded bipeds of either sex who ought to be working hard for a living.

In the course of my wanderings over the face of the globe I have visited many lands and seen many monasteries, and have heard and read a great deal about the life within; and it is remarkable how accounts agree everywhere as to the inevitable deterioration of morals that sets in, as the initial enthusiasm leaks out. It matters not one jot what the colour of the monk's habit or his skin, or the shape of his head, or the tongue he speaks, whether in Portugal or Pekin, the result is the same, the tend ever downwards. It seems, in fact, to be a law of nature, that when a community of human beings cuts itself off from the friction of the world, and screens the lives of its members from public scrutiny, deterioration at once sets in. Enthusiasm may be of service in delaying this, but no enthusiasm can be maintained at fever-heat by a life of mere contemplation; and directly it begins to cool down, the palsy of idleness sets in, followed by the creeping-paralysis of doubt; then comes indulgence and luxury; and last of all there sets in a reign of mere bestiality.

This is no figment of the imagination, but the stern verdict of history. 'Public opinion' may go wrong, and is not to be worshipped as a fetish; but at any rate it keeps human beings from lapsing into mere beasts.

Monasticism, like feudalism, has served its purpose in the economy of the world, and must now be classed with the 'played out' cults. We must search elsewhere for the highest expression of altruism.

Amongst sundry excursions we had planned was a drive to the old city of Coimbra (pronounced Queemborough), the great university town of PortugaL But the face of Nature, during our sojourn amidst these scenes of sylvan loveliness, wore a sad and tearful expression, too often gazing down with streaming eyes and a clouded brow; and as Coimbra is an eighteen-mile drive, we had to give up the trip.

Of course, the excursion can be accomplished by train; but our object was to see something of the intervening country, and perchance branch off, if the spirit moved us, to investigate some of the villages *en route*, rather than to burrow into class-rooms, museums, or lecture-halls, or to gaze on the contents of libraries, which have the same dry and forbidding aspect in all countries.

The interests of Coimbra are chiefly historical and scholastic. There are of course a number of ecclesiastical edifices and defunct monastic establishments which 'merit notice,' but as we felt no hankerings after churches, nor even a yearning for convent-cells after our enforced seclusion in the monastery of the Carmelite brothers, we contented ourselves with the lovely vista of the city that is obtained from the railway bridge over the Mondego *en route* for Lisbon.

The town is finely placed on high ground, with the river flowing below. And the Mondego is especially dear to the Portuguese, from the fact of its rising in, and flowing through, exclusively Portuguese soil. The alluvial plain through which it winds after passing Coimbra is extremely productive, and has been called 'the fruit-basket of Portugal,' its fertility being caused by the periodic overflowing of the river when charged with fertilising matter, and which thus performs the same useful office for the adjacent districts as the Nile does, on a far grander scale, for Egypt.

The chief reason we regretted the miscarriage of our projected trip was the loss of the only opportunity we should have of visiting the famous Fonte dos Amores, in the beautiful and historic gardens of the Quinta das Lagrimas—the scene of the dreadful tragedy of Inez de Castro, that lovely and unfortunate princess who was basely murdered, and whose body now reposes by the side of her dearly loved Dom Pedro I., in the silent aisle of grand Batalha.

That famous tragedy in high life has been immortalised in verse by Portugal's favourite bard, Camoens, of whose works there are now several excellent translations in English, notably that by Sir Francis Burton.

The story has been utilised by play-writers in many lands. And in old days, it was a very popular stage-play in Portugal, especially amongst the monastic orders. Beckford gives a highly entertaining account of a performance he witnessed at the royal monastery of Alcobaca, and explains that there was nothing unusual in this, seeing that in the golden days of the Portuguese monarchy, amateur theatricals were frequently resorted to at Mafra, 'to dispel the *ennui* of that royal and monastic residence.'

During the Peninsular War the Quinta das Lagrimas (House of Tears) was often occupied by British officers, one of whom wrote: 'The officers of our squadron were in high luck at the distribution of billets; we were quartered in the house of a nobleman, which was left in the care of his son, a colonel in the Portuguese service. Here the kindest attention was shown, and having every comfort we could require, a sumptuous mess was established, for which we had an abundance of plate and the best services of china.'

When Sir Nicholas Trant was governor of the province, he caused to be erected, by the side of the Fonte of so many sad memories, a stone, on which was engraven Camoens' exquisite lines, 'whose beauty and pathos,' says an English writer, 'no poet has ever surpassed.' Indeed, in the opinion of Portuguese of fine taste, the poet's best passages are 'untranslatably beautiful.'

There is another interesting connecting-link with the old Peninsular War days, in the neighbourhood of Coimbra, which must be ever dear to Englishmen—the Quinta of the Condeça d'A——. Here, not only was the great Duke 'hospitably and enthusiastically received by the family,' but wounded British officers of all ranks were admitted, and received the tenderest care during the whole period of the war.

The only allusion to this splendid domain, 'one of the wonders of Portugal,' that I have met with, in the course of a pretty extensive search amongst books on Portugal, occurs in some interesting letters written by an English lady from Lisbon, in 1821-23.

From this writer we learn that of the numerous estates of the A—— family, the one near Coimbra was the chief, and that there was introduced here 'a degree of comfort as well as magnificence, which assimilates very nearly with English taste and ideas.' The establishment must have been conducted on a scale of magnificence rare in Portugal; for, at the time this lady wrote, the Condeça had provided most nobly for the accommodation of those friends who might travel from Lisbon to visit her, by the erection of several houses at her own expense, 'furnished with every requisite convenience, and placed at the same points of distance with the common, horrible inns.'

The kitchen was 'of immense dimensions, and most superbly appointed'; and, like the famous 'temple of gluttony' at Alcobaca, was traversed throughout its length by a river, from which it was the common practice of the cooks to catch the fish which a few moments afterwards were prepared for the table.' It is said that the Duke of Wellington amused himself by fishing in it during his sojourn here.

'How much reason have many of the English to remember the genuine friendship of this family!' says the lady I have quoted, alluding to the amiable and accomplished owner. 'I am assured, by eye-witnesses,' she continues, 'that during the Peninsular War the princely mansion was ever open to our wounded officers; so much so, that the house resembled a hospital, and the lives of several individuals were preserved entirely through the kind and unremitting attention which they received from their really illustrious and excellent hosts.' Mark what follows. 'I ought not to omit that their example was followed in a more humble way by the peasantry, during the time of that great struggle; and after this latter proof of just and grateful feeling, who ought to suffer themselves to believe that the Portuguese are incapable of moral regeneration? And yet I hear this asserted every day of my life.'

It is, alas! too true that the behaviour of the Portuguese

Government and its tools, their disgraceful incompetence, their shameless greed, and the gross corruption which sapped every branch of the administration throughout the war, have blinded the eyes of Englishmen to the many fine qualities of the Portuguese people, causing them to forget the noble conduct of private individuals— the many acts of kindness and tender sympathy which did so much to alleviate the sufferings of our wounded soldiers. Even Napier has never allowed one word of acknowledgment of all this to slip from his facile and eloquent pen.

Romans and Moors have all in turn held sway in Coimbra. But it was good King Diniz, 'the Patriot King,' who, by the foundation of the university, in 1306, left the most enduring mark of his rule, and laid the basis of its present-day prosperity. It was not, however, till 1527 that the university was permanently located here, when it was finally removed from Lisbon in consequence of the frequency of the 'town and gown' riots.

Like everything in Portugal, the university was for several centuries under the numbing influence of the church, during which time it produced few shining lights of learning, orthodoxy being more esteemed than mental culture. In fact, after making their *début*, the students were in the habit of returning home till the time for the 'finals' approached, and certificates were never refused to 'good students,' the degrees being conferred without regard to scientific or intellectual acquirements.

And so matters went on till Pombal came on the scene, and, like every educational reformer, made himself highly 'unpopular.' His first measure was to sack the Jesuits— a step for which there was absolutely 'no precedent'; and having bundled out these scheming, self-interested clerics, with their 'orthodox' ways, and their degrees for 'good students,' this high-handed meddler proceeded to put the educational system on a sound footing, and to make things shipshape generally, a process which entailed treading on a great many 'worthy' people's corns.

It was at this juncture that several Englishmen were engaged as professors in various branches of learning. For Pombal, with all his hatred of the 'English influence,' was not above utilising Englishmen in the service of his country. 'And thus,' says Kinsey, 'without arrogance we may assume that the English have contributed in no small degree to the restoration of learning and science in Portugal.'

About 1200 young men are in residence at Coimbra during term-time, and I was given to understand that a student can obtain board and lodging at from two to three pounds per month, while most of the lectures are free.

A party of these young men, in their quaint academic dress, came up to Bussaco while we were there, on donkeys. The unwonted spectacle of a foreign lady and gentleman so astonished these *literati* that they stood dumfounded with open mouths; and at last, perceiving the lower extremities of my legs to be encased in stockings—I was wearing knickerbockers,—their intelligent countenances fairly beamed with delight; some of them laughed outright. Such a disregard for the conventionalities of decent society as was shown by wearing stockinged legs, as high as the knees, was quite too much for these *illuminati* of the higher learning. It is pleasant to know, though, that the Coimbra students are 'noted for their courtesy to strangers.' In some lands disapprobation would have found expression in ''eaving 'arf a brick' at the offender.

The Coimbra students have many of them arrived at an age when Englishmen are fathers of families, and would naturally look on the recreations of British students as essentially frivolous, scorning association with a fellow-graduate who demeaned himself so far as to kick a leather ball about, in a state of semi-nudity, and looking on a young man who made 'a century' at cricket as a fit subject for an asylum, while as for any self-respecting mathematician rowing a boat till he was breathless and perspiring, why such a fellow would be cut by every countrymen of Camoens. Needless to say, the mere suggestion of it being *chic* to absorb a pound of marmalade into the human system every morning, with breakfast, would shock the moral sense of the Coimbra undergrads beyond recovery.

I was glad to have made the acquaintance of these young men—the hope of Portugal; and though I have never been able to discover the humorous side of knickerbockers—possibly owing to a certain rigidity in my neck—it was delightful being able to afford amusement of a strictly moral nature to one's fellow-creatures, with so little exertion to oneself.

The leisure moments of these sedentary young men are largely devoted to politics and poetry. In their poetical flights the Mondego—the 'River of the Muses,' as it is often called, comes in for a good deal of apostrophising, and many are the glowing comparisons drawn between it and the classical goddesses of antiquity.

In connection with the political leanings of the students, it is interesting to turn to the forecast of an English visitor to Coimbra, in the 'forties, when Portugal was just beginning to recover from the effects of the disastrous civil war and the passions it had brought in its train.

Kingston resided many years in Oporto, was a Portuguese scholar, and on intimate terms with many prominent men, and had every opportunity of gauging native opinion. This is what he says: 'The general political principles of the university are, I regret to say, ultra-liberal, verging on, if not quite, republicanism. It requires no prophet to foretell that Portugal will become, or attempt to become, a republic before many years are passed.'

The spirit in which Kingston visited Coimbra may be gathered from the following:—

'It is not mere sightseeing which can afford most interest in such a place as Coimbra. As the University of Portugal, it is the nursery of the statesmen, the legislators, the professors of law, of medicine, the leaders of parties; indeed, of the talent of the country. It is by mixing among the students, by conversing with them, by learning their habits and ideas, that one may be able to prophesy, with some approach to accuracy, the destinies of the kingdom, in which most of them must perform some prominent part. The greater number of my Portuguese acquaintances have been members of the university, some of the younger ones still are so. They are one and all imbued with a liberal spirit—but, as is generally the case, when men have but lately thrown off the yoke, pressing for so many centuries on their necks, I fear they run much risk of falling into the opposite extreme, and that in shunning the galling goad of a despotic sovereign, they may bring themselves a heavier curse—the anarchy of a republic.'

I have quoted this writer because he is the only one of his day—or since—who has given attention to this particular phase of Portuguese life; and was, moreover, competent to form an opinion from his own observations and knowledge of the trend of political thought.

Kingston's forecast has a special interest at the present

moment in view of recent developments. His remarks help to explain much that has taken place within recent times.

To the 'intelligent foreigner,' Coimbra possesses a quite unique interest, from the threefold distinction it enjoys:—1st. It is the great seat of learning; 2nd., possesses the greatest number of illiterates in proportion to population of any city in Portugal;[1] 3rd., it is the centre of the toothpick industry. Now, a city which can boast of a threefold distinction of this description is well worth visiting.

To turn to lighter subjects.

There is a phenomenon to be witnessed at Coimbra, which must invest the place with a peculiar interest in the eyes of dabblers in the occult sciences; and the wonder is it has for so long escaped the attention of the scientific societies of Europe.

The authority is unimpeachable—to wit, a British Gazetteer. Now, according to this immaculate authority, —which, so the editor informs us, is 'intended for the special use of Englishmen,' and compiled for the purpose of 'supplying the inquirer with independent, and at the same time precise and well-authenticated information,'— I say, according to this authority, the monks of the S. Augustine Monastery of the city of Coimbra, 'mostly men of noble descent and polished manners, are often seen mounted on fine horses, splendidly caparisoned, being forbidden by the regulations of the monastery to appear on foot beyond its walls.'

The reader has only to keep in mind the solemn fact

[1] The actual figures, taken from official sources, stand thus:— Population, including the university, 316,624 : Wholly illiterate— males 105,582, females 166,256=271,838, equal to 85 per cent.

that this said bachelors' club was suppressed as a public nuisance in 1834—the existence of establishments of this nature being regarded as out of harmony with the spirit of the nineteenth century, which looks on marrying and giving in marriage as one of the chief ends of existence—and the well-nourished occupants let loose on the world, where doubtless many of these eligible but guileless young gentlemen 'of noble descent and polished manners' fell a prey to designing mammas. I say, the reader has only to keep all this in mind to realise the extraordinary character of the phenomenon.

There can be no mistake about it, the compilers having 'spared no pains to make the work worthy of the reader's confidence.'

TO LISBON

There is but one day-train to Lisbon, the journey from Pampilhosa Junction of 150 miles occupying nine hours, at the rate of about sixteen miles an hour—not a dangerous speed, or one calculated to bring an undue strain on the permanent way.

En passant, we laid in a stock of Coimbra bread—an excellent, light sort of bun, rather like our Coburg, and which with cheesecakes and illiterates constitute the specialities of the university city.

The route was not new to me, for I had traversed it twenty-eight years before; but as the trip was made by night, and in very festive company, my recollections of the scenery were not particularly vivid. As a matter of fact, the route is not attractive, and in the absence of any external objects to engage the attention, one's thoughts naturally wander back to former times and other scenes, and especially to the stirring days of the Peninsular War,

LISBON, FROM THE SOUTH SIDE

UNIV. OF
CALIFORNIA

when the country between Coimbra and Lisbon became one great battlefield.

In that stern drama two acts stand forth with a vividness which not even the lapse of ninety years has sufficed to blur. One was the gathering of the British army under Sir Arthur Wellesley at Coimbra, in May 1809, preparatory to its advance on Oporto, the passage of the Douro, and the expulsion of the French from Portugal. The other was the retreat of this same army, the following year, through this very city of Coimbra, onwards to the lines of Torres Vedras, sweeping before it the inhabitants not only of a city, but of an entire province.

The dramatist's wildest flight of fancy could scarcely have devised two more strongly contrasted situations; while the whole course of the war may be searched in vain for a parallel to the appalling misery of that retreat on the lines, in the autumn of 1810.

We are too apt to look on the story of the Peninsular War as a mere chronicle of brilliant victories, a glorious page of our own military history, forgetful of the frightful horrors that followed in its wake—the sickening tale of human suffering which a careful study of that great struggle would disclose. Our own histories gloss over the dark side of it all; and as no hostile foot has trod our soil for many centuries, the dwellers in our tight little island can never realise the full significance of a hostile invasion, and all that it entails on the inhabitants of a country. The full measure of the sufferings of the peasantry of Spain and Portugal during those six years of warfare with a fierce and relentless foe has never been grasped in all its hideous reality. No writer has ever attempted to grapple with the subject, for it is so vast in its scope and so absolutely revolting in the details which diligent search would disclose, that no one dare venture nowadays to draw aside the veil of oblivion which time has mercifully thrown over it. Still, the reader who seeks to inform himself on the subject may get a very fair notion of the horrors of those far-away days, if he will; though to get at facts he must search through the masses of long-forgotten war literature that lumber up old bookshelves—histories of the campaigns, officers' journals, and personal reminiscences, wherein, amidst much that is of purely antiquarian or professional interest, we come across ever and anon descriptive scenes which, for realistic power and gruesome interest, might vie with the productions of some of our most accomplished 'war correspondents' at the present day.

Jotted down while the impressions were fresh in the mind, those personal reminiscences carry one back to the days of the war, causing the very scenes to rise up before one in all their hideous reality. Once more we seem to hear the tramp of feet, the rumbling of the guns and carriages, and all the confusion of sound that accompanies the retreat of an army; while above all this we seem to detect that long-drawn wail rising from the throats of thousands of innocent, suffering creatures of all ages who are being urged on, day after day, by kindly British officers, who, appalled at the misery which hems them in and from which there is no respite—no, not for a moment —inwardly question the wisdom and justice of the edict which causes it all.

No traveller over this route who is conversant with the circumstances of that awful retreat—and certainly no Englishman should come to Portugal without having read up the subject—can gaze on the scenes of so much suffering and woe unless he be entirely devoid of sensibility, without his sympathies being touched, and a feeling of utter detestation being evoked for the author of it all —that truculent heathen, Buonaparte!

There is scarcely a rood of ground over which the line passes, between Coimbra and Lisbon, but is associated with some affecting or tragic episode in that enforced migration of a populace before the devastating legions of France. And yet, in spite of what transpired, the landscape smiles as it did of yore, for that kindly old nurse, Nature, has swept away every mark and scar; and, but for the imperishable record of printer's ink, nothing would remain to remind one of the ghastly tragedy enacted here.

And so the hours drag on, as if the journey was interminable. I know there are people who complain of railway travelling in Portugal as wearisome. And so undoubtedly it is—if you are in a hurry. But you must never be in a hurry in the Peninsula. For there life is still held to be worth living, and, on that account, worth prolonging to the uttermost. And of all the ways of prolonging life, commend me to a railway journey in fair Lusitania. To enjoy it, however, to the full, the roving and impatient Briton must drop all preconceived ideas concerning the 'eternal fitness of things' in steam locomotion. He must commence by erasing the twin words 'quick' and 'hurry' from his vocabulary. For the only reply a self-respecting Portuguese fidalgo would deign to give an individual who hinted at the word 'hurry' would be the exclamation, uttered in a slow and dignified manner, 'Amanha!' which, being interpreted, means 'To-morrow!' And the nation conscientiously acts up to this rule of life by never doing to-day what can be put off till to-morrow.

Now it came to pass, about seventy years ago, that a

bold British sailor called Napier—who was 'spoiling' for a fight of some sort—took it into his wild head to go campaigning in Portugal; and after fighting many battles against the usurper Dom Miguel, this bluff sailor bethought him of jotting down his experiences, wherein, amongst other brusque sayings, he had the effrontery to declare—in a moment of pique, begotten of some sad experience of native ways—that the Portuguese would never be a nation till the word 'amanha' was expunged from their language. But he was suffering from that essentially British complaint called 'restless energy,' which is anathema in southern lands.

To be sure, some folk might take exception to the number of stoppages and the apparent waste of time at small roadside stations where no one gets in or out of the train. But to me these halts are a never-failing source of delight. For, putting aside the question of sketching, or even of botanising, along the line while the train waits, there is both pleasure and profit to be derived from the spectacle of so many officials in gold lace and brass buttons, and with their caps decorated with miniature locomotive-engines wrought in gold thread, parading each station in a slow and dignified manner—almost bowed down with the burden of responsibility attaching to the duty of putting through one train a day each way. And then the mind wanders off into side-issues,—as, for example, how these magnificent functionaries employ their leisure moments—which, by the by, are neither brief nor infrequent; or how any railway company can manage to support such an incubus of officialdom and pay a dividend, supposing that it does pay a dividend, which in Portugal is too often to imagine a vain thing! *C'est magnifique, mais ce n'est pas la guerre!* or, as a

British railway official would put it, 'It's grand, but it ain't business!'

At most stations you hear a shrill little voice calling 'Agua fresca! agua fresca!' and behold, a comely damsel, with red water-jar and glass, dispensing her limpid store to thirsty passengers. I have occasionally, when the demand was brisk, seen these young ladies running!—yes, actually running! think of that!—though, to be sure, I trembled for the consequences, expecting every moment to see the juvenile delinquent led away by a gilded official and consigned to a dungeon. Oranges and other sorts of fruit are hawked about, according to the season. But civilisation has not attained here to the tea-basket stage.

After the lapse of a decent interval the station bell is struck, once, twice, thrice, the last stroke being the signal for departure; and the train having gone, the gold-laced officials retire to their several lairs for a few hours' rest. I never saw any business going on anywhere; but perhaps the parcel and goods traffic is conducted under the cover of night. It often struck me, though, that if there was more work to be done the officials would not look so terribly bored and overburdened with dignity—then certainly would not willingly carry about such a weight of gold lace.

All the navvy work on the railways of Portugal is done by women—fine, muscular wenches they are too, many of them; and they carry the little baskets of sand and dirt beautifully poised on the head with infinite grace of deportment, chattering like magpies the while. It would be an insult to the human form divine to speak of these ladies as belonging to the 'weaker sex.'

Of the civility of the railway officials I cannot speak too highly. The person who asks to see your ticket—there is no 'demanding' tickets here—does so with an apologetic air, as if he were begging a very great personal favour; and having looked at the ticket—perchance snipped a piece out of it—the courteous official, instead of shoving it back into your hand without a word of acknowledgment, makes the return of it quite a graceful little ceremony, and leaves you enraptured.

The Portuguese are certainly a courteous race, and even railway officials have surrendered none of their native polish by accepting the badge of servitude. But then, of course, they are not flurried by unsympathetic inspectors and impatient guards who are worried with time-bills. An average speed of sixteen miles an hour allows the dull routine of duty to be carried on with proper regard for the dignity of the human race.

The official time-tables are an interesting study, for they show you what the official conceptions of travelling 'facilities' are in the ancient realm of Portugal. Take the journey, for instance, between Lisbon and the Liverpool of the north—Oporto. There are three trains each way during the twenty-four hours, but not one express. Two are what the time-table calls 'mixed,' and are considered rather slow even by believers in the 'amanha' doctrine of life,—they take from thirteen to more than fourteen hours over the pilgrimage, at an average rate of fourteen miles an hour. There remains, then, only one train for people in a hurry, and this 'flier,' by dint of skipping a dozen stations, manages to accomplish the trip in the record time of eleven hours. But then, of course, two hundred and fifteen miles is a serious undertaking for a descendant of Albuquerque, and it would be inconsistent with his sense of dignity to rattle over the miles at the rate we do. The average speed of this particular train is nineteen miles an hour, which quite accounts for the serious and anxious cast of countenance I observed amongst the officials as the time drew near for the passing of the 'flying Scotsman' of Portugal.

Comparing this with our own poor achievements, I find the distance but a few miles in excess of the longest express run without a stop—Paddington to Exeter, one hundred and ninety-four miles: time, three hours forty-five minutes.

The only other record run worth mentioning is that between Barreiro, on the south side of the Tagus, and Faro, the southern commercial metropolis. The distance is the same as to Oporto, and is achieved at the rate of sixteen miles an hour, or just under twelve hours. In this case only a single train runs each way during the twenty-four hours, and stops at every station.

Now, a recent British writer on Portugal gravely informs us that the Portuguese are essentially an adventurous nation, fond of travelling and full of enterprise. I often wonder if this was 'writ sarcastic.' A few minutes' study of the railway time-tables will show how much is being done at the present time in the way of affording scope for the national fondness for travel. That the spirit of enterprise is alive, however, is shown by the up-to-date management of the Lisbon-Figueras line, which actually runs an 'express' two days a week to Caldas da Rainha during the season. What more could the most exigent tourist want?

One result of the existing system of management is that visitors are entirely debarred from making excursions to places of interest along the lines and returning the same day. No 'pleasure-seeker' cares to drag himself out of bed to go to a place, say, twenty miles off, at four o'clock in the morning, and not get home again till midnight. And yet, that is what you must do in some cases. So few are the trains on any of the lines, that it is never considered necessary to have time-tables spread abroad. Every one knows quite well the hour at which the only train leaves and arrives, and that is all any one cares to know; and so, out of Lisbon or Oporto, it is the exception to find a time-table in the hotels.

As a further incentive to travel, several pages of the time-table book are taken up with particulars of 'circular tours' in Spain and Portugal, itineraries of routes and prices, etc., tickets for which may be obtained by any one confiding enough to deposit a sum of 'ready' eight days in advance. Personally, I wouldn't trust a Portuguese railway company with my oldest pair of shoes as a deposit!

As few of my readers have ever had the privilege of gazing on a 'Guia Official dos Caminhos de Ferro de Portugal' (Official Guide to the Portuguese Railways), I venture to offer a brief extract from one:—'WATER-CLOSETS.—Nos comboios directos que circulam entre Figueira da Foz e Villa Formoso ha water-closets com lavatorios, no fourgon do conductor. Em Pampilhosa ha gabinetes-toilette com retretos reservadas para homens e senhoras, a 30 reis por pessoa.'

Not being a holder—thank goodness!—of shares in Portuguese railways, their dividend-paying capabilities are a matter which interests me very little. But it is worth mentioning that every one 'engaged upon the business of the State'—a delightfully elastic term—is allowed to travel free or at reduced rates, a privilege which has proved such a wonderful incentive to travel, that no less than ten thousand persons are said to hold free passes over the State railways of Portugal.

From time to time a clamour is raised in the British

Parliament on this very subject by patriotic M.P.'s, who desire to see free travelling for 'the chosen-of-the-people' introduced into our own benighted land. But just think of the whole six hundred 'wise men of Westminster' being let loose on our railways with their 'best girls'!— for, sure, no base Saxon Chancellor of the Exchequer, with a spark of chivalry in him, would deny the same privilege to 'their sisters and their cousins and their aunts'?— Begorra, no!

There is one thing which the peripatetic Briton will greatly miss here, and that is the poetry of the 'Pill-puff.' No big boards fleck the fair face of Nature in Portugal, bearing bewildering legends to cheer the traveller in his pilgrimage through the land. The simple inhabitants have not yet been educated up to that high pitch when the added beauty of the advertisement is felt to be essential to the complete enjoyment of Nature's charms. For, after all, Nature is a clumsy composer, and sadly needs helping along. Only the savage considers beauty unadorned as beauty still, and playfully chops off the heads of people who go about sticking boards on end.

When the fair Lusitanians have attained to a South Kensington system, and the croak of the art-student is heard in the land, and when all men can chatter 'art-jargon' for hours on end, and fall down and worship at the shrine of ugliness and decay, wear sad and bilious faces, and adopt the gait of the knock-knee'd and silly, and eschew the society of ordinary mortals of flesh and blood—why, then, they will be able to appreciate the dignity and beauty of the pill-puff, and will probably ordain that all their roads may be lined with illuminated texts, apropos of soap and other things. For of such is civilisation!

The shades of night had fallen ere we reached our goal. Our train was due at 8.30, but the Puffing-Billy and its Mahout were so worn out with their exertions that a quarter of an hour had to be whiled away within sight of the station before a stray locomotive could be pressed into the friendly service of pushing us into the terminus. Here our friend met us, and very soon we were in his comfortable quarters overlooking the Estrella, whose noble pile looked more lovely than ever, the graceful dome gleaming like a mass of white alabaster in the clear moonlight.

SPRING THE THIRD

A VISIT TO THE ALGARVE

WE had carried away such pleasant recollections of our visits to northern and central Portugal, that a trip to the extreme south seemed quite in the natural order of things; especially in view of the enticing rumours which had reached us of very beautiful scenery, hidden away in a certain Serra de Monchique, a mountain range running east and west through the province of the Algarve—the very vagueness of the report adding zest to our desire to explore it. Besides, a veritable halo of romance encircles all this part of the kingdom—its very name, 'Al Garb' (The West—so called from its situation relatively to the rest of the Moorish dominions), being suggestive of that warrior race who, in moments snatched from fighting, loved to dream away life amidst enchanting scenery, fruitful gardens, and well-tilled fields, with plenty of shade and running water—not forgetting a comfortable provision of fortified places to run to in case of need.

A French traveller, describing this province in 1766, referred to it as 'of little importance or utility to the Portuguese monarchy.' It is, nevertheless, dignified with the title of 'kingdom'—the Kingdom of the Algarves, as it is called—a relic of those far-away times when it comprised the entire coast from Cape St. Vincent to Almeria, with the opposite coast of Africa, and including Ceuta and Tangier, which were then in the possession of the Portuguese monarchy.

For centuries the Algarve was a battlefield, whereon was fought out the long struggle for supremacy between the Christians and infidels, in which, as usual, English help was solicited and rendered, and which only came to an end in the thirteenth century, when Portugal attained its present limits.

Three centuries later, when all Portugal went mad over foreign explorations, and nearly every one ran off to the newly discovered eastern Eldorado, and scarcely a labourer was left to till the soil, the great landlords imported African slaves in such numbers that the Algarve was said to be almost entirely repeopled by them. The effects of this unfortunate importation can be traced up to the present day, and may be held to account, in great measure, for the deterioration that has taken place in the Portuguese nation during subsequent centuries.

Before setting out on our travels, there were certain matters concerning which it was imperative to seek for information. For it is never safe, as I have already observed, to strike out a new line in Portugal without making careful inquiries as to accommodation. The most assiduous sightseer can hardly affect indifference to the ills this flesh is heir to, and, if he values his peace of mind—to say nothing of his body—he will, if wise, reduce the risks of disturbance to a minimum.

Now, as the better-class Portuguese never travel if they can help it—there are thousands of people in Lisbon, it is said, who have never set foot south of the Tagus, and the 'sunny south' is not yet the vogue—we found great difficulty in getting information about it. As far as roving Britons are concerned, the Algarve is a veritable *terra incognita*; and very few Portuguese go there from other parts, except on business, and even they can tell you very little worth knowing, seeing that their ideas of comfort have been formed in a somewhat Spartan school.

At last we got an introduction to a very charming Anglicised Portuguese gentleman, who had but recently returned from a visit to the south, and who most kindly gave us the benefit of his experiences, with much useful advice as to means of getting about, and places worth visiting.

'Of course,' said he, 'you must not expect accommodation such as you find in Lisbon, or even at Cintra, for it is only of late that anything that could be called, by courtesy, a hotel has been opened in those remote parts. You know, in Portugal, up to within recent times, no one travelled because there were no hotels; and there were no hotels because no one travelled. But now things are beginning to improve, and no doubt in a few years we shall have decent hotels at most places of interest. In the parts you are going to, although you won't find luxury, the hotels are clean, and the food good, though plain; and you will find the people everywhere simple and obliging.'

His accounts of the places of interest and descriptions of the scenery quite fixed us in our determination to see something of that particular kingdom wherein, as Lord Carnarvon wrote some seventy years ago, 'a British foot had ne'er or rarely been.'

Our arrangements were soon completed, and as there is but one train each way during the twenty-four hours between Lisbon and Faro, the capital of the Algarves, it may be supposed that the traffic between the metropolis and the extreme south is neither vast nor continuous. The terminus is at Barreiro, on the south bank, the same as we departed from for Setubal; and we took the afternoon steamer which connects with the 5 P.M. train. Steam, the great leveller, has swept away 'scaleras,' with their scarlet-clad rowers, and much else; but the prospects of river and shore are much as they were a hundred years ago—the same imposing city 'crowded with convents, towers, and palaces,' while, crowning an eminence, 'the huge mass of the convent of San Vincente looks dark and solemn'; and away over in the Setubal direction, the 'sunset was tinging the distant mountains of Palmella,' exactly as described by a traveller of old.

A short run brought us to the junction for Setubal, where a buffet drew forth the greater part of the passengers for the purpose of getting a 'square meal.' And on resuming the journey, we were relieved to find the occupants of the through-carriage consisted of but two passengers besides ourselves.

The journey to Faro, though but two hundred and ten miles, occupies just twelve hours, at a speed of eighteen miles an hour; but as an excellent first-class through corridor-carriage is provided, with the usual equipment, the journey, in spite of its tediousness, can be accomplished in perfect comfort; and as first-class travellers on this route are as rare as swallows in March, the five compartments of which the carriage consists afford ample room for stretching out at night.

Our fellow-passengers on this occasion were commercial travellers on business bent, who, on learning our intentions and destinations, regarded us with amused wonder, 'for,' said one, in excellent English, 'there is nothing whatever to see at Faro!' The idea of going so far to gaze on 'objects of interest' or scenery evidently tickled these kindly bagmen, whose want of sympathy arose from what an old writer describes as 'the total inability of the natives to comprehend the feelings which prompt an Englishman to forsake the comforts of his native land, and to prosecute a long and fatiguing journey through an uninteresting country.'

Having gazed on us with pitying looks for some time, they sought consolation in their brown-holland bags, supping heartily off the contents, after which they retired to another compartment and made themselves up for the night.

To be sure, there was little enough to gaze on without, for the country was particularly uninteresting,—a flat, unbroken expanse of moorland, covered with stunted scrub, like an unshaven chin, which struggled out of a sandy soil, stretching away in every direction, as far as eye could see. But the Alemtejo (literally, 'beyond the Tagus') is the poorest and most thinly populated province in Portugal, the poverty of soil and lack of water discouraging all attempts at cultivation, with the result that immense tracts are left as nature turned them out, in the first instance—a badly finished job, which man has done nothing to improve on.

Various schemes have been propounded from time to time for turning this barren and profitless heritage to account by 'skifting' the peasantry from the over-populated districts in the north; for there is plenty of elbow-room here, if little else, to attract settlers. But until some means can be devised for improving the water-supply, the inhabitants of the rich and fertile north are not likely to fall in eagerly with the proposed emigration scheme. And even if they did, there would still remain the difficulty of providing money; for it is certain that foreign capital will never flow into Portugal as long as the nation's finances are managed on existing methods. Meanwhile, the 'desolate wastes of the Alemtejo' are given over to herds of swine, which munch and grow fat on the acorns of the evergreen oak, and are converted in due course into hams, which are considered to equal in flavour and quality any in the world.

It is perhaps with the idea of hiding the nakedness of the land from the too curious stranger that the journey through these parts is ordained to take place by night. Personally, I grudge a night journey through a strange country, as, however uninteresting the landscape, one likes to carry away some impressions of the country; and, in the present instance, once you have traversed the Alemtejo, there is said to be some pretty scenery along the route, the greater part of which is passed at an hour when the arms of Morpheus encircle its victims in the firmest of grips.

And yet a night journey in such a climate has its compensations. The soft, silky air is heavily charged with aromatic odours, rising from the innumerable sweet-smelling shrubs which abound even on the wild moorlands of the Alemtejo—lavender and the gum-cistus might almost be called the weeds of Portugal, besides rosemary, juniper, myrtle, and innumerable species of bulbous plants which freckle Nature's fair face; while overhead, the heavens present a wondrous expanse of splendour, the stars flashing down on one like diamonds from a velvet setting. The coolness of the night air, too, is so delicious, so soothing, that one is tempted to lie with head out of window for hours, breathing in the refreshing fragrance.

Stations are few and far between. There is a longish halt at the junction for Evora, and again at Beja; but nobody seems to get in or out, and there is a depressing absence of stir anywhere. The quiet of our corridor-carriage was only once disturbed during the night, and it came about in this wise. At Beja a fine old country gentleman—one of the olden time—got in, and, settling into a corner, slept away most delectably till the small hours of the morning, when his 'beauty sleep' was abruptly terminated by an intruding rustic. It seemed that the old gentleman had forgotten to tell the guard to arouse him at his destination. Consequently, as the train was beginning to move out of a small roadside station, at about 3 A.M., a boor burst into the carriage, rushed frantically from compartment to compartment, and at length discovering his quarry, seized the old gentleman without a word, and bustled him along the passage and out on to the platform before he had properly realised what all the fuss was about.

We stayed awake as long as we could, for it seemed almost an insult to Nature to sleep through such an exquisite night. But Nature willed it otherwise, and soon after midnight we settled ourselves comfortably to rest—the commercial gentlemen snoring away like the porkers of the Alemtejo in an adjoining compartment.

Directly the first faint streaks of early dawn flushed the eastern sky, our ears were greeted with sounds of awakening life, and, gazing out, we were rejoiced to find that the hours of darkness had wrought a complete transformation in the face of Nature. We were now in a land of corn and wine and fruit-trees, where Nature, discarding the austerity of the preceding evening, was all geniality and smiles.

By 4.30 the sun was 'looking up' his old haunts; birds were in full song, and the labourers were afield—for, be it observed, the 'working day' in Portugal lasts from sunrise to sunset, with a couple of hours 'spell off' at midday, when the labourers literally 'flop down' in their tracks. I have seen men lying in the furrows, and masons coiled up in the litter of their work, as if enjoying the luxury of a feather-bed. The inspiriting cry for a 'living wage' and an 'eight-hours day,' with long evenings for 'improving the mind,' has not reached to the land of Camoens.

At 5 A.M., on as lovely a morning as it is possible to conceive in this unfinished world, we drew up at the haven we had longed for—the Faro station, which was a crimson blaze of geranium, the walls and even roof being almost enveloped in it. There was neither crowd nor confusion—we were the solitary arrivals! And in bright sunshine—the crisp morning air making us feel as blithe as larks—we strolled over to the hotel, a couple of hundred yards away.

Notwithstanding the unseasonableness of the hour, we found the senhora who presided here all smiles and anxiety to be kind, and we were at once invited to seek repose between the sheets. But just the least suggestion of a fragrance that was not of new-mown hay, or even of lavender, which had assailed our nostrils on entry, became convincingly apparent as we made a tour of the establishment; and by the time we had reached the very best bedroom of all, and exchanged confidences, we agreed that this was no haven to tarry in, and, to the astonishment of the hostess, not only declined her beds, but ordered our luggage to be left in the hall.

Os Ingleses were known to be eccentric, but that a lady and gentleman should reach the southern metropolis at 5 A.M. and not fly to bed instanter was a revelation of character which staggered the good woman. And when we ordered coffee, and went out for a walk to talk over plans, the senhora gave up the attempt to solve the enigma of the British character in despair, and, I have reason to believe, went back to bed.

We had come provided with letters of introduction, including one to the British Consul at Faro, which important official we decided on looking up as early as we decently could, seeing that he was a married man of mature age, whose partner would of course resent being wakened up at an unearthly hour by two peripatetic strangers. Besides, being a Portuguese, he would naturally be averse to transacting business before 'business hours'; so, to while away the time, we wandered off on a voyage of discovery, directing our steps, according to our wont, to the market, which was awake even thus early, but poorly supplied. We spied some ripe figs, though the month of May was still young; but fruit in the Algarves is a fortnight in advance of other parts; and, laying in a supply of oranges, we sought out a sunny seat on the esplanade near a miserable patch of ornamental garden. Here some sickly palms, with other semi-tropical plants, were dragging out a squalid existence under the depressing influence of dust and periodic waterings.

The prospect before us was not entrancing. We gazed across a vast expanse of mud—it might have been Weston-super-Mare,—which, at low tide, represents the harbour here, the horizon being bounded by sand-dunes, beyond which was said to be the sea. Midway across the mud-flats we discovered a Portuguese man-of-war, high and dry, reposing snugly enough on her self-made bed of mud. The truth of the commercial gentleman's remark began to dawn on us—that there was nothing to be seen at Faro.

When the clock struck eight, we could no longer control our impatience, being convinced that every self-respecting Consul, be he Portuguese or Jew, should be about his master's business by that time; and suiting the action to the thought, we set off on a search for this important official. After being directed here, there, and everywhere but the right place, we at last got hold of a policeman—one of the Guarda Civile—who, after a few moments' consideration, motioned us to follow, and away we went, though in quite the opposite direction to the one we had been going, and, after passing through many tortuous lanes and smelly alleys, arrived at a door where by dint of much knocking an inhabitant was roused up, who informed our cicerone that he had come to the wrong shop. Some further conversation took place, in an unknown tongue, and our guide, with profuse apologies, made us retrace our steps the whole way we had come, when, lo and behold! within a few paces of the very spot he had dragged us from, a board with the British lion on it, denoting the official abode of the Consul, was hanging over a doorway!

Our would-be guide had gone to so much trouble in his efforts to assist, and was so profoundly abashed at the wild-goose chase he had led us, that, out of sheer pity, I pressed into his unwilling palm a hundred reis note (fivepence). The poor fellow was so overcome with gratitude that he seized my extended hand with both of his own and pressed it again and again; and, not content with this public demonstration of regard, the good man must needs repeat the performance with my wife, exclaiming all the time, 'Obrigado, Senhor! muito obrigado!'

And now to business, said we. But many moments elapsed before any response came to our knockings. At length a small trap-door, which had escaped notice, lifted, and a most ancient and venerable head popped out and demanded our business. Having put our case, and explained that we were wandering Britons stranded in a strange town in need of advice, and presented our letter of introduction, the venerable head popped in again, the trap-door banged to, and there was silence for a while. Then a sound of drawing bolts fell on our ears; the official door was thrown open, and behold, the British Consul in his dressing-gown! and, doubtless, inwardly cursing such an unseasonable visit. We were waved to chairs, and after an exchange of compliments and apologies on our part, the old gentleman explained that he 'had very little English,' but that his chief clerk was a remarkably accomplished linguist; and although he had not yet arrived—ten o'clock being the usual hour of his appearance—he should be directed to wait on us at our hotel and arrange what was needed. We made our bows and retired; but it occurred to us that a British Consul, or rather Vice-Consul, who ' had very little English,' was somewhat of a *roi fainant*. Still, there was the chief clerk.

Now, it had been part of the programme to make Faro our headquarters for a few days, making excursions by carriage to the various places of interest within driving distance; and thence to work along the coast westwards to Lagos and Sagres, perhaps even to Cape St. Vincent. In any case, we hoped to have driven to the mouth of the Guadiana, not a great distance off, and which constitutes the frontier between Spain and Portugal, and up its west bank as far as Villa Real de S. Antonio—a town to which a very curious history is attached.

The story of the way in which this place came into being reads like an Eastern fairy tale, in which an all-powerful king or his vizier exclaims, 'Let there be a city!' and behold a city springs up there and then; and although Villa Real can hardly be said to have sprung up in a night, the circumstances of its origin throw such a curious light on the way things were managed under the régime of Portugal's greatest minister, the Marquis of Pombal, that the story will bear repeating, especially as it is unknown to Britons.

I have already explained, in a previous chapter, that one of the great Marquis's hobbies was the encouragement of native trade and manufactures, and this he rode without much regard to vested interests, or respect for the rights of those already engaged in commerce and manufactures. His efforts, however, in these directions, for want of knowledge and experience, were characterised by more zeal than discretion, and nearly all ended disastrously. So much so, that within a few years of his fall every part of the country bore marks of his ill-advised enterprises, in the shape of ruined buildings and impoverished landowners.

Now, amongst his grand schemes was a project for the development and encouragement of the sardine fishery—or, as writers of the last century call it, the 'pilchard' fishery—which, undoubtedly, under judicious management was capable of very considerable development, and of proving a source of wealth to the nation.

But, unfortunately, Pombal, like most despotic ministers, was much too proud to follow the advice of experts; and although he had directed a Dezembargador, or Judge, to examine and report upon the scheme, he no sooner discovered the report to be unfavourable to his project than he seized the Judge, and clapped him into a dungeon.

The result of this contempt for 'expert' advice is to be seen in the town of Villa Real, which has been instanced as a 'standing monument of the Marquis of Pombal's obstinacy and vanity.'

The facts may be thus briefly summarised. Pombal wished to encourage the sardine fisheries of the Algarves; but, at the same time, his vanity prompted him to build a fine new town in sight of his neighbours and rivals, the Spaniards, which would give him command of the river and trade. There was already a fishing-village at the mouth of the Guadiana, occupying a position admirably suited for working the sardine-nets, where the fish had been caught and cured for centuries past; and there, undoubtedly, was the proper place for the new town. It was on this spot, moreover, that the impartial Judge advised it to be built, adducing many excellent reasons in favour of his recommendation.

But Pombal thought he knew best; and, being confirmed in his opinion by a crowd of sycophants who were always ready to soothe his vanity the better to gain their own ends, he gave orders for the new town to be built where it now stands, nearly opposite to Ayamonte on the Spanish side, without any regard to the unsuitability of the situation for the particular purpose in view.

An English traveller who visited the town in 1778, within a short time of its completion, described it as beautifully situated, with plenty of deep water and room for shipping; an extensive quay with a spacious landing-place, and a handsome custom-house; the houses all built regularly on a uniform plan, with a neatness to be seen nowhere else in Portugal; the streets well-paved, built by the line, and crossing each other at right angles; two large inns for the accommodation of travellers, and a neat square in the centre of the town, with a church on one side of it, and a town-house on the other, and a large marble fountain, which threw up water to a considerable height, in the middle.

'Such was this new creation of the late Minister, which by its appearance at a distance had raised our curiosity,' wrote the Englishman; 'but on coming into it there was not a living soul to be seen in the streets, nor even in the town, if we except the Juiz de fora, and a sergeant's guard daily relieved from Castro-Marin.'

The most delectable part of the story remains to be told—namely, the way in which the funds for this expensive folly were raised; for it never cost the king a farthing!

Pombal, having obtained through his Viceroy a circumstantial account of every person of property in the province, directed him to call each one into his presence, and to inform him that his Majesty had formed the design of building a new town, with a view to encouraging the trade and fisheries on the coast of the Algarve, and would esteem it highly if he would contribute for that purpose.

Now, in those golden days of Portuguese monarchy, a hint of this sort was considered equivalent to a command; and terms of agreement being ready prepared for signing, each person was thus induced to sign a bond by which he bound himself, within a stipulated time, to raise a building upon the spot assigned him.

And in this manner S. Antonio was conjured into being.

To complete the full measure of his folly, Pombal ordered the fishermen to leave their old quarters at Monte Gordo, and take up their abode in the new town.

They obeyed the first part of the precept, but instead of coming to S. Antonio they passed over to Spain, where they remained till Pombal was turned out of office, and then returned quietly to their old habitations.

The story is a striking illustration of 'the ruinous consequences of uncontrolled authority lodged in the hands of a single despot.'

Perhaps Lord Carnarvon's estimate of Pombal's character as a statesman is the most just that has been made: ' His public conduct was not based on any public principles, and he entered into a most unrighteous war against the nobility, not because he thought their privileges incompatible with the well-being of other classes, but from a mean and rancorous jealousy of an order to which he did not naturally belong.'

At the appointed hour the Consul's chief clerk was announced; and to our surprise there was ushered in a dapper young gentleman, of pleasant manners, who spoke English fluently, and proved a very 'friend indeed,' for he threw himself into our plans with the most hearty goodwill, and arranged everything to our complete satisfaction, expressing himself at the same time as delighted beyond measure at having been afforded the opportunity of helping us.

As we had decided that it was not good for us to be here longer than could be helped—a peep into the rival establishment showing that there was only a choice of evils—the first part of our travel programme had to be cut out, and our obliging young friend assured us that our best plan would be to go straight to Monchique, where the hotel was known to be good, make that our headquarters, and from thence pay visits to Lagos, and other places of interest further westward.

To reach Monchique, however, it would be necessary to retrace our steps a short way up the line we had come by, to a place called Messines, the third station out from Faro, where a carriage could be procured for the drive to Monchique, our friend kindly undertaking to 'wire' orders for the carriage to be ready for us on arrival that very evening.

And so, all being satisfactorily arranged, there was nothing to be done but to while away the time by sight-seeing till the train left at 6.30 P.M.

A very cursory examination of the town, however, confirmed the truth of the bagman's statement, and we were by no means sorry when the hour of our departure was at hand.

Personally, I carried away anything but pleasant recollections of the place. I was extremely unwell, and in great pain all day, and derived but little consolation from the interesting reflection that Faro was the Ossonoba of the ancients, and was probably built by the Carthaginians.

Far more interesting is it to know that Faro was one of the many Peninsular ports that English fleets made havoc of, before and after Armada days, when Spaniards and 'Portingales' were all lumped together as a pack of murdering rascals who had to be taught respect for the English flag. The most notable pillage was in 1595-6, when, after taking Cadiz, the fleet came on here, and after plundering and burning the town, carried away the library of the celebrated Jeronymo Ozorio, Bishop of Silves, by way of a memento, or perchance as a means of beguiling the tedium of the voyage home, seeing that ships' libraries were not supplied till a couple of centuries later. This part of the plunder, says a writer of the last century, fell to the share of the Earl of Essex—it must have been dull reading for the tars,—and he passed it on to the University of Oxford. One wonders if the spoils are still there.

It was pleasing to reflect that by the bestowal of a hundred-reis note on a local policeman, I had done something to remove the bad impression left by British seamen in 1596.

The only mark of Moorish influence that came under observation here was one that is common to the whole of Portugal—namely, the dignity which petty officials contrive to throw into the performance of their duties. Here, at Faro, I had occasion to send a telegram to a friend in Lisbon. The telegraph-office was proportionate to the importance of the southern metropolis, and the customary air of *dolce far niente* prevailed throughout the establishment. After writing my message, I handed the form through a window to an official who was rapt in those profound meditations which engross the minds of all Government employés during working-hours, and who seemed annoyed at the interruption. After leisurely perusing the document, he handed it back, waving me to an office on the opposite side of the hall. Here another senhor had to be disturbed; nevertheless, he condescendingly accepted the paper, perused its contents, and informed me of the amount to be paid. The message was then stamped, and I was on the point of departing, feeling a perfect brute for giving so much trouble, when once more the document was thrust back. Under the impression that I had committed some grave breach of etiquette, I was about to apologise, when the official, with a magnificent air, waved me back to the other window again, where official number one was graciously pleased to re-accept the paper, and, having again examined it, banged to the window, and the little comedy ended.

To be sure, no Government but a Portuguese would have hit on the happy expedient of maintaining a duplicate establishment for the despatch of telegrams, for no object, as far as one could see, than as a means of providing a livelihood for a number of useless dependants. But Government offices in this functionary-ridden land are arranged with a view to finding food for the greatest possible number of vultures, all intent on pecking away at the rapidly decaying carcass of State.

Our young friend, the chief clerk, came to see us off, and at 6.30 we joyfully shook the dust of Faro from off our feet. The evening was lovely, and our route lay through what Costigan, who passed through the province more than a century ago, described as 'a beautiful flat country, consisting mostly of enclosed corn-fields, covered with almond-trees interspersed with the St. John's breadfruit-tree, pomegranate, fig, and olive.'

The run of thirty odd miles occupied over an hour and three-quarters, and it was dark by the time we reached Messines, where, to our surprise, we met our bagman acquaintances of the previous night, who, evidently, by their looks, thought us crazier than ever getting out at such a benighted spot instead of going straight back to Lisbon, like themselves.

Gazing into the gloom, we descried a 'shut-shay' and a pair of horses, whose driver was evidently on the look-out for *os Ingleses*. And after rattling over the cobble-paved streets of a small town, we plunged into pitchy darkness, only made blacker by contrast with the zone illumined by the carriage lamps, and soon began to realise that there was something amiss with the road; in fact, one would have thought from the motion that we were traversing a series of pits and mounds, suggestive of a cross-country track, or an 'obstacle race.' For three weary and most uncomfortable hours did we roll and pitch and labour over that unconscionable tract without even the satisfaction of knowing what all the fuss was about, until I began to imagine myself back once more in China, *en route* for Pekin, and was enabled to enforce, by means of an object-lesson, what I had often vainly sought to explain to the companion of my travels when describing a journey in a north China cart—namely, that after taking your seat, you lose it directly you start, and never find it again till the end of the journey.

The stars had become obscured, soon after starting, a few ominous patterings on the windows bespoke a change, and presently the rain came down in torrents, and lasted without intermission for the rest of the journey. Then one of the lamps went out, and as the other only emitted a sickly flicker, we expected every moment to end our travels in a ditch; and in true philosophic spirit we lay back, and, like St. Paul, wished for daylight.

At last there was a shimmer of lights ahead, a few isolated wine-shops were passed, and presently we were rattling through the dark and deserted streets of a town. 'Monchique at last,' thought we; and pleasant visions of supper, clean rooms, and comfortable beds revived our depressed spirits. At length, turning abruptly into a side-street, the driver pulled sharply up, and the carriage was at a standstill. 'Thank goodness, here we are!' we inwardly ejaculated, and a feeling of exhilaration came over us at the prospect of a good night's rest after thirty hours of travel and sightseeing. But alas! these pleasing visions were rudely dashed by a glance into the surrounding gloom. The rain was still falling in sheets; the driver, a dripping mass of humanity and wet clothes, was hammering at a door which appeared to lead into a wretched hovel in a blind-alley, and the prospect that slowly dawned on our wearied gaze was far from exhilarating. At last the door was opened by a slattern of a girl, disclosing a steep stair leading to what appeared to be the roof, and the driver invited us to alight. 'Well,' said we, 'if this is Monchique, the sooner we get back to Lisbon the better.' It was then we elicited the melancholy news that this was the *estalagem* at Silves, that the horses could go no further that night, that here was the usual stopping-place, and that next morning we could continue our journey to Monchique—if we wished. There was nothing for it but to make the best of things, and bad enough they were.

Climbing the stairs, we were received at the top by an aged hag, who did the honours of the establishment. First we were shown a room which combined the dirt of a native kitchen with the dismal meanness of a *sala de jantar*, and apparently fulfilled both purposes; and on asking to see the *quartos a dormir*, a door was thrown open displaying a large empty room, absolutely guiltless of everything but an iron bedstead, with straw mattress and pillow, and a broken chair. 'Outro!' we exclaimed, and away we were led to what was doubtless the best room in the 'hotel,' equipped in the same luxurious style, but with the additional comforts of a basin, a broken chair, and a table. The window was large, and opened on to the main street, and as the air seemed sweet, we ordered up our belongings. Meanwhile the ancient hag brought in the 'bed linen,' made up the bed, and placed a jug of water in the basin. The arrival of a towel provided with deep lace frilling completed the preparations, and gave quite an air of grandeur to the wash-stand.

Inquiries on the subject of refreshment having disclosed the nakedness of the land—black coffee without milk, at midnight, not being exactly calculated to promote slumber—we threw our wet and weary selves on to the bed 'all-standing,' and slept the sleep of the tired.

To have opened our luggage under such conditions would have been simply to invite an influx of little visitors; and as we had no particular desire to carry away more disagreeable reminiscences of our visit than need be, we kept everything tight closed, and, for the same reason, remained on top of the bed, instead of creeping inside.

Directly there was light enough next morning, I performed such ablutions as were possible with a saucer and a laced handkerchief for drying purposes, and sallied forth to investigate our surroundings.

Now Silves, as it happened, was one of the places especially commended to our notice, seeing that it had been the last resting-place of the Moors before their final expulsion from Portugal, and was said to contain many marks of Arab occupancy. Part of the old Moorish wall that encircled the town was visible from our window.

Sallying out before cock-crow, I climbed the steep ascent leading to the old portion of the town, which crowned a hill, and presently arrived at an open space on the hillside, where an early market was being held just without the principal gate. A collection of graceful water-jars and black and red pottery was spread out on the turf, around which many picturesque figures were grouped with the ease and grace of pose that comes so naturally to southerners. I seemed all at once to be transported back to Tangier. Never, in fact, since the days I spent in that fascinating Moorish city, many, many years ago, had Moor-land been brought so vividly before me. Those beautiful water-jars, with their long, slender necks and classic forms, seemed to carry one back for hundreds of years—connecting-links, possibly, with times more remote even than those of the Romans.

Having peeped in through the old gateway, and laid in a supply of bread and fruit, I hastened back to hurry up the driver, who had but just emerged from his lair. He was rubbing his eyes, and probably cursing *os Ingleses* for their confounded early-rising and bustling ways; and it was only by a frequent repetition of the nearest equivalent in the Portuguese language for 'hurry up,' that I succeeded in convincing him that we really wanted to be off.

In old days, before the introduction of railways and *trens de aluguer*, with their Jehu-like drivers, the Lisbon coachies were proverbial for their slowness and conscientious objection to hurry; and the story is handed down of an English lady-resident who, after exhausting all her powers of expostulation and sarcasm, at last exclaimed in despair: 'Is there nothing that will prevail on you to make haste?' upon which the driver, a well-known character called José, quietly pulled up his mules, and, looking round, replied: 'I never made haste when I was young; I am now seventy years old, and that is not the time of life to begin'; and turning round, he resumed his customary pace.

To breakfast in the pig-hole we had passed the night in was out of the question; and so, having replenished our commissariat from outside sources, we determined on getting away as soon as possible. Daylight had revealed the weak points of the establishment with a vengeance. Large rat-holes, which bore evidence of frequent use, afforded easy communication with the room below, which discovered itself to be a wine-shop; while the winds of heaven and earth ran in and out through gaping cracks in the boards of which wall and ceiling were constructed. Never since I passed a night in a Chinese caravansary, on the road to Pekin, had I rested in so squalid a shanty —and it was called an hotel! So novel, indeed, was the experience to one of the party, that all sorts of interesting possibilities were passed in review—midnight robbers, assassins, murder, and orphans! With such agreeable dreams does the fertile imagination busy itself.

I have gone into matters somewhat minutely because, as was subsequently explained to me, this particular *estalagem* is the usual stopping-place, a sort of half-way house, for travellers *en route* to the mineral baths of Caldas Monchique, the most famous invalid resort in south Portugal. I think it only right that intending visitors to that particular sanatorium should be forewarned of the accommodation provided, and thus escape the shock we experienced.

By eight we were 'all aboard' and *en route*, and, truth to say, in fairly good spirits; for, in spite of our decidedly damp clothes, the rain having penetrated the carriage pretty freely the night before, and the 'hard lying' we had experienced—for we had fallen on no bed of roses, —we had slept soundly; and as we drove through the crisp morning air laden with the scent of orange-blossom, and under a spotless expanse of azure blue, we did full justice to our bread and fruit, washed down with the wine of the country.

Most of all did we congratulate ourselves on having carried away no little reminders of our lodging, vowing inwardly, at the same time, that wild horses should not drag us up to that particular garret again, even if we had to coil ourselves up in the carriage.

In justice to the management, I must admit that the charges were reasonable ; though, to be sure, we had not subjected the resources to a severe strain.

The day was heavenly. Every vestige of last night's storm had been swept away. The sun shone brightly; and although at starting there was a very perceptible nip in the air, the genial sunshine soon warmed us through, and there was a delicious feeling of exhilaration in the sense of rapid movement through a lovely country, with anticipations of safe arrival at the haven we had longed for. All depressing recollections of the night's experiences soon vanished under these genial influences.

> 'Oh evil day ! if I were sullen
> While the earth herself is adorning
> This sweet May morning,'

as Wordsworth sang.

The first mile or two led through a cultivated valley of the utmost fertility, past a succession of well-kept orange groves, gardens, and fruit orchards, interspersed with cornfields.

The Moors knew what they were about when they made Silves their headquarters; and many a glance backwards did we steal towards the picturesque little town, perched on top of a conical hill in mid-valley, and glistening brightly in the morning sunshine.

In front rose a chaos of low hills, with higher ones

beyond, while in the blue distance towered up the peaks of the lofty Serra de Monchique, whither we were bound.

On entering a tangle of valleys cultivation ceased, and here Nature was allowed to exercise her own sweet sway, clothing hills and valleys with an unrelieved expanse of the gum-cistus in all its varied colourings—yellow, rose, and snow-white streaked with purple; but the beauty had fled from the flowers, and we could only judge of the splendour that once was theirs from patches of bloom that clung to the trees in sheltered spots.

Lord Carnarvon, who traversed this same district a few weeks earlier in the season, was entranced with the beauty of the scene. He describes how one passes 'for hours together through mountain defiles, and over plains covered as far as the eye can reach with the tall and unvarying *cistus ladaniferus,*' and goes on to describe how 'the graceful form of this plant, its green glistening leaves, its large, white, sleepy-looking flowers heavily spotted with purple, and meeting the sight in every direction, are not without their influence on the mind. There is a fascination in the gorgeous monotony and universal stillness of the scene, in the solemn splendour of the never-clouded sun and sky, and in the heavy and almost enervating fragrance with which that all-prevailing cistus loads the air.'

The road, which had been really excellent so far, now came to an abrupt end a quarter of a mile short of a very ancient bridge of many arches, spanning a river. Here we had to leave the raised causeway and 'make tracks' across country, pitching and plunging in a way that threatened destruction to springs, and then dash up the embankment again, on to the bridge, over which we bumped and rattled in glorious style, and so on for another few hundred yards till we picked up the road again. Was it any wonder that the driver 'bucked' at the prospect of facing this 'trap' the night before?

Why the enlightened administration with which Portugal is at present blessed has shrunk from completing this half-mile of road I could get no one to explain. All I ascertained was that matters had been in this state for several years past, and were likely to remain so.

I felt inclined to exclaim with Southey, 'Almost I regret the Moors: what has this country gained by their expulsion?' It is only when we begin to locate the 'golden age' that we find it recedes ever further back, like a will-o'-the-wisp!

And now for some miles we followed the banks of a river—a sluggish stream of dirty water, so different to the north-country rivers,—reminding one of the sluggish streams at home so aptly characterised by the oft-recurring name of 'Ouse.' Still, the banks were prettily fringed with graceful tamarisk; and strips of garden with oleander hedges, through which the crimson pomegranate flower gleamed, relieved the 'lulling influence of the great cistus wastes.'

At length our ways parted, the river taking a bend to the southward, soon to drown its sorrows in the Atlantic, and our road commencing the long and gentle ascent which winds through the cistus-clad hills to the beauteous regions beyond.

The road was admirably engineered, and, strange to say, in good repair, and the near prospect of a good square meal and cleanliness at our journey's end made us take a less jaundiced view of things than had been the case a few hours earlier.

Slowly the range of view widened out on emerging from the valleys; while in front, peeps of the jagged peaks became more frequent, and we could even discern habitations high up on the mountains.

We seemed to be clinging to the side of a deepish gully running up between two spurs of the main serra, and at length, on turning a corner, came plump on to a hamlet of scattered houses sunk in a narrow ravine ending abruptly on the mountain-side.

A smart villa or two, run up in that garish, tasteless style which endears itself to the modern Portuguese, stood out from the rest; and while we were marking well their towers, the carriage suddenly swerved from the road, and, following a steep and narrow track, plunged downwards. In another moment we pulled sharply up in a quagmire of mud at a mean-looking building, where some natives were hanging listlessly about, their faces wearing the expression of half-amused wonder that invariably suffuses the countenances of the better class Portuguese at sight of foreigners.

'Well,' thought we, on observing the mean and squalid surroundings, 'this is a queer "turn-out" for a fashionable "thermal establishment"; still, appearances may be delusive. Let us hope that things are better than they seem.' Picking my way through the filth I saluted the assembled crowd, presenting at the same time my credentials, in the shape of a letter to the agent for the property, which our kind friend the Consul's clerk had provided me with.

After the address had been well studied and the letter passed from hand to hand, there was a general response of 'Nao sei, senhor!' I afterwards learned that the addressee had long been gathered to his fathers, showing that the Consul's clerk was a bit of a humorist!

There was nothing for it but to play my trump card in the shape of a letter of introduction to the medical gentleman at the head of the establishment. The effect was immediate, and in another moment I was chatting away pleasantly with Doctor C—— B——, who, after the manner of 'the friend in need,' proved a truly courteous and kindly 'friend indeed.' To be sure, his English was limited, but he spoke French and German fluently, and with his help we selected our room, disposed our belongings therein, and proceeded to refresh the inner man. And really, all things considered, I am bound to confess the place was not nearly so bad as might have been inferred from appearances.

And now, a brief sketch of the 'establishment' will enable the reader to follow our movements and enter into our feelings, even if it should fail to excite a longing to follow in our footsteps.

The mineral springs, whence the place derives its fame, gush forth at the head of a narrow gully, which terminates abruptly on the mountain-side like a 'blind-alley.' The 'establishment' is designed on the most primitive, almost squalid, scale, and consists of a long low building, following the downward course of the stream, and containing baths and various offices. Closely adjoining this is another wretched-looking building, dignified with the name of 'hotel,' the lower part of which is occupied by village shops.

All this huddle of buildings stands in a sort of pit, facing south, and I should imagine the want of ventilation must render the place unendurably stuffy in hot weather.

There are neither 'grounds' nor gardens, though a sort of jungle-walk of a hundred yards or so along the side of the stream is dignified with the name of 'paradise'—which is anything but complimentary, one would think, to the real thing!

To be sure, there is the mountain-side to roam about on; but precipitous slopes, granite boulders, and a dense undergrowth, hardly constitute an ideal airing-ground for invalids.

This particular Caldas has been frequented from very early times: even now Roman coins are turned up with the spade, and the fact of one of the early kings of Portugal having derived great benefit from the waters is proudly cited in proof of their virtues. The existing establishment was founded by the Bishop of Silves in the last century; and although improvements have found their way here since those primitive times, the original baths are still in use, and are of interest as examples of early art applied to tubbing.

As will be found the case at all thermal establishments in Portugal, a large portion is reserved for the use of the very poor, the accommodation provided being sufficient, if plain—for the poor tub *en masse*, and prefer it: they were ever gregarious. Patients of this class are treated with every kindness and consideration, and it was most gratifying to observe the esteem in which our worthy cicerone, Doctor C—— B——, was held by them, and the respect shown to him.

For paying-patients more modern appliances are provided. Those who are content with simple fare and a total absence of luxury find accommodation in the 'establishment.' The hotel, which is under separate management, being resorted to by people accustomed to the average comforts pertaining to a low state of civilisation—there are no luxuries even here.

The spring from whence the baths are supplied is copious, and rises at a tepid heat: the waters are especially beneficial in cases of rheumatism. Senhor C—— pointed out some quite miraculous cures amongst his poorer patients—men who had been carried in as hopeless cripples, and were now able to walk. One could only regret that where Nature had done so much in the way of providing the raw material, man had assisted her so little in the supply of accessories for the poor specimens of afflicted humanity who come to worship at this particular thermal shrine.

The establishment, until within the last year or so, has been under Government management. What that means, the reader who happens to be acquainted with Portugal can surmise! It is now leased to a company, the management being vested in Senhor C——, who, if I mistake not —and if the needful funds are forthcoming—will presently work a transformation. For Senhor C—— is a man of enlightened views, has travelled, and is ambitious, and was kind enough to confide in us some of his schemes for regenerating the place and placing things on an up-to-date footing. And assuredly there is ample room for improvement. Senhor C—— is in his second term of office here. The first he held many years ago, when it was a Government concern. Since then, Senhor C—— has travelled in Germany, where he made the acquaintance of all the physicians of repute in the particular branch of cure he is interested in, visited all the important waters, and made himself thoroughly familiar with the arrangements in vogue at the best establishments in that land of scientific tubbing. He even visited Pastor Kniep, and after a careful study of his system became a convert, and is now so thoroughly convinced of its soundness that, since his return, he has become an enthusiast for cold water, plain diet, and bare feet, and has made several proselytes.

We derived a vast deal of amusement from watching the worthy senhor and his disciples plodding about in the filth and sticky mud which abounds here in wet weather, with all the fervent zeal of converts to a new form of belief. To be sure, the soles of the feet were protected by grass sandals, but no sandals are proof against the mud of this delectable spot, and the consequences were not nice.

Now, I have studied the system of Pastor Kniep as set forth in his book, but I can find no reference to mud as a factor in the cure; and for that reason—to say nothing of having arrived at an age when mud-larking seems frivolous and the body is susceptible to chills.—I have remained deaf to the voice of the charmer and the persuasive eloquence of an enthusiast. I even ventured to turn up my nose at the Kniep bread which was provided, in the shape of a half-baked, sticky mass of brown stuff, suggestive of the nasty little bread pellets that schoolboys manufacture from new bread.

I was assured by one of the proselytes that the benefits accruing from the practice of going barefooted are indisputable, and quite palpable to the eye. The first thing is improved circulation, and after a few days the bad blood, or poison, in the system 'erupts,' in the form of red spots, and you begin to feel better—inwardly ejaculating, 'It is doing me a lot of good!' All of which, said the fair enthusiast—for it was a lady who confessed—goes to prove that the human extremities were never intended to be enveloped in warm wrappings. To all of which one might rejoin that we have a much more venerable precedent for perambulating the earth as nature made us—with the simple addition of fig leaves; but even savages find an extra leaf or two convenient when the thermometer drops below freezing-point.

Well, it is refreshing to see human beings acting up to their belief, however absurd the form it assumes. For my own part, not even the author of 'Logic' would convince me that 'splodging about' in filth is otherwise than nasty, if not disreputable, however sweet may be the sensations arising from contact with dewy grass, according to the *régime* of the inventor, the late Pastor Kniep, who—strange coincidence !—left this world for other fields while we were at Caldas de Monchique, and, for aught we know, may be gazing down at this very moment and inwardly chuckling on his disciples in Portugal.

Considered as a health resort, the shortcomings of the place are only too palpable. To begin with, there is no place within easy reach where invalids, accustomed to the simple usages of civilised existence, can walk about or even sit down, without being confronted with a great deal of 'matter in the wrong place.' To step out of the door, in wet weather, at any rate, is to plunge into a very slough of despond—even strong shoes threatened divorce in the attempt to extricate them from the sticky soil. True, there was a courtyard, measuring a few feet each way, where a seat or two adorning the sides invited the weary to rest; but suggestions of decaying vegetables, and even animal matter, from sundry nooks and corners—the sight of which at once reminded one of many runnings backwards and forwards at certain hours of the day, and of furtive emptyings of pots and pans and other kitchen utensils, by the people belowstairs, who were intent only on quick despatch—somewhat marred the enjoyment of even this sylvan scene.

An old woman with a broom, say once a month, or, if the funds of the establishment would admit of so much extravagance, once a week, would have worked wonders. But every one seemed pleased and happy; and it would have ill become a stranger to have tempted the inhabitants of this happy valley to taste of the fruit of the tree of knowledge of good and evil, or even to have instilled a 'healthy spirit of discontent,' which wise men assure us is at the root of all progress in this world.

'Where ignorance is bliss, 'tis folly to be wise,' says the copy-book maxim; but the proverbial 'exception,' in this case surely applies to matters sanitary, where 'ignorance,' with its attendant evils, brings about a state of things the reverse of blissful.

Meanwhile, dirt and litter and *dolce far niente* prevail everywhere in this charming 'health resort.' And it is most fervently to be hoped that the company will soon find the funds for enabling their energetic and enlightened director to give shape to his many schemes of 'betterment'—otherwise there must be a catastrophe ere long. For, without going into details which would be out of place anywhere but in a sanitary inspector's report, I may say that incongruities exist here which would 'make a cat laugh,' and over which the 'polite letter-writer' must perforce draw the veil of oblivion.

A word or two concerning the 'hotel.' On the whole, and relatively to its surroundings, it might be described, in the words so often on the lips of a canny Scot when he fears to commit himself to a definite statement that might be used against him, as 'no' that bad'! Our bedroom—the best in the house—was well enough, roomy, clean, with even a sprinkling of furniture. Yes, this is quite true; for, on referring to my notes, I find mention of a washstand, chairs, and even a table was forthcoming, after some hunting about; and what more could the most exigent of British travellers want? But when it came to a bath, surprise, indignation, and dismay, all in turn, manifested themselves on the countenances of our attendants—we had quite a good congregation, considering it was the usual hour of *siesta* when we began turning the establishment inside out,—and there was dire consternation when we explained that life was not worth living without a morning tub, and that we should not be happy till we got it. A long consultation followed, resulting in the despatch of an envoy to the director, who, by way of solving the difficulty, proposed we should bathe at the 'establishment,' and kindly placed all the baths at our disposal. But the horrors of the 'middle passage' to be faced every morning, in a state of deshabille, did not strike one of the party as a particularly exhilarating prospect, and we declined with thanks. At length there was a shout from the bottom of the stairs, and, amid peals of laughter, a bath, big enough to have accommodated quite a large party *en famille*, was triumphantly carried in. Whether it was a relic of Roman times, or had been dug up, or simply rediscovered in some long-forgotten nook, history recordeth not, but we expressed our delight, and all went swimmingly afterwards.

The preparation of the morning tub was quite an interesting event. The water, drawn fresh from the mineral spring, warm and sparkling, was brought across in an immense 'forty-thieves jar' by a labourer, who, on arrival at our door, was relieved of his burden by a laughing damsel, installed as our guide, philosopher, friend, and most devoted slave.

Happily, the beds were irreproachable, the linen was of spotless whiteness, and the mattresses were spring.

The Sala de Jantar was chiefly remarkable for a Puritanical simplicity. The walls had once been whitewashed; the floor consisted of rough planks with interstices through which the winds of heaven, charged with the odours peculiar to a village 'store,' where fish, onions, and groceries fought for precedence, percolated pretty freely, together with scraps of conversation from the village wits assembled beneath.

By way of decoration a clump of oranges hung from the centre of the plank ceiling, and a few vile ornaments and rank oleographs, of the semi-humorous description which delight the vulgar of all nations, spotted the walls. The horticultural tastes of the proprietor found vent in a couple of imitation plants, composed of paper and eggshells, which reposed on brackets; while in a corner a sickly creeper, growing out of an old meat-tin, climbed along the wall by the aid of nails and string.

The place was heavily stocked in the spittoon line—a necessary precaution in view of native customs, which are curious, but not nice. The table appointments were rather below than above the average, which is all that need be said.

The advantages, or disadvantages, according to the point of view of the critic, of the system of flooring in vogue here was illustrated the very afternoon of our arrival; for, on entering the sala, we discovered a merry crowd of damsels on their knees, in a circle at the far end —not at their devotions. On closer investigation we found they were exchanging compliments through an aperture with the occupants of the shop beneath, and with a peal of laughter they pointed to a broken pitcher which had just surrendered its contents on to the counter below.

But this was not the only use to which the interstices were put; for next day, the charming young lady who ministered to our wants, after satisfying herself that all was as it should be, suddenly plumped down at the very same hole, and after hallooing, up shot a sheet of notepaper and an envelope; and then with a merry laugh and *obrigado* she sat herself down at the far end of the table and indited a letter—perchance to some love-sick swain in the far Alemtejo. Evidently that hole was too useful to be stopped up; and if any of my readers should chance to visit this far-away spot in years to come, the aperture, no doubt, will still be found fulfilling its many uses. For this is a land wherein all things always are the same.

A door in the centre of one side led direct to the kitchen, without the agency of a passage, wherein, to the best of my belief, founded on careful observation, every department of domestic economy pertaining to a large and young family was concentrated, not to mention the cooking. The lessee of the hotel was a woman with a long tail of bairns—I never discovered a senhor—all of whom lived and moved and had their being in the kitchen, and, when not assisting mother, or prying into pots and pans, or stealing furtive glances through the half-opened door, varied by occasional predatory excursions into the sala, disported themselves in the adjacent mud. Nevertheless, the family were devout, for as the party bedded in a corner immediately under our room, and the floor was provided with the usual interstices, we could distinctly hear the 'patter' and infantile accompaniment of prattle as the elder ones recited their beads.

The eldest daughter, who appeared to do all the waiting and house-maiding, and had constituted herself our particular guardian angel, was a remarkably fascinating young person. She had an exquisite complexion, lovely eyes, and the most perfect set of ivories that ever adorned the human countenance, and really handsome features; and when her face was framed with the neat coloured handkerchief, the usual head-covering of the poor, she looked decidedly piquant. She exercised quite a sisterly authority over us, was cheery, good-tempered, and obliging, desperately anxious to please and make us comfortable, and always ready with a merry laugh if anything went wrong—in fact, she was the one bright spot in a desert of dirt and 'fecklessness.' I may say that the women of this province were handsomer than any we had met with in other parts of Portugal. One of the bath-women had a really beautiful face, of a clear olive complexion.

Our every action was interesting to the dear child of nature afore-mentioned: it was a pure joy to her examining my wife's clothes and toilette appointments, and there was neither vulgarity nor rudeness in this. Certainly no disrespect was intended—it was just the curiosity of a child finding itself in new surroundings.

Perhaps our eating had the greatest fascination for the natives: indeed, for the first few meals, the entire *personnel* of the establishment would gather round, openmouthed, as if we were visitors from another world—as indeed we were, in their estimation,—pressing the food on us, and constantly asking how we liked it, followed up by explanations of the ingredients.

We found the country-people just as they had been

described by our Lisbon friend—merry, good-natured children, ever kind and obliging, and free from the 'grasping' tendencies of dwellers in towns.

Possibly there are travellers who would resent so much solicitude in their welfare; but we rejoiced at the possibility of affording so much innocent amusement with so little effort to ourselves, and cordially entered into the spirit of the play.

The cuisine was far better than might have been expected—in fact, some of the dishes were excellent. There was a particular way of cooking French beans, for example, which suited our palates to a nicety; and the curious habit of mixing up all sorts of meats in one dish excited our curiosity and lent variety to the entertainment. The compotes of fruit, too, which at most hotels were simply half-cooked things swimming in liquid sugar—the Portuguese sweet-tooth being abnormally developed,—proved an excellent dish. We even had strawberries, and there was a particularly toothsome condiment made of quinces, which we had met with elsewhere.

The bread, I am fain to admit, was quite the very best I ever tasted in Portugal or anywhere else; and the baking being performed in a primitive, dome-shaped oven, standing on the rough hillside, and within sight of our window, we watched the process with interest. The oven was heated with green boughs cut from the undergrowth around, lighted up during the afternoon, and left burning all night. Early next morning the *débris* was cleared out and the batch of bread put in. One would have thought that so much green kindling, with its dense, fetid-smelling smoke, would have tainted the bread, but it was not so.

Such was the *ménage*. I have described it with some

minutiæ, as I was assured by a lady resident that the hotel was considered the best in the Algarves; that it was patronised by very wealthy people, who were *extremely* particular, and not content to put up with the accommodation provided at the 'establishment': what that was like we never dared inquire, much less investigate.

Nevertheless, as a specimen of a fashionable watering-place, Caldas de Monchique is well worth visiting; while for people who love simplicity of life combined with the prattle of infants, and like the little angels to be toddling around at all times, the place has much to commend it.

A good night's rest put us in excellent spirits—even a disordered liver is not insensible to the charms of new surroundings; and after early coffee we set off to spy out the land and get a whiff of mountain air, for the stuffiness of the pit wherein the establishment lies was already very noticeable.

Crossing a sparkling stream of clearest water, which was playing hide-and-seek round enormous granite boulders, we struck up the mountain-side, following the direction of a newly made path through a pine wood, and bordered with rare and beautiful flowering shrubs of infinite variety. Strolling on for half a mile we came out on the bare mountain-side, from whence we could realise the altitude of the spot, and were able to admire the vast extent of country spread out below.

Observing a cottage in course of erection, we strolled up to it, and to our surprise were courteously received at the door by a French gentleman, who bid us welcome to his domain, and immediately launched out in praise of the beauty of the view and the many charms of the site he had selected for his house.

We were soon on friendly terms, and I really think this

exile from *la belle France* was sincerely glad to meet with travellers from other climes, for with the courtesy and *bonhomie* of his countrymen he soon made us feel at home.

It appeared he was a merchant residing at Lagos, which he presently discovered to us shimmering through the blue haze that half concealed the far-off coast, and was consul for France at that port. Every summer he came up to the Serra with his wife and family to enjoy the cool breezes and to develop his little estate, for 'I have bought all the mountain-side, you see,' said he.

He was enthusiastic about the salubrity of the climate at this altitude. 'Here, on the southern slope, it is the finest in the world—it is never too hot nor too cold. Snow is unknown, while the summer sun is always tempered by the breezes blowing straight from the Atlantic. We find it so healthful,' he went on, 'that I have bought a property for a very small sum, and am busy, as you see, building a little house to come up to. All those paths you saw, and the one you came up by, were laid out by me, and I am planting, by degrees, the whole of the property with rare shrubs and trees. I have already put in several thousands.'

In reply to a suggestion that the expense of doing all this must be very great, he said: 'Yes; but, you see, it is my hobby. Moreover, the soil is so fertile, you have only to scatter seeds about, and they spring up without further trouble.'

The mountain-side, within easy reach of the cottage in embryo, was seamed with newly made paths, bordered with trees and evergreen shrubs in endless variety: the graceful mimosa contrasted by the rich dark green of the arbutus being particularly noticeable, and all giving promise of infinite beauty in years to come—a sort of paradise in the rough.

'Might we continue our walk?'

'Go where you will,' said our host, waving his hand with a majestic sweep embracing the entire mountain; 'if you take that path it will bring you to a point where you will get a magnificent view—there is not such another in Portugal!'

A hundred yards off, a diminutive structure, hardly worthy the name of cottage, confronted us, and on approaching it, to our surprise two gaily attired females, equipped with Japanese parasols, emerged, chatting and laughing loudly, the younger of whom scampered up the mountain-side in most un-Portuguese style. As our path led close to the fair apparitions, we saluted them in Portuguese, and the salutation was returned. Then the elder lady made some remark, and as they evidently wished to be friendly and to converse, we essayed our best Portuguese; but the result not being entirely satisfactory, we asked them in French if they understood that language. The effect was electrical—'Je suis Français,' exclaimed the elder, with a merry peal of laughter, and the flow of words was immediate. 'That is my husband you were talking to just now; and this,' pointing to a comely, merry-faced damsel, 'is my daughter.' It seemed they had come over for the day to look after the house-building, and, inviting us inside the little 'crib,' feasted us with wild mountain honey, taken from under a boulder close by, and in course of boiling-down for the wax. This exactly accorded with our tastes, and was in fact equal to the best heather honey. A long chat ensued; and after a pressing invitation to 'come again,' we resumed our ramble.

Clambering on a short distance, we chose a comfortable resting-place, and sat down to enjoy the superb panorama spread out in front—unsurpassed in Portugal, our French friends declared it to be..

There, almost at our feet, the sun glistening on its waters, was Portimao; there Lagos; there, further west, Sagres; and there, but dimly outlined through the haze, famed St. Vincent, the Cape which has lent its name to two of the greatest victories in naval history.

How many glorious memories are called up at sight of these classic spots! The very winds seemed charged with messages from the past, and whispered to us of Drake and Fenner, of Jervis and Napier.

It was in the month of May 1586, the year before the departure of the great Armada, that Drake, finding Lisbon too strong to force, brought his fleet into these waters and, seizing Cape St. Vincent, there established his headquarters, with a view to severing the fleets at Cadiz and Lisbon, and intercepting all supplies for the latter. Reporting his proceedings to Walsingham, he wrote: 'There have happened between the Spaniards, Portingals, and ourselves divers combats, in the which it has pleased God that we have taken forts, ships, barks, carvels, and divers other vessels more than a hundred, most laden, some with oars for galley-planks, and timber for ships and pinnaces, hoops and pipe-staves for casks, with many other provisions for this great army [intended for the invasion of England]. I assure your honour the hoops and pipe-staves were above sixteen or seventeen hundred tons in weight, which cannot be less than twenty-five or thirty thousand tons if it had been made in cask ready for liquor, all which I commanded to be consumed into smoke and ashes by fire, which will be unto the King no small waste of his provisions, besides the want of his barks. The nets which we have consumed will cause the people to curse their governors to their faces.'

This mention of 'nets,' says a commentator, refers to the destruction of the Algarve fisheries, upon which, since the loss of the Newfoundland and North Sea fisheries, the Spaniards chiefly depended for providing the Armada with its stores of salt fish.

The nets, together with some fifty or sixty fishermen's boats, were burned on Cape St. Vincent, 'near the Friary,' and doubtless made a fine blaze.

'The 4th of May we drew into the Bay of Lagos,' wrote Fenner, in his delightful letters to Walsingham, where next morning they 'landed about a thousand men,' and marched to the town. On nearing it, 'there presented in sight of us divers troops of horsemen, whereat we being nothing amazed, but always bending upon their greatest troops, they with courtesy gave us passage; so as before we came unto the town they had above four hundred horse, which seemed brave but bad masters.'

After a careful survey of the town, the Englishmen, finding the place stronger than they had expected, 'thought it more meet upon some pause, the place being surveyed honourably and tractably, to depart than rashly to attempt the hazard of our companies.' A few shots were exchanged, by way of compliment, in which two horses and one of the horsemen were killed; 'and so we spent in stands expecting their valours the most part of the day, before we drew aboard, and boarden in good sort without the loss of any one man.'

The fleet drew off the same afternoon, a portion of the ships going eastward, where a party of four hundred men was landed at Albufeira (now a station on the Lisbon-

Faro line), 'where the houses and village were presently fired with some barks and boats,' and the men re-embarked, the main body proceeding to Sagres, which was a pretty hard nut to crack. Here a landing was effected the same evening, a small castle captured, the garrison taking refuge in another and stronger one standing upon Cape Sagres— 'a place,' says Fenner, who helped at the taking of it, 'of great strength, having but one way to come at it, environed with the sea and a marvellous high upright cliff on three parts, the front only to approach, with a wall battlemented of forty feet in height and a gate in the midst.'

But Drake and his merry men were not to be frightened by the sight of walls forty feet high; though, to be sure, his vice-admiral, William Borough, 'an old-fashioned officer grown grey in the naval traditions which Drake was making obsolete,' proved a regular wet blanket— always ready to prove that Drake, who he naturally regarded as a novice in naval warfare, was undertaking operations that were 'without precedent,' and which set at defiance all 'the recognised rules of warfare.' The poor old gentleman could see no further than his nose ahead, and admitted afterwards that 'as touching the landing at Cape Sagres, it is true I did dissuade from it, by my letter, for the reasons therein alleged.' Old gentlemen are quite out of place in the navy: they are always for caution; 'precedent' is their shiboleth, and 'recognised rules of warfare' their god.

Drake's motto was 'God helps those who help themselves,' and in this spirit he 'went straight' for Sagres Castle. Hear what Fenner says: 'God stirred the minds of the General and his company to approach it; and he summoned the governor, whose answer was, as he was to assault on the behalf of his lady and mistress, he was to defend in the behalf of his lord and master.'

There was nothing for it now but to go in and win. As Fenner wrote: 'It was meet and most necessary for us to win the place for divers causes': chief amongst which were the watering and cleansing his ships, and refreshing his crews by a run ashore. Besides, the bay was a good 'road for our fleet, and withal a great "pray" against the enemy.'

So at it they went. The attack was made in true scientific style, 'about two of the clock,' and in a couple of hours the Spaniards had had enough of it. Their captain, who was hurt in two places, 'grew to parley,' with the result that the castle was surrendered on the condition that the lives and baggage of the garrison were saved, 'which was granted and perfectly performed.' Altogether, a very good day's work. 'But God,' says our authority, 'who is the giver of all good things, giveth strength unto His, and striketh with fear those whom He meaneth to chastise'—in this case, the Spaniards.

Then they took a rest. But there was still work ahead; so, on the sixth day, making an early start, 'the General marched to another castle of good strength, and took it, and so the Friary and Castle of Cape St. Vincent, and took the same'; then returning to Cape Sagres the same evening, they threw the guns over the cliffs, 'which were not left there, but with great pain and trouble boarded into our boats and brought away,' and, setting fire to the castle, 'boarded our companies' before night.

But Drake was not the man to tarry while there was work to be done; so next morning, 'very early, we landed at the first castle, which we razed and burned, and brought away the ordnance,' and the ships in the meanwhile having been watered, 'by one of the clock the whole fleet set sail to prosecute further action.'[1]

This capture of Cape St. Vincent, with its four castles, was as daring an exploit and as smart a piece of work as the British Navy ever accomplished. Its importance will be realised when it is understood that in those days, as Fenner tells us, 'all shipping that come out of the Straits for Lisbon,' as well as 'any that come from the northward, anchor there until convenient wind serve them.'

As long as Drake lay there he held the key of the situation, for the ships at Cadiz, and others coming through the Straits, could not join the rendezvous at Lisbon. As Fenner neatly put it, 'We lie between home and them, so as the body is without the members, and they cannot come together.'

The rest is told in the story of the Armada.

But Sagres has older and far nobler associations than I have mentioned so far.

In the eyes of every patriotic Portuguese, as well as of all people interested in the history of maritime exploration, the chief interest of Sagres lies in its association with the father of maritime discovery, Prince Henry 'the Navigator.' It was in this storm-lashed spot he matured those far-reaching schemes which resulted at last in one of the grandest exploits in the history of navigation—the discovery of the passage to India round the Cape of Good Hope. Sagres, in fact, may be regarded as the cradle of maritime discovery.

It was to this savage and isolated rock that Prince Henry, the famous son of John I. by his English wife, Philippa of Lancaster—'the generous and noble-hearted Philippa'—retired from the attractions and dissipations of the Court

---

[1] The reader who is interested in dashing exploits should read the story as told *in extenso* in a recent publication of the 'Navy Records Society.'

in 1418, more than a century before Drake was heard of, for the purpose of maturing his high designs, and devoting himself entirely to the study of maritime exploration.

Here he built an observatory and established a school of navigation—the first one, probably, in the world's history; and having immense wealth at his command, he gathered together learned mathematicians and astronomers from all parts of Europe, by whose aid and advice charts were compiled and great improvements made in the construction of the mariner's compass.

The one idea which dominated all his schemes was the possibility of reaching India round the south of Africa, concerning which many legends had drifted down from ancient times, but of whose truth there was no proof forthcoming. Still, of its feasibility he seems to have been convinced by one of those curious intuitions which have inspired all great explorers in the world's history; and though he never lived to witness the consummation of his hopes and desires—he was not even vouchsafed a sight of the promised land—he undoubtedly, by means of his scientific researches, 'unswervingly pursued in calm and studious retirement,' laid the foundation of those maritime explorations which eventuated in the glorious achievements of Bartholomew Diaz and Vasco da Gama, in 1486 and 1497 respectively.

The strange thing is that the father of maritime exploration, Prince Henry 'the Navigator,' never went on a voyage of discovery in his life, though he made several warlike excursions to Africa. But though essentially a man of theory and of studious habits, his agents were all practical seamen. Indeed, he is said to have collected together all the most daring captains and navigators he could find, and, having imbued them with his theories, and doubtless imparted to them something of his enthusiastic faith in the reality of his dreams, he sent them forth on their romantic missions; and they all regarded him as their superior in all matters of scientific navigation.

It was from the bay of Sagres that these daring seamen set out to explore unknown seas, and it was to Sagres they returned after facing the perils and awful privations of long voyages undertaken in craft which were little better than half-decked boats, and of wretched construction.

After forty years of continuous study and research Prince Henry passed away, leaving it to his successors to reap the fruit of so much unselfish endeavour, and to profit by his exertions in the cause of maritime discovery.

In accordance, however, with the law of contrast which governs all human endeavour, the glory of Prince Henry's achievements was somewhat dimmed by his connection with the slave-trade. He has been called the father of the slave-trade; and it came about in this way.

Slavery was already a flourishing institution amongst the Moors of Morocco; and the Portuguese explorations along the west coast of Africa soon opened up vast possibilities in that abominable traffic, which Prince Henry and his coadjutors at once perceived might be applied with advantage to the cultivation of the thinly populated provinces of Alemtejo and Algarve.

The idea 'caught on,' as we say. Lagos became the headquarters of the trade, and in course of time the two southern provinces became nearly peopled with blacks, the far-reaching consequences of which are discernible at the present day—they have extended far beyond the 'third and fourth generation,'—for the black strain, once imported into a nation's blood, is with difficulty eradicated. It may be held to account for much that is otherwise inexplicable in the Portuguese character at the present day. Where, it may be asked, are the Albuquerques, the Vasco da Gamas, the Joao de Castros amongst the present generation? Gentle shepherd, tell me where!

The shuffling of Time's cards is ever prolific of surprises. But surely the irony of fate was never more curiously exemplified than in the ultimate disposal of the fruits of Prince Henry's labours! He had scarcely lain for a hundred years in the silent 'aisles of Grand Batalha' when a rough English sailor called Drake—one of fate's ruthless instruments for working out its ends—came sailing along the coast of Portugal, and seizing the classic rock of Sagres, stormed its castles, fired their contents, and, behold! every memento of 'the Navigator's' sojourn in these wild parts is 'wasted,' to use the expressive term of those days. These unsentimental English Jacks made such a clean sweep of the antiquities as, to use Drake's own felicitous expression, 'will cause the people to curse their governors to their faces.'

But, mind, Drake had no quarrel with the 'Portuguese. To quote his own words: 'The Portingals I have always commanded to be used well, and set them ashore without the wanting of any of their apparel, and have made them to know that it was unto me a great grief that I was driven to hurt of theirs to the value of one real of plate, but that I found them employed for the Spaniards' services, which we hold to be our mortal enemies, and gave some Portingals some money in their purses and put them to land in divers places, upon which usage, if we stay here any time, the Spaniards which are here in Portingal, if they come under our hands, will become all Portingals and play as Peter did.'

All of which goes to show that Drake was a diplomatist

as well as a sailor, and by no means the vulgar pirate he is popularly supposed to have been. His guiding principle was the 'singeing of the King of Spain's beard'; and this exploit at St. Vincent, and the results arising therefrom, might be described in the words used by a writer from Morlaix about this time, with reference to another of Drake's exploits: 'It will be such a cooling to King Philip as never happened to him since he was King of Spain.'

Even the Spaniards blessed Drake and wished him good luck! 'There is a Spaniard here,' wrote the same person from Morlaix, 'who was twenty years in captivity in the galleys (at Nombre de Dios) and now triumphing here, with continual prayers for Sir Francis Drake for his delivery.'

But Time's 'lucky-bag' had still stranger surprises in store. For out of all the fruits of Prince Henry's labours, namely, the Portuguese possessions in India, but little Goa now remains! England has won the whole of them. So inscrutable are the workings of fate!

And yet, there is a fitness in it. For Prince Henry's mother was an English lady of royal blood; and, but for that marriage, those noble sons, under whose wise auspices Portugal achieved such greatness as she ever attained to, might never have been born. The English alliance, which was 'sealed by the marriage' of John I. to the daughter of John of Gaunt, was fraught with vast consequences to both countries.

The presence of the English in India is of course distasteful to good Portuguese patriots. But they preserve their 'face,' as the Chinese say, by appointing a 'Viceroy of India' from time to time, who holds his court at Goa.

The mention of Lagos reawakens some of the most glorious memories of the British Navy. It was into this port that Drake, while holding Sagres, drove the ten Spanish galleys from Cadiz who had come to 'look him up,' and he vainly challenged them to come out and fight. And from that day onwards its associations with the British Navy have continued to the present time. It was to Lagos that our fleets retired in the old wars for water, rest, and refreshment. And it was to this same snug anchorage that Jervis brought his fleet and prizes after the memorable 'Valentine's Day' he spent with the Dons off Cape St. Vincent in 1797, in the course of which he administered another of those 'coolings' to the King of Spain.

And here again, some forty years later (July 1833), another British officer brought in a conquering fleet with its prizes—this time under the constitutional flag of Portugal. It was Admiral Napier—whose three cousins all fought for Portuguese freedom—who, chiefly with British officers and seamen, had just won another battle off St. Vincent, with greatly inferior forces, over the fleet of the usurper Dom Miguel—a feat of arms which made the world ring, and for which Dom Pedro, the lawful sovereign, created Admiral Napier Viscount of Cape St. Vincent.

Admiral Napier, in his interesting account of the war, says, with reference to their arrival at Lagos: 'We were received with the greatest joy by the inhabitants, who vied with each other in showering down blessings on the people (the English officers and seamen) they were pleased to call their deliverers from the most unheard-of tyranny that ever oppressed a nation.' The following British officers, who laid down their lives in the cause of Portuguese freedom, together with thirty men, were buried at Lagos the next morning, viz. Captains Macdenough, Goble, and Blackstone; Lieutenants Wooldridge, More, and George. 'They were followed to the grave,' says our author, 'by all the principal inhabitants, who vied with each other in providing comforts and accommodation for the wounded officers and men.'

The modern Portuguese show their gratitude by calling us 'pirates' and 'land-robbers.' But we must remember that black blood runs in their veins!

In such language did 'earth's many voices' whisper in our ears, as they sped up on the wings of the wind from the wild Atlantic shore.

Oh that one could

> 'Summon from the misty past
> The forms that once have been'!

Familiar as is the form of Cape St. Vincent to the modern mariner, how few of those who go down to the sea in ships are aware of the tragedy from whence it takes its name! It was here the martyred saint met his death, whose body was escorted to Lisbon in the bark that bore it by crows, whose descendants are still, it is believed by the faithful, preserved at the Sée Church in Lisbon. I myself have seen them, but whether the birds were in direct descent or not, I cannot take on me to affirm, in the absence of a pedigree-book.

The remains of a monastery, perched on the verge of a stupendous cliff, against which the Atlantic breakers have dashed their fierce and lofty crests in fruitless conflict these centuries past, is all that reminds one of the labours of man hereabouts, at the present day. Here, too, on a seat cut from the solid rock by spiritual agency, is the reputed resting-place of the saint.

There is a tradition that the Portuguese mariner of former times was accustomed to waft up a prayer to the saint, whom his imagination pictured seated on this lofty throne, to extend over him his protecting arm.

Putting aside the vexed question of saintly intercession, might not the modern voyager who rounds Cape St. Vincent, without loss of self-esteem, lift his hat in token of respect to 'the grand old man' of navigation—Prince Henry the Navigator?

I shall always regret the miscarriage of our plan to visit Sagres, a place of so many glorious memories. For having made the passage round the Cape to India, rendered possible by Prince Henry's labours, I felt a longing to visit this classic spot, the Mecca of the sailor, and there pay my respects to the home of 'the Navigator.'

Our Lisbon friend had particularly enjoined us to visit Monchique, a small town at a great altitude, in a situation of singular beauty—'that glorious valley of Monchique,' Lord Carnarvon calls it, 'which in point of picturesque scenery, is preferred by many of the Portuguese to Cintra itself.' We had been further enjoined, if the weather was propitious, to extend our excursion to the summit of the loftiest peak of the Serra de Foia, which overhangs the village of that name, from whence the view was described as being superb, commanding the greater part of the Algarves and far away into the Alemtejo.

Accordingly, the first day that was bright and sunny, with promise of a clear view, arrangements were made for us by our obliging friend, Senhor C——, so that we might accomplish the arduous excursion with the minimum of fatigue. A carriage was ordered from Monchique, the nearest livery-stable, and donkeys were to be in readiness there for carrying us to the summit.

Some curiosity was felt as to the sort of vehicle forthcoming from such a remote spot; and our surprise was great on discovering a smart landau, newly painted, and done up in the best style of upholstery, with an excellent and well-groomed pair of horses, and a smart, active coachman to match. The cushions, too, were well stuffed, the springs good—as indeed they needed to be,—and we agreed, that it was quite the best turn-out we had met with south of Lisbon.

Monchique is four miles from the Caldas, and though it is an ascent the whole way, the gradient is so easy that a carriage might trot up it. To our disgust, however, we had covered but a quarter of a mile when the road came to an abrupt end, and for the remainder of the way existed only in the rough—the authorities having contented themselves with shaping it, leaving to future generations the task of completing it.

The approach to the town is singularly beautiful: olive-trees, orange-groves, fertile gardens, and a luxuriant vegetation clothe the entire surface of the mountain, completely embowering the place; and our impressions of it exactly accorded with Lord Carnarvon's description: 'It is eminently beautiful; the vegetation in the valley is most luxuriant, and refreshed by streams of the clearest water; upon their banks the rhododendron grows profusely amid the lotus, the jonquil, and many varieties of the scilla, while the hills above are covered with chestnuts of an immense growth, and orange-trees bowed down by the weight of their golden fruit.'

We were surprised to find so large and well-ordered a town, with clean, cobble-paved streets, many shops, and prosperous-looking inhabitants; for it is one of the loftiest towns, if not the loftiest, in Portugal—cut off by miles of indifferent roads from every other place. All the intercourse with the outside world appeared to be conducted on pack-mules and donkeys.

Here we left our carriage, and presently a couple of 'mokes,' with merry lads to attend them, put in their appearance; and off we set, our path winding through a labyrinth of lovely lanes and fruit orchards, until at last it came out on the bare mountain-side, degenerating into a rough track with an almost precipitous slope on one side. The prospect was magnificent, while far above and in front the jagged peaks of the Serra de Foia towered skywards.

The last half-hour had unfortunately wrought a change in the weather. Heavy masses of rain-laden clouds were driving up from the Atlantic, and soon the peaks above were enveloped in mist; the wind freshened, and presently a downpour drove us to a cave for shelter. The cold, too, at this breezy altitude asserted itself unpleasantly, and forced us regretfully to abandon the ascent of the Foia, for even if we escaped a drenching there would be no view to repay the trouble of a further two hours' climb.

A lovely valley running in between two spurs of the mountain in front terminated in a deep and narrow gorge, and this inviting spot we determined to explore before retracing our steps; for the shower had passed off, and it would have been disappointing to have come thus far without seeing something of the beauties of the district. Faint voices of running water were wafted up to us from the dark, hidden depths below, wherein we presently discovered a mountain torrent of the purest transparency romping over the boulders in full song.

The chief attractions of this particular part of Portugal are the magnificent chestnut woods—not the stunted telegraph poles grown for kindling and other uses around Cintra, but forest trees of truly regal proportions and of immense antiquity, bearing marks of the fierce onslaughts to which they are exposed at this height. For the Atlantic gales blow home here with awful force. Some of the oldest and grandest of these monarchs of the glen are so torn and shattered that little but the bare trunk remains; and yet how magnificent they are even in their ruin! It was sad to see such evidence of Nature's destructiveness: a tender mother she can be, as we all know, but woe to those who obstruct her path on the mountain-tops! The sight of these grand old trees alone repaid us the trouble of the ascent.

Torrent and path gradually converged on a partially cleared spot at the head of the glen, and there, close to the ruins of an ancient mill, where the track crossed the stream, before beginning the ascent to the romantic village of Foia, we dismounted, and, greatly to the astonishment of our guides, expressed our firm intention of going no further. 'Not even to Foia?' they cried. 'No, not even to Foia,' much as they tried to persuade us to venture on.

But heavy clouds to windward, and driving mist overhead, discouraged any loftier aspirations. And so, after wandering about the wood for a while, we remounted and set off again for Monchique, reluctantly giving up the only chance we should ever have, in all probability, of seeing the 'finest view in Portugal.'

Our ride was accomplished *à la Portugaise*. That is to say, in the absence of saddles we rode as the natives of the country invariably do, sideways, exactly like the Holy Family as depicted in pictures of the Flight into Egypt. Now this is all very well in the desert, where sand makes soft falling, but on the bare mountain-side, with your legs dangling over a precipice, the experience is wont to be more exciting than pleasant; and although we tried to shape our countenances into a look of complete indifference as we skirted any dangerous parts, we were by no means sorry to get on to broad roads once more.

Though we had been balked of our goal, the excursion had been a delightful one: the recollection of that romantic valley, with its marvellous chestnuts, will ever linger pleasantly in the memory. The season of spring, too, is delicious everywhere in Portugal, and to lovers of natural beauty, as has been truly said, 'a Portuguese heath is, at that time, a scene of indescribable beauty.' The ground is so liberally bestrewn with aromatic plants, that the very air seems charged with the scent which rises as you crush them in walking. Amongst the many fruit-bearing trees and shrubs that adorned our path, we noticed the bramble, nearly ripe; almonds and walnuts in the same stage; the Caruba bean well formed—the natives distil a spirit from it; the gum-cistus already in seed, and the lauristinus in bloom and smelling sweetly. There was also abundance of the *Osmunda regalis*.

We had a long wait at Monchique, for the driver, not expecting us back for several hours, had betaken himself to his friends. This gave us an opportunity of looking about the little town and admiring the charm of its situation and surroundings.

The scamper down the long incline to Caldas was speedily accomplished, the donkey-boys, mounted on their steeds, cantering beside us, and keeping up a running chaff with our driver, until, at length, putting on a spurt, they soon out-distanced us, disappearing over the crest of a precipitous slope—a short-cut to Caldas, from whence, it seemed, they had been sent on in advance that morning.

The rest of our brief stay here was spent in wandering about the mimosa-edged paths of the Frenchman's estate, and excursions on the mountain; for, alas! we found it impossible to extend our travels as far as we had intended. Lagos, Portimao, and Sagres had been named by our Lisbon friend as places to visit, but our experience of hotels in south Portugal—even those frequented by 'very particular people'—was not such as to encourage further experiments, and we decided on returning to Lisbon forthwith, and after a rest there to revisit Cintra.

We often amused ourselves watching the boys playing a complicated sort of hop-scotch—called by the Portuguese 'man-game,' a rude outline of a man being first traced on the ground, and the game consisting in kicking a bit of wood successively from limb to limb.

We much regretted quitting these fashionable baths without carrying away pleasanter impressions; but, in spite of a real desire to please on the part of the hotel management, and the never-failing good-humour of our guardian angel, there were sundry discomforts which disinclined us from prolonging our stay. We most fervently pitied the poor martyrs who had been sent there for the benefit of their health!

The charges, though low compared with English hotels, were certainly high, having regard to the many shortcomings of the establishment. And we were amused, when the bill was presented, at the half-apologetic remark that it had been necessary to charge us rather more than customary, owing to our having had *four meals* a day, whereas only two were usually provided.

The fact is, on taking up our abode here we had explained that we could not keep the native hours, and had arranged to have early coffee and a twelve-o'clock breakfast, and dinner at seven. And it seemed that the early coffee and a cup of tea or chocolate at five constituted the extra 'meals'!

It is lamentable to think of the reputation for gluttony we must have left behind. Doubtless the tradition of the faddy English, with their 'four meals,' has become one of the stock legends of the establishment.

A carriage had been ordered up from Silves, the nearest 'posting town,' and at 2 P.M. we bade adieu to our most kind and helpful friend Senhor C——, and departed. The parting with our little maid was most affecting: the usual kiss was bestowed, and I felt more than ever convinced of the partiality with which these favours were conferred; and then, off we set on our thirty-three miles drive to Messines. For, although Saboia de Monchique station is nearer as the crow flies, there is no road to it.

The first stage of sixteen miles to Silves, chiefly downhill, was soon covered, and the day being delightful, we thoroughly enjoyed the run down—although, to be sure, some anxiety was caused by the driver's fixed determination to work off arrears of sleep *en route*. And seeing that the road abutted on to the steep and, in parts, precipitous mountain-side, and was without protecting parapet, and the horses from force of habit—under the delusion, may be, that they were going up instead of down hill—zigzagged from side to side in a rather alarming manner, we momentarily expected to discover the bottom of a ravine.

Certainly I was unkind enough to poke Jehu with the point of a stick when he lurched further than usual over the edge of the seat. But, in time, he got so used to these little marks of esteem, while the horses seemed so thoroughly able to take care of themselves, that I let the poor fellow sleep on until his hat fell off.

I am thoroughly convinced, from what I have seen of Portuguese drivers, that there is a strain of lizard blood in their veins, the result possibly of intermarriage during the jelly-fish stage of our common ancestry. But breeding will out! and it is remarkable how uniformly all drivers manifest the tendency to a condition we have been taught to associate with the fat boy in *Pickwick*. For no sooner do they get well settled to their work, under a warm sun, than down goes the head, the body begins to oscillate, and forthwith they sleep the sleep of the just.

Fortunately, Portuguese horses have been trained to these habits from infancy, and, but for 'the cursed gift of imagination,' which tortures the stranger with visions of mangled remains and sorrowing parents, there would be no occasion to notice the habit.

As we neared the river, with its unfinished bridge, the driver woke up by instinct, and from this point rattled us on to Silves in dashing style, pulling up with a flourish at the scene of our late nocturnal adventures, to which we gave the 'cut direct,' and marched off to investigate the town.

There was a full hour to spare, and right glad were we to have the chance of seeing a place invested with so many historical associations.

Silves is not only one of the most ancient towns in Portugal, but it was here that the Moors made their last halt before being driven from the kingdom in 1263, when Alphonso X. took the title of King of Portugal and Algarves.

Perched on top of a conical hill, the town at a distance resembles, as Lord Carnarvon justly observes, 'a city of other days'; an impression confirmed on nearer inspection by its massive walls, its overhanging houses, and old-fashioned windows.

The enterprising traveller and most graceful writer above-mentioned must have been singularly susceptible to female charms; for he never meets a member of the softer sex without launching out in praise; and he has left it on record that 'the women of Silves, and indeed of all the Algarve, are in face, and often in figure, extremely beautiful: their complexions are pale but clear, their eyes, shaded by long lashes, are always fine, and generally distinguished by a soft and pensive expression which pervades the countenance and even characterises the smile. The beauty of the Algarvian, less full of fire than the Spanish, but fraught with more tenderness, sinks not, however, less deeply in the heart.'

After so splendid a certificate of beauty it would be sheer impertinence in mere visitors of an hour to pass further criticisms. Our one regret was, that none of these visions of loveliness condescended to cross our path here.

The walls of Silves are singularly perfect, the old Saracenic towers still domineering the town, which even now seems haunted with the spirit of its old masters; for an air of dreaminess pervades every part, not excepting the cathedral, a building of no great size, and of quite striking plainness.

The only Moorish relic we forgot to examine was the reservoir, which, I believe, is still in use; but the question of water-storage had no fascination for us at the moment. We preferred to saunter through the quaint, silent streets, admiring the crimson carnations and avalanches of bourganviliers and other flowering plants which lolled their bright faces over the walls in gorgeous masses, from the hanging gardens which the Moors so dearly loved and left as legacies. At every turn here one expects to meet the veiled and turbaned figures that once walked the streets of this quaint old town.

But what must ever invest Silves with a deep interest in the eyes of English travellers, is its association with a most gallant feat of arms performed by a little band of Cockney warriors seven hundred years ago. The story, as recounted by Mr. Morse Stephens, may be thus summarised :—

In 1189, Sancho I., the 'City-builder,' as the Portuguese christened him, being engaged in one of the many wars with the Moorish interlopers, and in need of help, one of those bands of Crusaders bound for Palestine put into Lisbon. These dashing soldiers were easily persuaded to break their journey, and 'get their hands in' for the more serious fighting ahead by striking a blow at the infidel foes in the Peninsula. Sancho at once 'requisitioned' these Crusaders, amongst whom was 'a well-equipped force of Londoners,' with which welcome addition to his army he not only swept the Arabs out of Alemtejo, but captured Silves, the capital of Algarves. But Yakub, the Arab chieftain, was not the man to sit down quietly after a reverse, and biding his time he made an attempt to retake Silves, but 'was foiled by a hundred young London Crusaders'—those 'boy-soldiers' concerning whom so many disparaging things are said by 'old fogey' critics at the present day.

Guide-books and other entertaining works of fiction tell us a great deal about styles of architecture and dimensions of churches, but they too often forget to mention the one thing needful; and, although seven hundred years have rolled by since that gallant defence of Silves, one cannot, even now, gaze on the walls without experiencing, as an old writer puts it, 'that pleasure which is natural to a thinking mind, at being on a spot famous for any historical event.'

Since those far-away times, how many hundreds of Englishmen have laid down their lives in preserving the liberties of the Peninsular peoples! And how has this been rewarded?

The last stage of eighteen miles—from Silves to Messines—was new to us, in a way, seeing that we had traversed it on the last occasion in the dark. But there is nothing attractive about it. There is not even nowadays the exciting prospect of encountering a 'Black Company,'— mounted ruffians, who, in the days of civil troubles, now happily gone by, were wont to range the country, perpetrating horrid outrages, and living by the plunder of the peaceful inhabitants.

The road was abominable—exactly in the state the remembrance of which inclined the Scots in after years to 'bless the name of General Wade.' Would that the mantle of that energetic road-maker had descended on the authorities of the Algarve!

We reached Messines as the sun was rougeing the opposite hills, and having an hour to spare, we had an excellent opportunity of studying twilight effects on a landscape of no great interest.

The weighing of our impedimenta must have been quite a godsend to the station staff—the result supplying a curious illustration of the eccentricities of railway management on the 'Sul E Sueste' line. The 'excess' charge from Lisbon to Faro, two hundred and ten miles, was forty reis (about 2d.); from Faro to Messines, the same (though only thirty-two miles); while from Messines to Lisbon it was sixty reis; the amount of luggage being the same in every case. But as scientists tell you the human body increases in weight at certain times of the day, irrespective of eating, so, no doubt, human luggage varies in the same way. At least, such is the inference to be drawn from the curious phenomena I have described, and which the stationmaster confessed an utter inability to explain. As it was only a matter of farthings, it wasn't worth making a fuss about—or even writing to the *Times*, that champion of wandering Britons' grievances!

We were the sole occupants of the corridor-carriage to Lisbon, and passed a very comfortable night. Next morning the sun rose in the utmost splendour, converting the 'dreary wastes' of the Alemtejo into a fairyland, and, as we ran through the fringe of cultivated ground bordering the Tagus side, the country was looking its best. At 7 A.M. we left Barreiro in the steamer for Lisbon, rejoicing in the near prospect of comfort and cleanliness, and the lovely vistas from our friend's house at the Estrella.

Although we had not seen all we wished, our experience had been an interesting one; just sufficient to encourage a longing to revisit the southern parts when civilisation has made greater strides, and the science of sanitation has penetrated to the wilds of the Algarves.

Lest any of my readers should infer from what I have stated that we were exceptionally fastidious and hard to please, let me add that, since our visit, I have heard of a Portuguese family who went to Monchique for the waters, but were driven away instanter by the lack of conveniences and the exorbitant charges.

I was given to understand that my wife was the first Senhora Inglesi who had set foot in this Elysium.

IN THE DREARY WASTES OF THE ALEMTEJO

UNIV. OF
CALIFORNIA

TABLE ETIQUETTE

'When you are in Rome, do as the Romans do' is one of those wise saws which are more honoured in the breach than in the observance; and it is well that it is so, for although the maxim contains a certain amount of worldly wisdom, the individual who obeyed it too literally would return to his own country a more offensive member of society than when he left it. Does not old Fuller say: 'Travel not beyond the Alps. Mr. Ascham did thank God that he was but nine days in Italy: wherein he saw in one city more liberty to sin than in London he had ever heard of in nine years. That some of our gentry have gone thither and returned thence without infection, I more praise God than their adventure.'

There are habits in all countries which every self-respecting Briton would do well to avoid; and no matter how desirous he may be to humour the prejudices of the people amongst whom he moves, he should be careful never to demean himself by acts of vulgarity or coarseness. There are many ways of enjoying life without expectorating about the carpets, talking at the top of the voice at meals, or eating like a beast of the field; and the individual who would derive pleasure from his travels, and return home a wiser person than when he set out, will note peculiarities and remain at peace with all men.

These sage reflections were suggested by excursions over the face of the globe generally, and by sundry visits to Portugal in particular, and will doubtless be scoffed at by the intelligent reader, as all wise counsel is when presented gratis.

There are few matters of greater interest to the traveller in search of novelty than the 'table-manners' of a people;

and, as it was my good fortune to enjoy many opportunities of studying these in Lusitania, it has occurred to me that the knowledge thus amassed ought to be made available for my fellow-sufferers in this probationary state.

Let me premise this essay by observing that the Portuguese always travel *en famille*: and as private sitting-rooms would add to the cost of hotel life, these sensible people appear at *table d'hôte en famille*. In fact, as far as I could discover, without unduly peering into the sanctity of family life, the Portuguese eat, sleep, and live *en famille*; and no doubt, if they could arrange it so, would die *en famille*; they would naturally prefer to go to heaven *en famille*;—but that is looking rather far ahead.

Now, hotel life under these homely conditions has naturally a picturesque side to it; and although, happily, the hotel 'season' had not begun when we were moving about, yet, from time to time, families would come to stay, and from what took place we could form a tolerably clear idea of what a Portuguese hotel would be like later on.

The particular feature of family life which most forcibly impressed us was the inhuman way in which the *meminos* were dragged about, from morning to night, with their parents, from whom indeed they were scarcely separated for a moment. In the matter of games, or indeed of any occupations for their leisure moments, which were neither few nor infrequent, they seemed to be absolutely resourceless—as indeed were their elders; and when not eating, or shrieking, would just hang about the rooms and passages, waiting for something to turn up—a manner of life which struck one as being almost as unprofitable as gazing into space, the lifelong diversion of their elders. And the worst of it was they never went to roost before the rest: a practice which, I have been assured by people well acquainted with the home-life of the Portuguese, has most injurious effects on the children, and is accountable for their delicacy in after-life.

Now the ways of childhood have a distinct fascination for most of us. We all like to see how we behaved and looked during the early stages of life. Still, fond as one may be of the gambols of babies and the innocent prattle of childhood, there are moments when the thoughts take a serious turn and you yearn for the silence of the cloister, or, at least, for a few moments' relief from the infernal clatter of noisy, uncontrolled brats. It is safe to aver, moreover, that if the Portuguese went to bed earlier in youth, ate fewer sweets and drank less water in middle age, and abstained from the practice of gazing vacantly into space all through the after-period of life, they would be less burdened with what a caustic writer calls 'churchyard fat'—that particular casing which imparts such a flabby, unwholesome look to the Portuguese of the well-fed classes. There might even be a reappearance of Albuquerques and De Castros!

I am afraid, however, that this sort of advice, when proffered to a nation already on the downgrade, is rather like trying to arrest a waggon running down-hill by putting peas under the wheels!

Dining *en famille* being *de rigueur*, and the party comprising children of all ages, and even nurses, there was much to amuse at this particular function, if not to edify; more especially as, between courses, the juveniles would rush out to work off their superfluous energies by a romp. In fact, a very brief experience of the *messa redonda* (*table d'hôte*), sufficed to impress one with the delightful absence of the frigid conventionality, miscalled decorum, which renders our hotel dinners so stiff and formal a parade in 'review order.' There can be no doubt, as the poor snail remarked when a cart-wheel ran over him on the highway, that 'travel expands the mind.' One's little insular prejudices begin to melt away under the disintegrating influence of repeated shocks, until at last one begins to wonder why people at home allow themselves to be hampered by so many absurd restrictions as to the use of implements in eating.

'I think the fair ones of Portugal are very dexterous in the use of the knife,' I once remarked to a friend who had long resided in the land. 'Yes,' he quietly replied. 'I used to think so too, until I beheld a Russian lady taking her soup with a knife. I was dining at the table of an ambassador, and the marvellous way in which this *grande dame* lapped up the scalding liquid with the point of her knife—keeping up a continuous stream—was such an astonishing feat of *léger-de-couteau* that it absolutely fascinated me. And now nothing surprises me.'

There is no hard-and-fast rule as to the use of implements here; even Nature's provisions are brought into play, after the fashion of our lightly attired ancestors, who—happy people!—had no 'plate' to keep clean, or to lock up when they left home. For example, I have a very vivid recollection of a fashionable lady, dining with her child and its nurse at a much-patronised-by-society hotel, not a hundred miles from Lisbon, who, after taking the edge off her appetite, was observed lolling contentedly over the table—on which her elbows reclined, the sleeves rolled well above these useful joints—gnawing a bone, supported in both hands.

On another occasion, and in another place, a well-dressed lady—the owner of a husband, and the mother of some nice girls and a boy—arrived at the dinner-table in a hot and flushed condition, and with the dew sparkling on her matronly face, plumped down, and proceeded to wipe her nose, mouth, and face with the dinner-napkin in a solemn and workman-like way before attacking the food, which she then proceeded to do justice to in a style that became a wife and a mother.

But it is in the use of the delicate little lance, yclept toothpick (which crops up everywhere on a native dinner-table) that the fair Lusitanians do chiefly excel. There rises up before me at this moment the form of my *vis-à-vis* at the dinner-table in a fashionable health-resort—a fair creature of some fifteen or sixteen stone, whose piquant face was adorned with a fine moustache and an incipient beard—reclining gracefully over the table on both elbows, head erect and slightly inclined backwards, mouth thrown open, and the pick travelling leisurely round the entire range of Nature's grindstones. It was magnificent, but ——! The display was thrown away on me, as I am no admirer of other folk's jaws.

How we English worry about trifles! What a lot of time and trouble, for instance, we waste over butter—rolling it up into balls or crinkles, and then putting these into dishes of water which are scattered broadcast over the table. There is none of that nonsense in Portugal, where time is so precious. The butter for the table—which, by the way, is always salted, never fresh—invariably appears in its original tin. And, in the intervals between courses, every one within reach dives into the tin with his or her knife, and conveys the small portion extracted direct to the bread, which it is *de rigueur* to hold aloft in the left hand, the elbow resting on the table.

The exercise of this graceful cult opens out endless possibilities of fun; it is extremely amusing, for example, trying to dodge other people's knives, and 'cutting in' betweenwhiles. A little harmless diversion of this sort is absolutely necessary to break the dreary monotony of the prolonged banquets of Portugal.

The practice has its drawbacks, to be sure; for, after being pecked at with dirty knives for a meal or two, the butter-tin is wont to assume rather a squalid aspect, and on this account, when we fed by ourselves, we generally managed to persuade the waiter to wash and prepare a small ration of butter for our own particular and private use, which naturally confirmed people in the conviction of the eccentricity of *os Ingleses*.

The Portuguese of both sexes undoubtedly enjoy the heartiest of appetites; and it was a real pleasure to see the ample justice they did to the good things provided by a liberal management, as well as the enjoyment they derived from the exercise of eating. I am aware that English travellers have taken exception to what they consider the inordinate voracity of the natives; but the fact of only two 'square meals' being provided during the twenty-four hours necessitates somewhat of a gorge, and may be pleaded in excuse of what might otherwise be mistaken for an unreasonable attachment to the pleasures of the table.

The Briton abroad can hardly be instanced as a fair example of a light feeder: quite the other way. And when he visits Portugal, and finds there a people who can beat him on his own ground, he is seized with jealousy, and falls into the error of describing their gastronomic feats as unmitigated gluttony. Now this may be held to account for the jaundiced view so many wandering Britons have carried away with them in regard to native appetites. Even the kindly Beckford has been misled in this matter, and in many a felicitous passage describes the 'feeds' he assisted at, so as to make the unsophisticated reader picture scenes of most unedifying gluttony. Speaking of the old Marquis of Marialva, the most influential noble in Portugal, Beckford says: 'Having a more than Roman facility for swallowing an immense profusion of dainties, and making room continually for a fresh supply, he dines every day alone between two silver canteens of extraordinary magnitude. Nobody in England would believe me if I detailed the enormous repast I saw spread out before him; but let your imagination loose upon all that was ever conceived in the way of gormandising, and it will not in this case exceed the reality.' Nor were the ladies of the palace in any degree less remarkable for their gastronomic achievements. Describing a royal supper-party, he says, ' on entering we found the Camareira Mor (Lady of the Bedchamber) and five or six other hags of supreme quality feeding like cormorants. I never beheld eaters or eateresses lay about them with greater intrepidity.'

My own opportunities of study were rather more restricted, nevertheless they entirely confirmed the hearty and businesslike way in which the Portuguese are said to consume their meals. A short account of a spectacle I was privileged to witness one Sunday afternoon, in a fashionable hotel near Lisbon, may be cited in evidence of the faith that is in me on the particular subject of *table-d'hôte* manners and customs in this ancient realm.

The room in which the feast was held was long and low, and by dint of very close packing might seat a hundred diners. We made our *entrée* at about half-past six—

dinner had commenced nearly two hours earlier—and by dint of great exertion reached the table that had been reserved for us, and while our repast was being dished up took the opportunity of studying the *mise-en-scène*. Every inch of table-space was occupied, the room being so tightly packed that the waiters could hardly move about. The company comprised the usual proportion of nurses with children in arms, some of whom had already begun to manifest symptoms of that comfortable sense of repletion which is supposed to be the sequel to a hearty meal on a healthy stomach, by those infantile 'struggles to be free,' which the admonitions of a nurse at meal-times invariably provoke: while other infant prodigies were giving vent to their feelings in songs and shouts which delighted the fond parents. The weather being decidedly warm, every door and window was, of course, tightly shut, while every chink by which the raw air could penetrate was jealously sealed. The oil lamps were in full blast: prolonged 'stoking' had raised the temperature of every member of the distinguished company to the 'flushing-point,' the hard exertions they had undergone being evidenced by the streams of perspiration which coursed down many a kindly face.

Here and there signs of exhaustion were beginning to manifest themselves; but the majority were still 'hard at it'—there is no other term that so exactly expresses the busy scene which met our astonished gaze at this moment.

Having completed a general survey of the room, our attention was attracted to a male member of the community seated within a yard or two of us, whose outward form and enthusiastic devotion to his victuals at once suggested a comparison with the fat boy in *Pickwick*, say on attaining the age of fifty—supposing him to have lived so long. The fat lay round his neck and chin in ponderous wrinkles, while his face fairly beamed with pleasure from the results of his labours. How that fat-encased gentleman enjoyed his food! He had come there to dine, and it was only meet that nothing should be allowed to interrupt the enjoyment to be derived from a dinner of many courses and three hours' duration! Not a single item in the way of food escaped his eagle glance. No waiter dared to skip him; for he refused nothing, and was always ready and impatient for more. But, somehow, as the end drew near he dropped a little behind, perchance from dallying too long over a favourite dish, or from attacking it a second time. Be that as it may, dessert had been in full swing for some moments before our friend signified his desire for a clean plate and a change of food. He began with an orange or two, and then toyed with some loquats; and when the plate could no longer contain the wrecks of his enterprises, and he had attained to the felicitous state so aptly expressed by the schoolboy phrase as 'fit to burst,' he bethought him of the pleasant light refection which had been reserved as a sort of *bonne-bouche* for the last, to fill up any stray crannies that had escaped observation during the stowage of more substantial goods, and called for strawberries. But alas for the vanity of human hopes, while his attention had been concentrated on weightier matters the strawberry-dish had been cleared!

And now there ensued a scene.

In a very old number of *Punch* there is a picture entitled 'The Baffled Voluptuary,' showing a stout and elderly gentleman who has provided himself with a 'pottle' of the luscious berries, tramping up a steep hill under a broiling sun, with a view to ensconcing himself on a seat under a tree where the berries can be consumed in quiet, being arrested in full career by the offensive legend 'Wet paint.' Well, now, the expression on that old gentleman's face was mildness compared to the face and feelings of the poor hungry Portuguese fidalgo when the solemn truth broke in upon him; for, unlike the old gentleman of *Punch*, he had not even attained to the 'possessive case.' He fairly howled—like a spoilt and greedy child.

Never, in the course of my wanderings, did I gaze on such a scene as now ensued. To yell for the waiters was the work of an instant; and when these patient and overworked slaves attempted to soothe this descendant of De Castro by assuring him that an ample supply of strawberries had been provided, his wrath knew no bounds. 'Call this a dinner!' he shouted, in stentorian tones, in his own sonorous mother tongue: 'call this a dinner, and no strawberries!'

Conversation had ceased. Every eye was directed sympathetically on this poor victim of misplaced confidence who was making the room echo to the cry of 'morangao,' for the Portuguese are *mui sympathica*, and there was not a man or woman in that assemblage but would have willingly torn the strawberries from his or her mouth to have stayed the cravings of their fellow-countryman—and stopped his jaw. This sudden explosion was the more surprising, seeing that the fidalgo had scarcely opened his mouth during dinner, except for ingress. Yet his strength of lung was unquestionable; and his face shone as he shouted, until it seemed to have caught some of the fire of his own eloquence. I am not sufficiently versed in Portuguese expletives to analyse the language he used; but the reader will admit that to be done out of your share of strawberries is enough to make a saint swear, to say nothing of a Portuguese fidalgo who looked ' a little lower than the angels ' !

Finding that apologies were but pouring oil on the flames—there was no music, alas, to soothe the savage beast!—the waiters retired for a brief space as reappeared with a dish of the much-coveted fruit. The sight was magical; the storm fell as quickly as it had arisen. A smile stole over the face of the fat fidalgo, as, relapsing into his wonted silence, he proceeded to fill up a large tumbler with the berries, smothered them in sugar, filled up the glass with generous Colares, and ' swilled off' the contents without a wink.

Such was the scene enacted on a Sunday afternoon at a hotel of fashionable resort, near Lisbon.

The comment of a travelled friend was: ' Really, such a beast ought not to be allowed to feed in public,' adding an adjective I omit. But this was mere prejudice. Why on earth shouldn't people enjoy themselves in the way that suits them ?

The sequel to it all was, that when *our* dessert appeared, the strawberry ration was below the average, and the waiter was profuse in his apologies. We assured him we quite understood; and, as he was a firm friend of ours, and would have cut off his right hand, metaphorically, to serve us, we spared his feelings by avoiding all further allusion to the matter.

．　．　．　．　．　．　．　．

' The contemplation of a fallen country,' as Southey truly observed, ' is very melancholy,' and when this distressing spectacle is aggravated by the thought that the carcass of State is rotting away for lack of such commonplace qualities as honesty and common-sense, sadness gives place to indignation; and, but for a firm faith in an intelligence at the heart of things, one might well wonder what useful purpose is served by prolonging the death agonies of such countries as Spain and Portugal.

Happy the tourist who travels through the Peninsula in ignorance of the dark side of the beautiful picture which everywhere meets his gaze. And where ignorance is bliss, 'tis folly to be wise!

Portugal was the first foreign land on which, as a boy, I set eyes. I have paid many visits to the country since, and each time I quit it my feelings are precisely those of Southey's: 'I am eager to be again in England, but my heart will be very heavy when I look back upon Lisbon for the last time.' I can honestly say, 'Portugal, with all thy faults, I love thee still!'

INDEX

ALCACER DO SOL, 149-150.
Alcantara aqueduct, 40.
Alcobaca, history of, 43-44; visit to, 60, 65-67; Murphy and Beckford, 67-75; literary treasures, 76; Lord Carnarvon's visit, 77; desecration of, 78; present day appearance, 79; kitchen at, 80-81.
Alemtejo, 319-20; 'dreary wastes' of the, 378.
Algarve, a visit to the, 315.
Aljubarrota, victory of, 44; memento of the victory at Alcobaca, 79; battle of, 83; English archers at, 84.
Architecture, Belem Castle, 15; abbeys of Alcobaca and Batalha, 43.
Arcos dos Aguas Libres, 40-41.
Arrabida Mountains, 143, 153.
Art in Portugal, 59.
Art Pottery, Caldas ware, 56; whistles from Matosinhos, 207.
'Art-product' of Portugal, the only, 56.
Avenida da Liberdade, 26; the king on horseback, 27.

BARREIRO TO FARO, by rail, 311, 317; to Setubal, 144.
Batalha, history of, 43-44, 85-96; Beckford at, 86-87, 90-93.
Baths at Caldas da Rainha, 53-55; at Caldas Monchique, 337-342.
Bay of Biscay, crossing fifty years ago, 3.

Beckford, William, 3; at Caldas, 54; description of Alcobaca, 62-65, 68; Convent of Batalha, 86-87, 90-93.
Beja, 320.
Belem, health officer at, 15.
—— Castle, 15.
'Bell-frog,' silvery tones of the, 241.
Black Horse Square, 17.
Blakeney, General Sir R., 120.
Bom Jesus, 225, 228-229, 235-237; great festival at, 257-262.
Bombarral, 49.
Bombay, dowry of Catherine of Braganza, 168.
Braga, 225, 227, 243-244, 253; in Roman times, 254; cathedral and relics, 254.
Braganza, Catherine of, 168.
—— Hotel, Lisbon, 18.
Brazil, Prince of, and the Franciscans, 119.
British soldiers and the legions of France, 49-51.
Bull-fight, 31-38.
Bussaco, 263; monastery at, 271-280; Wellington at, 275; Fonte Fria, 287; custom of carrying everything on the head, 288-289; donkey-riding at, 291; a hot-weather resort, 292; visit of Coimbra students, 300.

CAES DE SODRE, 28-29.
Caldas da Rainha, 44-45; waters of, 53-55, 96-101.
—— de Monchique, 353.
—— ware, 56.

391

Camoens, Portugal's favourite bard, 296-297.
Campo Pequeno, cricket on, 30; now a bull-ring, 31.
Cape Espichel, 143.
Cape Roca, 10.
Cape St. Vincent, Drake at, 356; Jervis, 365; Admiral Napier, 205, 365.
Carnarvon, Lord, at Alcobaca, 77; at Setubal, 155.
Carriages and tramways of Lisbon, 19.
Cascaes, the Lisbon Margate, 28.
Cavado, river, 246.
Central Railway Station, 27.
Cetobriga, 149.
Charles II. and Catherine of Braganza, 169.
Chubb's safe, a, and the Custom House, 196.
Church, near Caldas, containing votive offerings from seafaring people, 100.
Churches at Lisbon, 39; at Oporto, 183.
Cintra, consumptive patients at, 2.
—— mountains, 10.
Clerigos, tower of the, struck by lightning, 185.
Coimbra, 263, 295-303; British army at, 305.
—— gate, 280-282.
Convent of Nossa Senhora da Arrabida, 153.
Convent of S. Antonio, 187.
Convents in Portugal, 22, 23.
Crawfurd, Oswald, on Portuguese art, 59; *Round the Calendar in Portugal*, 237.
Cricket at Oporto, 180-181.
Cruz Alta, 285.
Cupressus Lusitanica, 271, 283.
Customs officials courteous, 16.

DINIZ, King, 'the wise lawgiver,' 264, 299,

Docks and quays at Lisbon, 28.
Douro, ' bar ' at, 160; Customs' officials, 161; finest views of town and river, 162.
—— bridge of boats, a tragedy, 199.
—— passage of, by Wellington, 202.
Drake at Vigo, 7; at sunny Cascaes, 10; at Peniche, 103; at Cape St. Vincent, 356; Sagres Castle, 358.
Duas Portas, 47.

ENGLISH ARCHERS AT ALJUBARROTA, 84.
—— Crusaders at Lisbon, 106, 150, 376.
Estoril, a pleasant afternoon excursion, 28.
Estrella Square, cable tramway to, 20.
Evora, 320.

FABRICA DE FAIANCAS, 56.
Faro, 317; journey to, 318; arrival at, 322; British Consul at, 323; sacked by the English fleet, 330; telegraph office, 331.
Fish-market, near the Caes de Sodre, 39.
Fonte dos Amores, Coimbra, 296-297.
—— Fria at Bussaco, 287.
Foz, S. Joao da, 191, 204; a pleasant way of reaching, 206.
Franciscans at Mafra, 119.
French soldiery at Batalha, 93-94.

GALLINHA HOTEL, Alcobaca, 65.
Glass factory established by William Stephens, 265-266.
Gradil, 114.
Grand Hotel, Bom Jesus, 229.
—— —— Lisbonense, Caldas, 96.
Grande Hotel do Porto, 162.
Guadiana river, 325.
Guerrita, the bull-fighter, 37-38.
Guimaraens, precious relic at Braga, 254.
Guzman, Pedro de, 104.

INDEX

HOSPITAL AT OPORTO, 192.
Hotel, country, description of a, 107-110; table etiquette, 379; at a fashionable hotel, 385.
Hotel da Matta, Bussaco, 270, 279.
Hotel Dos Cocos, Torres Vedras, 101.

INEZ DE CASTRO, 75, 296.

JESUITS' COLLEGE, Oporto, 192.
John I. defeats the Castilian army, 83; Batalha erected to commemorate the victory, 84, 86.
John I. and Phillipa, 83-86, 166-167.
John II., body of, desecrated by the French soldiery at Batalha, 94.
John V. in a convent, 23; builds a church and convent at Mafra, 115-118.

LAGOS, slave-trade at, 362; Jervis at, 365; Admiral Napier, 365.
Lecca, 204.
Leiria, extensive pine forest near, 264.
Leixoes, harbour of, 160, 161; railway to Oporto, 162.
Lima, Roman remains at, 251.
—— the 'river of oblivion,' 242
Lisbon, consumptive patients at, 1; best description of, 12; beauty of its situation, 13; landing at, 17; carriages and tramways in, 18-19; a contrast, twenty-five years ago and now, 19; public gardens, 21; fountains, a pleasant feature, 40; S. Antonio fêtes, 128-142; priest-baiting, 135; to Setubal, 144.
Lisbon and Oporto, a contrast, 163-164; railway journey between, 310.
Lisbon-Leiria railway, 44-46.
Lusitanian Mrs. Grundy, 25.
Luso, 270.

MAFRA, Pass of, 47-114; the 'Escurial of Portugal' at, 114-115; British occupation of, 120; monastery converted to national uses, 121.

Manners and customs at a fashionable hotel, 385.
Market, fruit, 39; fish-market, 39.
Marinha Grande, forest of, 265.
Matosinhos, 204; steam tramway to, 191; religious festival at, 206, 220-222; quaint pottery, 207.
Messines, 332, 377.
Methuen Treaty, 168, 171, 196.
Miguel, Dom, Oporto besieged by, 198.
Milheada, 268.
Mineral springs, Caldas da Rainha, 45, 53-55; at Torres Vedras, 101-102; Caldas Monchique, 342-353.
Mint of Portugal, 195.
Monasteries of Portugal, 185; pillage of, by French troops, 189; lead to deterioration of morals, 294.
Monchique, 330, 367.
Mondego, river, 295, 301.
Monte Agraca, 113.
Moorish castle, 48, 53, 99, 156.
—— influence, 179.
—— remains at Silves, 335-336, 374-375.
Murphy, the architect, at Alcobaca, 67-70, 81, 91; at Oporto, 182.

Napier, Captain Charles, 154-155, 205.
Napier's 'ever-victorious army,' 252.
Napier on Soult's capture of Oporto, 199.
Nime Junction, 226.
Nossa Senhora da Arrabida, convent of, 153.

O SENHOR DE MATOSINHOS, church of, 210-213.
O Senhor do Monte, commonly called Bom Jesus, 226, 228-229, 235-237; great festival, 257-262.
Obydos, castle of, 53, 99.
Octroi, at Lisbon, 126; at Oporto, 197.
Odivellas, convent at, 23.
Oporto, how to get there, 159, 160;

from an artistic point of view, 163;
inhabitants, 164; sight-seeing at,
165; colony of English at, 170-179;
old town, 172-173; Oriental influences, 174; principal streets,
176-177; markets, 177; churches,
183; English cemetery, 188; tramways, 191; the octroi at, 197; few
towns the scene of more stirring
events, 198.
Oranges at Setubal, 148.
Overland route not recommended, 4.
Oxen ploughing, 247.

PALMELLA CASTLE, 143, 156.
Pampilhosa Junction, 268, 304.
Passeiro da Copa, 53.
Peasantry of Portugal, 223.
Pedro I. and Inez de Castro, 75, 296.
Pedro, Emperor Dom, 203, 205.
Peniche, Drake at, 103.
Peninsular War, battlefields, 46, 48-49; Portuguese lack of gratitude to her deliverers, 52; horrors of the war, 305.
Pero Negro, 47.
Pine woods around Caldas, 99; an extensive forest north of Leiria, 264.
Pilgrims to the annual *festa* at Bom Jesus, 260.
Pinheiro, Senhor, 56-57.
Pombal, Marquis of, friend to the fair sex, 21; promotion of marriages, 24, 26; proof of the prescience of the great minister, 27; and the Franciscans, 118; and William Stephens, 265-266; builds Villa Real, 326-327; Lord Carnarvon's estimate of his character, 329.
Ponte de Lima, 242; Soult at, 252.
Port wine, 180.
Portimao, 356.
Portugal, one hears nothing about, nowadays, 'our ancient ally,' 1; country for consumptive patients, 1; sea route, 4; overland route not recommended, 4; mineral waters, 53-55, 342-353; neglect of the fine arts, 57-59; a country of great interest to Englishmen, 46.
Portugal, derivation of the word, 163.
—— north, 159; south, 317.
Portuguese, a nation of big ideas, 28, 192; have no love of natural beauty, 30; remarkable for their courtesy, 146.
Portuguese railways, 312.
Post office, Oporto, 194; at Lisbon, 194.
Pottery at Matosinhos, 207.
Praca de Camoens, 20.
Praco do Commercio, 17, 128.
Priest-baiting at Lisbon, 135.
Prince Henry 'the Navigator,' 166; at Sagres, 360-362.
Public gardens, scheme for making flirtations easy, 21.
Purses, pretty native product, 178.

RAILWAYS, navvy work done by women, 309; civility of railway officials, 309; railway travelling, 123-127, 304-314, 317-322.
Ribaldiera, 47.
Rocio, 19, 39, 42, 128.
Roman Catholicism in Portugal, 139, 218-219, 256.
Roman remains at Lima, 251; at Braga, 254; Troja, 149.
Royal mail steamers, 5, 159.
Rorica, 49; British soldiers at, 51.
Rua dos Clerigos, Oporto, 176.
Runa, 47; hospital at, 105-106.

SAGRES, Drake at, 358; Prince Henry 'the Navigator,' 360.
S. Antonio fêtes, 128-142.
S. Lorenzo, river, 114.
S. Mamede, 49.
S. Vincent, story of the martyred saint, 366.
Santarem, King of Castile retreats to, 83.

INDEX

Serra convent, Oporto, 198, 202-203.
Serra de Bussaco, 268, 292.
Serra de Foia, 369.
Serra de Gerez, 226.
Serra de Monchique, 315.
Setubal, 143-158.
Sierra de Chypre, 114.
Silves, 334; Moorish wall at, 335, 374; beautiful women of, 375; London crusaders at, 376.
Sobral, silk industry at, 113.
Soccorro mountain, 47.
Soult's capture of Oporto, 199.
Springs, at Caldas da Rainha, 45, 53-55; at Torres Vedras, 101-102; at Caldas Monchique, 342-353.
Stephens, William, glass factory of, 265-267.
Strawberries, how eaten by Lisbon fashionables, 110.

TABLE ETIQUETTE, 379.
Tagus, arrival at the, 11; a noble river, 12.
Tangiers, history briefly stated, 168.
Tapada, or Royal Park of Mafra, 114.
Time-tables, lack of, 312.
Torres Vedras, 47-48, 101-105; cemetery at, 122.
Trains, travelling by, 123-127, 304-314, 317-322.
Tramways, at Lisbon, 19; worked by cable to Estrella, 20; at Oporto, 191; steam tramway to Foz and Matosinhos, 191.

Trant, Sir Nicholas, 297.
Treaty of Windsor in 1386, 85-86, 167.
'Tree of Heaven,' 21.
Troja, 149.

VIGO, Bay of, 5; a veritable Eden, 6; long-sunken treasure, 8.
'Vigo plates,' 9.
Villa Nova de Gaia, the port-wine town, 173.
Villa Real de S. Antonio, 325.
Vimiera, battlefield of, 49.
Vineyards of north and south Portugal, 244-245.
Vasco da Gama, 15.

WARBURTON, ELLIOT, voyage in an 'aboriginal' P. and O. steamship, 3.
Waters, Colonel, story of, 202.
Wellesley, Sir Arthur, at battle of Rolica, 99.
Wellington, Lord, 47; at Vimiera, 49-50; at Batalha, 96; at Torres Vedras, 103; at Oporto, 172, 192; passage of the Douro, 201; at Ovar, 264; at Bussaco, 275; at Coimbra, 297.
Whistles from Matosinhos, 207-208.
Women of Lisbon, 35-36; during the 'dark ages,' 25; of Silves, 375.

ZIBREIRA VALLEY, 47.
Zizandro, river, 48.

Printed by T. and A. CONSTABLE, Printers to Her Majesty
at the Edinburgh University Press

www.ingramcontent.com/pod-product-compliance
Lightning Source LLC
Chambersburg PA
CBHW020739020526
44115CB00030B/631